GOOD GREEN KITCHENS

W9-BDL-146

Greater Victoria Public Library

AUG 1 0 2006

Juan de Fuca

GOOD GREEN

KITCHENS

614135863

GOOD
GREEN
KITCHENS

The Ultimate Resource for Creating a Beautiful, Healthy, Eco-Friendly Kitchen

JENNIFER ROBERTS

WITH PHOTOGRAPHS BY LINDA SVENDSEN

Gibbs Smith, Publisher
Salt Lake City

Greater Victoria Public Library

AUG 1 0 2006

Juan de Fuca

First Edition
10 09 08 07 06   5 4 3 2 1

Text © 2006 Jennifer Roberts
Photographs © 2006 as noted on page 158

All rights reserved. No part of this book may be reproduced by any means
whatsoever without written permission from the publisher, except brief
portions quoted for purpose of review.

Published by
Gibbs Smith, Publisher
P.O. Box 667
Layton, Utah 84041

Orders: 1.800.748.5439
www.gibbs-smith.com

Designed by Catherine Lau Hunt
Printed and bound in Hong Kong
Endpaper photographs by Emily Hagopian

Library of Congress Cataloging-in-Publication Data
Roberts, Jennifer, 1962-
  Good green kitchens : the ultimate resource for creating a beautiful,
healthy, eco-friendly kitchen / Jennifer Roberts ; photographs by Linda
Svendsen.
—1st ed.
     p. cm.
Includes bibliographical references.
ISBN 1-58685-700-2
1. Kitchens—Remodeling. 2. Green products. I. Title.

TH4816.3.K58.R63 2006
643'.3—dc22

2005033877

The products, companies, resources, and techniques described
in this book are provided for information purposes only and are not
endorsed by the author or Gibbs Smith, Publisher.

Contents

3

4

5

Cabinet exteriors are FSC-certified cherry finished with Osmo Hardwax Oil, a wood finish made from vegetable oils and waxes. Cabinet boxes are FSC-certified plywood.

An IceStone counter made from 75 percent recycled glass, including at least 30 percent post-consumer content.

Introduction

If you are as keen on kitchens as I am, you know that there are enough books, magazine articles, and TV shows about home design to provide inspiration, information, and entertainment around the clock.

So do we really need another book on how to refurbish, remodel, or design a new kitchen? I think we do. Something vital is missing from most discussions about kitchen design. More often than not, design is treated as if it were merely a question of style, function, and budget—as if our kitchens, and the materials and methods that go into creating them, are somehow set apart from the larger contexts of human health and environmental sustainability.

With *Good Green Kitchens* my hope is to expand the conversation so that when we design our kitchens, we're more likely to consider not only personal matters of taste, function, and cost, but also global concerns such as demand for energy and natural resources.

I can practically hear the groans. If you're embarking on a kitchen redo, you've already got way too much to think about, and now I come along saying you should be fretting about the state of the world too—the melting Arctic ice fields, the vanishing rainforests, the declining fisheries, the industrial chemicals in mothers' breast milk. I wouldn't be surprised if the daunting scale of these environmental messes makes you want to retreat to the kitchen and cook up a storm.

Go for it! In my view, the world would be a better place if we all spent more time baking, grilling, kneading, roasting, blending, chopping, sautéing, braising, and serving up heaping platters of goodness. Let's just make sure that the homes where we do all this good cooking and eating are healthy for people and the planet.

Open shelves provide easy access and require less wood than cabinets with doors. See more of this kitchen on page 145.

IS IT EASY BEING GREEN?

Here's the reality: paying attention to eco-friendly design adds a level of complexity to any kitchen-improvement project.

Creating a healthier, eco-friendly kitchen requires extra research. You may need to do some reading to get grounded in the principles of green design. You may need to learn about products and construction techniques you're not familiar with. And if you're going to hire pros, you'll want to identify designers and builders in your area with experience in creating eco-friendly homes. All of this will take extra time. But if you have the skills to manage a kitchen renovation project, you have the skills to make it green.

My hope is that *Good Green Kitchens* will inspire you to incorporate eco-friendly design into your next kitchen-improvement project. But even if you're not ready for total immersion, this book offers dozens of small solutions that will contribute to a healthier planet: simple actions like putting a low-flow aerator on the kitchen faucet to save water and water-heating energy, or using the toaster oven rather than the main oven to cook a small dish, or replacing incandescent lightbulbs with energy-saving compact fluorescents.

Once you're in the habit of taking small steps, larger actions such as choosing certified wood, recycled-content products, or high-performance windows will come more easily.

▲

A bamboo cabinet made by AlterEco with a recycled glass countertop by Counter Production.

▼

Open shelves turn everyday cookware into works of art in this home built of timbers salvaged from an old warehouse.

STYLE AND SPIRIT

If an eco-friendly countertop looks as sexy as a brown paper bag, you're not likely to invite it into your kitchen for a long-term relationship. Fortunately, you don't have to sacrifice style for the sake of sustainability. Green kitchens can and should look great.

In fact, eco-friendly, healthy kitchens come in every style: traditional, modern, rustic, high-tech, country, eclectic—you name it. Creating a green kitchen is not a question of taste, politics, geography, demography, or budget. It's a matter of using energy and natural resources wisely and creating a space that's healthy and pleasurable to spend time in. There are myriad ways to accomplish this.

Green building or green remodeling is quite simply an improvement on conventional practices—with an emphasis on energy efficiency, conserving natural resources, and creating a healthy home. These fundamental issues cut across all styles. So when it comes to creating your own green kitchen, don't feel like you have to imitate any particular look you see in this book or elsewhere; you can have a dream green kitchen that satisfies your soul and your unique sense of style.

I can't emphasize enough that, despite the beautiful floors, cabinets, and countertops you'll see in these pages, living green doesn't mean going out and buying all kinds of new stuff. It's important not to confuse buying green with living green.

To my mind, buying green is a

◄ ▲

The cabinets and island are made from salvaged sycamore trees that were cut down as part of a flood control project. Cabinet boxes are formaldehyde-free wheatboard. The vintage range is a restored O'Keefe and Merritt.

▼

Vegetable trimmings can be swept into a slot in this island's salvaged sycamore top; a compost container within the island catches the scraps.

materialist approach to solving environmental problems—it focuses on buying products with eco-friendly attributes. There's nothing wrong with that. In fact, I'm an advocate of using our purchasing dollars to effect positive change by rewarding companies that are doing good things for the environment and refusing to support those that aren't.

But living green is not about buying a brand-new kitchen or owning particular products or appliances. Living green is about opening the spirit, or the heart, to ways in which we can direct our energies toward creating places that are healthy, vibrant, and joyful.

The core of this book focuses on the material aspects of creating a green kitchen. It offers advice on choosing flooring, cabinets, counters, and appliances; after all, if you're designing a new kitchen you need to think about those things. But in your hunt for the greenest and most gorgeous countertop, don't forget that it's your heart and intention that matter most, not the stuff you buy.

Green Design: Trendy or Timeless?

In this world nothing can be said to be certain, except death and taxes and—with apologies to Benjamin Franklin—the fact that kitchen styles will change. The cherry cabinets, granite counters, and pro-style stainless-steel appliances so beloved today will someday be about as chic as gold-speckled laminate counters and avocado refrigerators.

What about green design? Is it a fad destined to cycle out of style, like panini presses and fondue fountains? Or is it here to stay?

Both, I dare say. Green design is a fad in the sense that it's a relatively new wave to have reached the shores of kitchen design. Eventually, I predict, the fad will peter out. But it won't be because people grow tired of it and move on to the next new thing.

Green design will fade away because eventually it will no longer be distinct from good design; ecological awareness will be thoroughly integrated into standard design and construction practices. In the future, our homes will be free of toxic materials. In the future, our homes will produce more energy than they consume. In the future, our homes will be made of materials that are 100 percent reusable or recyclable, so that everything is endlessly renewable, with no waste.

Impossible, you say? Not if we set that as our intention and take a step on that path today.

COOKING AND EATING YOUR WAY TO A GREEN KITCHEN

I'll let you in on a secret. You can ignore all my advice in this book and still have a good green kitchen. What's paramount is to use your kitchen to prepare healthy food

Leslie Spring and Geoffrey Gainer in their modernized Victorian kitchen. See more of their kitchen on page 145.

A custom-made Vetrazzo countertop by Counter Production.

and serve it with love. At its core, the green-building movement is about taking care of ourselves, each other, and the environment. Where better to start than with what we eat?

There are many paths to eating well, of course. Grow some of your own food, if you have the desire and opportunity. Purchase locally grown food at farmers markets or from community-supported agriculture associations. Choose organically grown food that's not treated with harmful pesticides; you'll be safeguarding your health and that of farmworkers, as well as keeping pollutants out of the soil, air, and waterways. Eating lower on the food chain also eases the burden on our bodies and the environment.

As much as I'm an advocate for green building practices and products, if you can make only one change toward a greener kitchen, my heartfelt advice is to pay attention to cooking and eating for a healthier body and a healthier planet.

While nothing about this kitchen interior shouts "green," it was designed and built to be green from the ground up. Eco-friendly elements include FSC-certified and engineered framing lumber, cellulose insulation made from recycled newsprint, a 2.5-kilowatt solar electric system, and solar water heating for the pool and domestic hot water. The builder reused or recycled roughly 75 percent of the construction and demolition waste.

Neil Kelly Cabinets' standard cabinet box is wheatboard; they also offer boxes of FSC-certified plywood or medium-density fiberboard with no added formaldehyde. FSC-certified and reclaimed wood are among the options for cabinet exteriors.

1 green building: the big picture

What makes a kitchen green? There's no single definition of a green, eco-friendly, or sustainable kitchen. It may be helpful to think of greening the kitchen as a continuum that's shaded from light to dark green. At the light green end are the easy-to-do strategies such as choosing low VOC paints, replacing incandescent with fluorescent lightbulbs, or selecting energy-efficient appliances. At the dark green end are strategies like using only FSC-certified or reclaimed wood, consciously choosing to simplify and downsize, or using the kitchen project as a launching point for greening the whole house.

Where you fall on this spectrum, and indeed how you define the spectrum, is not particularly important. What matters is to embrace the idea of a continuum, knowing that wherever you are right now, you can always go greener. While some might view this as a recipe for dissatisfaction or frustration, for me it's analogous to a life well lived: it's possible to be fully satisfied in this moment while still being conscious that there is room in one's life for more living, more loving, more learning—and more greening.

The first part of this chapter lays out the three fundamental principles of a green kitchen: energy efficiency, resource conservation, and health. The second part of this chapter provides the larger context, outlining whole-house green-building concepts that are beneficial to understand even if your current project is confined to the kitchen. The final part of this chapter gives an overview of general kitchen-design strategies, including planning and layout issues, and describes how they relate to the world of green building.

CREATING AN ENERGY-SMART KITCHEN

When it comes to energy use, the ideal approach is to consider the performance of the whole house rather than individual rooms. Whole-house green design involves orienting the building and its windows to take advantage of natural heating, cooling, daylighting, and ventilating opportunities; creating a tightly built, well-insulated, weatherproof structure; and installing energy-efficient heating and cooling systems.

While whole-house issues are beyond the scope of this book, the list of whole-house green-building priorities starting on page 26 will give you an orientation to these issues if you're not already familiar with them. Of course, even when you're focusing solely on the kitchen, there's plenty you can do to be smart about energy use. Here are the basic principles:

Choose high-performance windows. If your plans call for replacing or adding new windows, choose good-quality insulating windows (typically double-pane, although in extreme climates triple-pane may be warranted). Choose windows with an appropriate low-e coating for your climate to keep heat inside the kitchen in the winter and keep the sun's heat out in the summer. The Efficient Windows Collaborative has helpful information on window technologies at efficientwindows.org.

Insulate well. If you're remodeling your kitchen, that's a perfect time to improve comfort and save energy by beefing up insulation in perimeter walls and ceilings. Check out today's eco-friendly insulation options, including batts made from denim and other textile scrap, spray-in or loose-fill cellulose insulation made from recycled newspapers, and recycled-content fiberglass batts with no added formaldehyde.

Prevent air leaks that waste energy. Stop air leaks around exterior doors with easy-to-install weatherstripping products available at any home-improvement store. Caulk cracks around windows. Check the heating and cooling systems' ductwork to make sure that all joints are connected and well sealed with a mastic sealant (don't use duct tape; it loses its effectiveness after a few years).

Choose energy- and water-efficient appliances. The kitchen accounts for a large portion of a home's energy use. Choosing more efficient appliances is one of the easiest ways to put your kitchen on an energy diet. See chapter five for details.

Provide good daylighting. Design the kitchen to be well illuminated by daylight even on the cloudiest days. Besides saving energy by reducing the use of electric lights, a daylit kitchen is more enjoyable to spend time in. Read the next section for more about daylighting.

Choose energy-efficient electric lighting. Effective kitchen lighting is paramount for comfortably and safely preparing food, and for creating an enjoyable, attractive space. For energy-efficient lighting that won't heat up your kitchen, choose high-quality fluorescent lighting for general lighting and many task-lighting purposes. See below for more about efficient electric lighting.

Provide summer shade. The hot summer sun striking west- or south-facing windows and walls can drive air-conditioning costs through the roof. And if you don't have air-conditioning, it can make the kitchen unbearably hot in the late afternoon and evening. The best strategy for keeping the kitchen cool without excess energy use is to keep the summer sun's rays off the building. Plant shade trees on the west and south sides, put in a trel-

◄

A second floor was recently added to the upper apartment of this 1970s duplex (this page and opposite). In an inversion of the normal living/sleeping arrangement, the kitchen, living and dining areas are on the top floor to make the most of views. The dining area's central bay has full-height glass doors to provide daylight. The south-facing doors are shaded by a trellis over the deck (left). Inside, the walls and ceiling are painted white to illuminate the space with indirect reflected daylight. The open-plan space has windows on three of its four corners, allowing for good natural ventilation. Appliances are Energy Star approved.

lis with leafy vines, or install awnings or overhangs to keep sun off windows.

FOCUS ON ENERGY: DAYLIGHTING & ELECTRIC LIGHTING
Daylighting

Daylighting is the controlled use of natural light to illuminate a room. It's a good green strategy that saves energy and money by allowing electric lights to be kept off during the day. But daylighting's benefits go far beyond energy savings. A good daylighting design can vastly improve your enjoyment of the kitchen by animating the interior, providing connections with the changing rhythms of the day, and perhaps even helping keep spirits up.

The key with daylighting design is to provide even light while keeping out excessive glare and heat. Too much direct sunlight can make the room uncomfortably bright; glaring shafts of sunlight striking work surfaces can make it difficult to perform tasks such as chopping vegetables or reading a recipe.

For balanced light in the kitchen, provide daylight from at least two directions. White or very light colored surfaces—walls, ceilings, floors, counters, cabinets—help reflect light, making the kitchen brighter. A window located close to a corner or the ceiling helps spread daylight by illuminating adjacent surfaces.

Skylights are an excellent way to provide daylight, although be cautious about using units that are overly large or have clear glazing—they might allow in too much hot harsh sunlight. Consider a skylight with translucent or prismatic glazing so the light is diffused rather than uncomfortably bright. Another good option is tubular skylights. They let in daylight without the excess heat; they're also relatively easy and inexpensive to install in existing homes.

Windows on the north side won't present a glare or overheating problem. East-facing windows are usually welcome in the kitchen because they cheer up the space with morning light that in most climates isn't excessively hot. South-facing windows can be shaded on the exterior with an overhang or awning; this keeps summer sun off the windows while allowing in some warming sunlight during the winter when the sun is lower in the sky.

The most problematic exposure for kitchen windows is the west side; hot summer sun striking west-facing windows can turn the kitchen into an oven. If possible, minimize the number and size of windows on the west side. Overhangs aren't very effective on west windows because the late-afternoon and early-evening sun is low in the sky. Exterior shutters can help, as can a window glass coating rated for a low solar heat gain coefficient (check the window label or the manufacturer's Web site for SHGC ratings). If it's not possible to keep heat off the exterior of the windows, use interior window coverings to keep the kitchen cooler.

Electric Lighting

Kitchen lighting must be functional—it needs to provide safe, effective illumination for cooking, cleaning, eating, reading, and any number of other activities. It should also be beautiful, with attractive fixtures and a well-considered design that provides an inviting quality of light. Good-looking lighting is especially important these days because we spend more time in our kitchens than ever before and our kitchens tend to be more open to other areas of the house.

Of course, kitchen lighting ought to be energy efficient too; after all, lighting accounts for roughly 9 percent of energy use in homes. The most energy-efficient option for kitchen lighting is fluorescents; they use two-thirds less energy than incandescent lights, generate 70 percent less heat, and last eight to ten times longer. The lights you use most often in your kitchen should all be fluorescent.

Go easy on the incandescent lights, including halogen lights. Incandescents are quite inefficient, with as much as 90 percent of the energy they consume ending up as wasted heat rather than producing usable light. That wasted heat creates a double energy burden because it causes air conditioners to work harder.

Options for energy-efficient residential light fixtures used to be limited to those old fluorescent tubes that flickered and hummed. Fortunately, fluorescent lighting technology has improved greatly in recent years, so you no longer have to sacrifice style and lighting quality in your quest for energy savings. However, quality does vary from brand to brand. Be sure to choose Energy Star–approved fluorescent lamps and fixtures; these are guaranteed to meet the U.S. EPA's criteria for color temperature, color rendition, and efficacy (measured in lumens per watt, which describes how efficiently a light source converts electricity into light).

The color temperature should be listed on the lightbulb's package. For warm lighting that's similar to the yellowish glow of an incandescent light source, choose fluorescents with a color temperature in the range of 2,700 to 3,000 degrees Kelvin. These bulbs are often marketed as "warm white." If you want whiter light (often marketed as "cool white") that's more comparable to daylight than to incandescent light, choose fluorescents with a color temperature of 4,100 degrees Kelvin or higher.

The color rendering index (CRI) indicates how accurately the light renders color. For more natural color rendering, choose fluorescents with a CRI of 80 or higher. (Old-style fluorescents that gave skin tones a sickly cast had a low CRI of 50 to 60.)

One downside to fluorescent light sources is that they contain minute amounts of mercury. That mercury con-

tent is dwarfed, however, by the amount of mercury emissions from coal-burning power plants. So even though the fluorescent lights themselves contain mercury, using them actually reduces mercury releases in the environment because it reduces demand for electricity from power plants. Don't throw spent fluorescent lamps in the trash; take them to your community's household hazardous waste facility. Since fluorescents last up to ten times longer than incandescent bulbs, you'll rarely have to dispose of them.

When designing your kitchen lighting system, think about providing lighting in layers so that you can switch lights on or off depending on the activities taking place in the room and available levels of daylight. These layers of lighting can be grouped into three categories: ambient, task, and accent lighting, as described below.

Ambient lighting. To provide general illumination in the kitchen, use lighting fixtures with linear (tubular) or compact fluorescent bulbs (screw-in or pin-based). Good options include fixtures mounted close to or on the ceiling, or linear fluorescents installed above cabinets, behind valances, or on top of or behind exposed beams. For linear fluorescents, choose T-8 fixtures rather than the older-style, less efficient T-12 fixtures. T-5s are also a good energy-efficient option; they're very

slender, making them ideal for narrow spaces. Also, choose linear fluorescent fixtures with electronic rather than magnetic ballasts. Electronic ballasts start up rapidly, and are flicker-free and quiet.

If you want dimmable linear fluorescents, you will have to pay more for a special dimming ballast. Some screw-in compact fluorescent lamps (CFLs) are dimmable, but most are not; check the product packaging. Dimming switches used with incandescent light sources will lengthen the service life of the bulb but won't provide significant energy savings.

Task lighting. To illuminate work surfaces such as the sink and counter, choose recessed ceiling fixtures or pendants with CFLs, or under-cabinet linear fluorescents. Position the light source so that it is in front of you when you're standing at the work surface; light coming from behind will cast shadows on the counter. Fluorescent under-cabinet fixtures are available that are sleek and unobtrusive. Position under-cabinet lights close to the cabinet's front edge to illuminate more of the work surface.

Recessed ceiling lights are very popular for kitchen lighting. One potential drawback is that the kitchen is a very moist environment, and moisture vapor can travel through the recessed light assembly into the ceiling cavity, where it can condense.

Under some circumstances, this can lead to mold and rot in the ceiling and roof. Choose recessed fixtures labeled "IC-AT"; these are designed for airtight housing and for direct contact with insulation. Also, the fixtures should be Energy Star approved for CFLs.

Accent light is used to highlight art, architectural features, and decorative elements, and to make the space more visually appealing. Good choices include CFL sconces and downlights, or perhaps a few halogen spotlights. Try to keep halogens and other incandescent bulbs to a minimum, however, because they waste energy. Keep in mind that "low-voltage" halogen lamps are not low-energy lamps. Low-voltage halogen lights are only marginally more efficient than standard incandescent lights, and are substantially less efficient than fluorescents.

CREATING A RESOURCE-SMART KITCHEN

Environmental impacts occur at every stage in a product's life cycle, from extraction or harvesting the raw materials to manufacturing and transporting the product, from installation in your kitchen to day-to-day use and eventual disposal. As a result, every design decision we make has an effect on the environment.

The goal of green design is to make more decisions that have a neutral or positive impact on the environment, and fewer decisions that will cause harm. This is becoming easier than it sounds. There are now many alternative products that use natural resources more wisely while still meeting our expectations for style, price, and performance.

Here are general guidelines for creating a kitchen that doesn't squander natural resources. Subsequent chapters provide more specific guidance.

Keep size in check. It takes more natural resources to build, furnish, and maintain a large kitchen than a smaller one. Design your new kitchen so that it's not overly large. Chances are it will be more efficient and enjoyable to work in too.

◄

In this remodeled kitchen (this page and opposite), the new door and windows were custom-made from salvaged old-growth redwood. New exterior siding is FSC-certified redwood chosen to match the original siding. Cabinet boxes are FSC-certified plywood. The walls are insulated with cotton batts made from recycled denim.

Simplify. An overabundance of consumer goods takes its toll on the environment by spurring resource extraction and manufacturing energy use. Think twice about whether multiple ovens, refrigerators, dishwashers, and a plethora of one-trick-pony appliances will actually improve your quality of life.

Don't throw it away. Reuse as much of the existing kitchen as you can, including structural elements, cabinets, flooring, counters, and appliances. Donate or recycle what you can't reuse. And when buying new goods, look for salvaged building materials and vintage furnishings.

Choose good wood. In environmentally vulnerable forests around the world, illegal and damaging logging practices continue, driven by our hunger for wood. To avoid increasing demand for unsustainably harvested wood, buy wood with the Forest Stewardship Council certification, or buy reclaimed wood from a reputable source. See below to learn more about choosing good wood.

Choose recycled and recyclable products. Recycling reduces the need to extract or harvest virgin resources, and reduces the need to build new landfills or incinerators to deal with ever-growing quantities of waste. Favor products with the highest post-consumer recycled content available; post-consumer content comes from materials that would otherwise wind up in the landfill, such as beverage containers and newspapers. And close the loop by choosing products that can be recycled when you're done with them.

Choose rapidly renewable resources. These are resources grown, harvested, and replanted on a relatively short rotation compared to trees. They include bamboo and other grasses, cork, soy, hemp, and cotton. Rapidly renewable resources also include agricultural waste products, such as particleboard-type panels made with straw instead of wood. Using products

These cabinet doors are bamboo, a fast-growing grass that matures in three to five years.

made from fast-growing renewable resources eases demand for slower-growing resources such as trees and nonrenewable resources such as petroleum.

Buy local products. Give preference to products that are harvested, extracted, and manufactured within 500 miles of your home. Using local or regional resources reduces transportation energy use and supports local enterprises. It may also help people make a stronger connection between their purchasing habits and the environmental impacts of product manufacturing.

Conserve water. Protect freshwater supplies and reduce stress on wastewater treatment systems by reducing water consumption. Choose a water-efficient dishwasher and low-flow faucets, and consider reusing gray water. See chapter five for more information.

Make less waste. Excess packaging needlessly wastes natural resources and burdens landfills. Avoid overpackaged products. Reuse or recycle packaging waste. Compost food scraps.

FOCUS ON RESOURCE
CONSERVATION: CHOOSING GOOD WOOD
As a building material, wood's got a lot going for it. It's renewable, abundant, reusable, biodegradable, versatile, easy to work with, and beautiful.

But unless carefully managed, logging operations can cause a host of ecological and social problems, including deforestation, landslides, stream sedimentation, and destruction of wildlife habitats, as well as displacement of indigenous people and threats to their livelihood.

Ninety percent of plant and animal species depend on the earth's forests for life, yet more than 50 percent of the planet's original forests have been lost to development, agriculture, and logging, according to Natural Resources Defense Council (NRDC), an environmental nonprofit organization that works to protect forests. Much of that loss has occurred in the past thirty years. Urgent action is needed to safeguard our remaining forests.

Many people seem content to leave forest protection to governments and the large eco-advocacy groups. Yet the truth is that our individual purchasing decisions drive much of the global demand for wood. Every one of us who buys wood for our homes, whether it's framing lumber, cabinets, hardwood flooring, or a kitchen table, has the power to protect forests or whittle them away. If you're on the side of protection, here's what you can do:

Use less wood. When remodeling your kitchen, reuse as much of the existing structure, cabinets, flooring, and other wood materials as possible. Keep size in check when designing a new kitchen—larger spaces require more materials. Frame new kitchens and additions using advanced framing techniques (also known as optimal value engineering, or OVE). This is a set of building practices—such as placing wall studs twenty-four inches apart instead of the more common sixteen inches—that can reduce wood use by as much as 15 percent. Consider buying vintage chairs, tables, and other wood furnishings rather than buying new wood furniture.

Choose reclaimed wood. Reclaimed or salvaged wood includes wood taken out of dismantled buildings or other structures, such as water tanks and wine barrels. It also includes wood from noncommercial logging sources that would otherwise have been chipped for mulch or chopped for firewood, such as wind-felled trees on private properties and logs from urban tree-thinning activities. When buying reclaimed wood, make sure you get it from a reputable source, and question the retailer closely. Many products are advertised as being made from reclaimed teak and other tropical hardwoods, but it's a claim that's almost impossible for a consumer to verify.

Choose FSC-certified wood. Whenever possible, use wood certified by the Forest Stewardship Council (FSC), an independent international organization that has established voluntary standards for responsible forestry management. Buying FSC-

labeled products rewards good forest management. It also gives consumers assurance that old-growth trees, biodiversity, water quality, and ecologically sensitive areas are being protected, and the needs of local people who depend on the land are being respected. More than 123 million acres in more than sixty countries have been certified according to FSC standards. FSC-certified lumber and other wood products are increasingly available and cost competitive. Learn more at fsc.org. For a directory of FSC-certified products, go to fsc-info.org. A number of other wood-certification schemes exist, but FSC is the only credible one and the only one recognized by the U.S. Green Building Council's LEED Green Building Rating System. Don't be hoodwinked by distributors or retailers who bandy around the terms *certified* or *sustainable*. If there isn't an FSC logo stamped on the wood, or printed on the packaging or the supplier's invoice, it's probably not FSC certified.

The FSC logo identifies products that contain wood from well-managed forests certified in accordance with the rules of the Forest Stewardship Council. © 1996 Forest Stewardship Council A. C.

Choose species that are unlikely to be endangered or logged from ecologically sensitive forests. If FSC or reclaimed wood isn't available, consider abundant species from second-growth forests or plantations. Give preference to species native to your region. Depending on where you live, good choices might include ash, beech, birch, black locust, cherry, Douglas fir, larch, maple, oak, pine, and spruce. Another option is to choose engineered wood products such as parallel strand lumber, glued laminated timber (glulam), laminated veneer lumber, and oriented strandboard. Engineered-wood products are made from fast-growing plantation trees, and they use wood fiber very efficiently with little waste. A few engineered-wood manufacturers offer FSC-certified products.

Do not buy large-dimension solid-sawn timber unless it is FSC certified or reclaimed. In general, large-dimension lumber that is free of knots and larger than two by eight inches is most likely from an old-growth tree. If you need large-dimension lumber for structural purposes, choose engineered, FSC-certified, or reclaimed wood. Be aware that reclaimed wood usually doesn't have a grade stamp, so local building codes may prohibit its use for structural purposes.

Do not buy tropical hardwoods, unless FSC certified. The *New York Times* reported that in 2002, Peru exported 45,000 cubic meters of mahogany to American ports, twenty times the total in 1992, and that as much as 90 percent of that mahogany was logged illegally. And mahogany is just one of dozens of tropical tree species that have been classified as vulnerable or endangered. WWF, one of the world's leading environmental protection organizations, says that if you buy tropical wood that doesn't have the FSC logo, it is likely that you are contributing to the destruction of tropical forests. WWF recommends avoiding products made with tropical woods, unless they bear the FSC logo; from their Web site, panda.org, you can download a photographic "Good Wood Guide" to help you identify tropical hardwoods in the store.

THE FULL SPECTRUM MYTH

Some companies used to tout the healing powers of their so-called full-spectrum lightbulbs, which sell for a hefty price premium over regular fluorescent bulbs. Don't be fooled. Nearly twenty years ago the Federal Drug Administration issued a Health Fraud Notice stating that the health claims made by manufacturers of so-called full-spectrum lights were "a gross deception of the consumer." While full-spectrum lamps offer very good color rendering, which can be useful for specific tasks requiring highly accurate perception of color and details, no health benefits have been scientifically substantiated.

CREATING A HEALTHY KITCHEN

On the average, Americans spend 90 percent of their time indoors. And whether we live in a bungalow or a mansion, the room where most of us spend most of our at-home time, apart from the bedroom, is the kitchen.

What if we approached the design of our kitchens as if our health and our family's health depended on it? How would that change our choice of lighting and daylighting? Our selection of surfaces that come into contact with food and our hands? Our perceptions of the colors, sights, and scents in the space?

There is much talk these days about the kitchen as a multifunctional space, where we do everything from checking e-mail to watching the news to entertaining our friends. At its heart, though, the kitchen is where we nourish ourselves. Ideally, a healthy kitchen would be designed to encourage healthy habits such as regularly preparing nutritious, appetizing meals and eating fresh, whole foods. But even if you use your kitchen mainly to brew coffee and down a bowl of cereal, why not design it to be beautiful and enticing so that you'll be tempted to slow down and really enjoy that coffee and cereal.

Besides eating well and creating a pleasing space, many other issues affect the healthfulness of the kitchen. Indoor air contaminants can pollute the kitchen, whether their origin is chemical (such as chemicals offgassing from building products) or biological (such as mold and mildew, pet dander, or dust). Good ventilation, daylighting, and electric lighting play a key role in contributing to good indoor environmental quality. Finally, safety, acoustics, and accessibility all should be considered when designing the kitchen.

The basic principles of healthy kitchen design are touched on here and fleshed out further in subsequent chapters.

Keep pollutants out of the kitchen. Avoid building materials, finishes, and furnishings that offgas noxious chemicals such as formaldehyde. Use zero or very low VOC paints, stains, finishes, and glues. Avoid polyvinyl chloride (PVC) products, if possible (read more about PVC in chapter two). Don't use synthetic pesticides inside or outside the house. If the kitchen has a door to the exterior, make sure there's a doormat inside and outside the door; as much as two-thirds of the dust and dirt in our homes is tracked in on our shoes.

Evaluate existing hazardous materials. Lead and asbestos are two unhealthy legacies from past construction practices. Older homes should be evaluated for these potential hazards. Lead from plumbing pipes is discussed in chapter five. Lead-based paint and asbestos are addressed in chapter two. Radon is another potential health hazard in new and existing homes; find out more in chapter four.

Ventilate. Adequate circulation of fresh air is critical to a healthy kitchen and a healthy home. On some days, opening a window is all it takes. But in the dead of winter or on a steamy day in summer when the air conditioner is running, an open window isn't the best strategy. Many newer homes that are built to be energy efficient incorporate mechanical ventilation systems that regularly introduce fresh outdoor air. In addition to providing fresh air, it's important to control moisture, especially in the kitchen, where cooking and dish washing can cause moisture to build up and encourage mold growth. One key strategy is to install and use a range hood that vents to the outside; just be sure the blower is not so powerful that it causes backdrafting (see chapter five for information).

Design for good daylighting and connections to the outdoors. A kitchen that's well illuminated by daylight without introducing glare or excess heat can be a delight to spend time in. Exposure to daylight may even help keep our spirits up. During the short days of winter, some people experience a form of depression called seasonal affective disorder, or SAD, which has been linked to daylight deprivation. People may even be more productive in daylit environments. Studies show that children in classrooms with good daylighting perform better on standardized tests than children in classrooms with little or no daylighting. For more about daylighting, see the previous section, Creating an Energy-Smart Kitchen.

Incorporate universal design principles. Universal design makes the kitchen more user-friendly for everyone, including children, the elderly, and people with diverse physical abilities. A faucet with a single lever is easier to use than a faucet with separate hot and cold handles. A dishwasher that is raised off the floor may be more comfortable for people who have difficulty bending. Appliance drawers are often more accessible than full-sized appliances. Heavy-duty drawers for pots and dishes make it easy to access items compared to deep cabinets. Open storage is more accessible than closed cabinets. Cabinets with glass doors make it easier to see what's inside without opening them.

Counters can be built at different heights to accommodate standing and seated cooks. A height of thirty-one inches works well for many people in wheelchairs as well as people who can't be on their feet for a long time. For disabled people who are

GREENWASHING

When a company tries to burnish its reputation or increase sales by making misleading claims about its environmental performance, that's called greenwashing or greenscamming. Sadly there's too much of it going on. Making sense of environmental product claims can be confounding for even the most well-informed building professionals and homeowners. For example, companies' marketing materials sometimes refer to LEED, the U.S. Green Building Council's Green Building Rating System (usgbc.org). Be aware that LEED does not certify or recommend particular products or companies.

A handful of credible green-products certification programs exist today. These programs play an important role in helping people separate the green from the greenwash.

CERTIFICATION PROGRAM	PRODUCT CATEGORY	WEB SITE
Energy Star	Energy-efficient appliances	energystar.gov
Forest Stewardship Council (FSC)	Wood from well-managed forestry operations	fsc.org
Green Label Plus	Low-emitting carpets and rugs	carpet-rug.org
Green Seal	Paints and coatings, windows and doors, cleaning products, and other product categories	greenseal.org
Greenguard	Low-emitting interiors products	greenguard.org
Rediscovered Wood	Forest products operations that use reclaimed, recycled, and/or salvaged wood materials	rainforest-alliance.org
Scientific Certification Systems	Recycled content, biodegradability, indoor air quality, and other single-attribute environmental claims	scscertified.com

Mark Feichtmeir and Karen Boness have surrounded their new home with intensely productive edible gardens. Farther away from the house, they are restoring the property's native plant population to provide wildlife habitat. See their kitchen on page 70.

ambulatory, thirty-five inches is a comfortable height. Electric appliances are safer for people with limited mobility or people with an impaired sense of smell who might not smell a gas leak.

For wheelchair users, basic design strategies include providing adequate space for wheelchair maneuvering even when cabinet and appliance doors are open, but not so much space that too much effort has to be expended moving from one work zone to another. Choose an oven with a door that opens to the side rather than down. Position the oven and microwave at accessible heights. Choose a cooktop with easy-to-use controls on the front so the user doesn't have to reach over the hot burners. Provide a twenty-four-inch-deep recess under the sink, cooktop, and at least one food-preparation area for the person's knees. Put light switches and electrical outlets within easy reach.

Pay attention to acoustics. While some people thrive in bustling kitchens, others find that high noise levels exacerbate stress. To create a more peaceful kitchen, choose appliances designed to be quieter. Choose cabinet drawers with self-closing slides that don't slam shut. Insulate walls and choose double-pane windows to reduce transmission of noise from the outside. Minimize hard surfaces that reflect sound, such as metal, concrete, tile, and stone. Favor sound-absorbent surfaces such as cork and natural linoleum. Include quiet nooks set apart from the main activity area for reading, conversation, and relaxing. Open plan layouts position the kitchen as the hub of the house, but if you prefer more tranquility, a traditional design with greater separation between rooms might be the ticket.

Play it safe. A healthy kitchen is a safe kitchen. The National Kitchen and Bath Association recommends these steps to a safe kitchen: provide glare- and shadow-free general lighting as well as task lighting on all work surfaces; use slip-resistant flooring; keep a fire extinguisher handy; keep electrical switches, plugs, and lighting fixtures away from water sources and wet hands; regulate water temperature (some new faucets have internal anti-scald dials to prevent water temperatures from rising to dangerous levels); choose a safe cooktop with controls in the front or along the side and with burners either staggered or in one straight row; lay out the space with safety in mind; traffic flow shouldn't interfere with the cooking zone; don't put the range near an entrance or exit; use slide-out bins and drawers to eliminate bending; design storage space to keep hazards such as cleaning supplies, knives and other sharp utensils, and appliance cords out of the reach of children.

Focus on Health: Improving Indoor Air Quality

Many modern building materials and furnishings, including some types of insulation, plywood, particleboard, paint, and even textiles, are made with chemicals that are released (outgassed) over time into the air we breathe.

Volatile organic compounds, or VOCs, are a major source of indoor air pollution in the home. VOCs are chemicals with a carbon-hydrogen bond that readily offgas, or evaporate into the air, at room temperature. Many VOCs exist in nature, and many more are synthetic chemicals manufactured from petroleum products.

You're likely familiar with the names—and even the distinctive odors—of dozens of VOCs, including propane, formaldehyde, acetone, benzene, butane, paraffin, and toluene. These are all useful chemicals, but not the kind of stuff you want to be sucking up in significant quantities. And yet VOCs are being released by hundreds of products in our homes, from paints and wood sealants to insulation and carpets to particleboard and plastic tubing.

Not to worry, our government protects us from harmful chemicals in consumer and building products, right? Yes and no.

Take paints, one of the most common home-improvement products sold. Certain VOCs in paints are known as smog precursors because the chemicals they offgas can react with nitrogen oxides (NOx) in the presence of sunlight to form ground-level ozone, or what most of us call smog. The federal government, charged with improving outdoor air quality, has established VOC-content limits for many products, including architectural coatings like paints, stains, and sealants. Almost all architectural coatings sold in the United States must comply with these content limits; allowable levels of VOCs vary by product category.

If a product such as a floor sealant or paint is labeled VOC-compliant, all this means is that the product complies with U.S. law. That's well and good, but is it good enough?

Remember, the federal VOC limits for architectural coatings were established to address smog, not indoor air pollution, so they only limit VOCs that are smog precursors. A manufacturer can claim that their paint is low VOC (which is indeed a step better than just VOC-compliant) or even zero VOC, and yet that product can still contain many VOCs.

I liken this to food manufacturers who print "FAT-FREE" in bold letters on their cookie packages. If you read the nutrition label, you find out the cookies are loaded with sugar and calories. They may be fat-free but you'll still wind up with love handles if you scarf down too many. *Caveat emptor.*

One manufacturer, AFM Safecoat, makes a full line of paints and coatings specifically geared toward reduc-

Neil Kelly Cabinets offers three types of finishes for their wood cabinets: a clear, water-based finish; plant-based oils and waxes; and low VOC paints. Cabinets are available with wheatboard interiors and FSC-certified or reclaimed doors.

ing chemicals that are toxic to human health. Years ago we sold AFM Safecoat products at the environmental general stores I helped launch in San Francisco. Besides selling the products, we used them when we built the stores, and I used them in my house. They worked great. Back then the main drawback was that the paint came in every shade you could want as long as it was white or off-white. Today, AFM Safecoat distributors can mix paints in a rainbow of colors, and they're all the more beautiful because the company has our health in mind when it formulates its products.

There's so much we don't know about the effects of indoor air pollution on our health. Our bodies are quite resilient, and if a home has good ventilation, we may never notice any effects from breathing in these pollutants day after day. But for the small number of people who develop severe sensitivities to chemicals commonly found in our homes, poor indoor air quality can be debilitating.

The most effective way to combat indoor air pollution is to keep out the offending materials in the first place. In many cases, there are healthier substitutes for suspect building components and materials. The subsequent chapters describe effective strategies for keeping indoor air pollutants out of the kitchen.

GREENING THE WHOLE HOUSE

Good Green Kitchens is just about kitchens, but when planning your new dream green kitchen, don't lose sight of the bigger picture. Much of what makes a home healthy and energy and resource efficient relates to whole-house building issues such as foundations, framing, electrical, plumbing and heating systems, insulation, roofing, and landscaping. It helps to understand the whole-house context so that you don't miss opportunities that may arise when you're revamping the kitchen.

This section provides an outline for key whole-house green-building strategies. To learn more, check out my book *Good Green Homes*. Another good resource is the LEED for Homes Green Building Rating System developed by the U.S. Green Building Council (usgbc.org). While geared primarily to developers of new homes, a read-through of the LEED for Homes checklist and accompanying literature is an excellent way to get a grounding in general green-home construction issues. Another helpful resource is StopWaste.Org's (stopwaste.org) green home checklists and guidelines for new construction, remodeling, and multifamily housing; while geared primarily toward California climates, most of the strategies are widely relevant.

Whole-House Green-Building Priorities
Land Use and Site
+ Avoid buying or building in ecologically vulnerable areas, such as floodplains, wetlands, wildfire-prone regions, prime farm-land, or areas known to be habitat for threatened or endangered species.
+ Consider remodeling an older home rather than building a brand-new home.
+ If building a new home, favor infill sites rather than building in an undeveloped area. Infill sites are urban or suburban lots where public infrastructure, including sewer and water service and paved roads, is already in place.
+ Choose a location that lets you leave your car at home often or even do without a car.
+ Consider higher-density living, such as apartments, cohousing communities, or other compact developments.
+ When building new, design in harmony with the site. Analyze how the site's features and microclimate will interact with the building. Consider ecologically responsive design strategies such as passive solar heating and cooling, daylighting, natural ventilation, shading, and solar orientation for renewable electricity generation.
+ Keep the building's footprint compact to preserve undeveloped land.
+ Minimize site disturbance by protecting mature vegetation, controlling erosion, and avoiding compaction of topsoil.

Layout
+ Bigger houses use more energy and materials; favor quality construction and good layout rather than bulked-up square footage.
+ Don't add a lot of formal space if you lead a casual lifestyle. Consider eliminating rarely used spaces such as formal dining and living rooms or overly large foyers.
+ Choose floor plans that will be flexible over time as the household's needs change.
+ Design rooms to serve more than one function. A guest room that's only used occasionally, for example, can double as a home office.
+ Design and orient the home so that all rooms can be well illuminated by daylight from windows, skylights, or both.

Structure
+ Reduce construction and demolition waste. Construction of an average 2,000-square-foot home in the United States today results in about 8,000 pounds of construction waste. Good waste-management practices can cut this waste in half

by focusing on reducing, reusing, and recycling.

+ If tearing down part or all of an existing house, deconstruct rather than demolish the structure to salvage usable building materials.

+ Use advanced framing techniques, also known as optimal value engineering, or OVE; they can reduce wood use by 15 to 20 percent compared to conventional framing.

+ Consider alternative construction methods such as structural insulated panels (SIPs), insulated concrete forms, or straw bale construction.

+ Follow proper design and construction techniques at the foundation, roof, walls, and windows to protect the building from water intrusion.

+ Follow regionally appropriate design and construction methods to withstand fires, earthquakes, hurricanes, flooding, or whatever natural disaster your region is prone to.

+ Provide superior insulation.

+ Minimize unnecessary air leakage.

+ Choose high-performance energy-efficient windows.

+ Choose durable siding and roofing materials that will last for decades with minimal maintenance.

+ Design the home to be comfortable without air-conditioning.

+ In climates with hot summers, keep the house cooler by choosing roofing materials that reflect heat (typically white or light-colored) and that have high emissivity, meaning they're able to shed heat readily.

Systems and Equipment

+ Choose energy-efficient equipment for space heating and cooling as well as water heating.

+ Design and install efficient, effective air-distribution systems. Properly design and install ducts to ensure adequate airflow and prevent air leakage.

+ Use linear and compact fluorescent lighting to the greatest extent possible.

+ Use motion sensors on outdoor lights. Reduce light pollution by using full cutoff fixtures on outdoor lights to direct light downward instead of toward the sky.

+ Choose energy-efficient appliances.

+ Install water-conserving faucets, showerheads, toilets, clothes washers, and dishwashers.

+ Consider renewable energy systems, such as photovoltaics, solar hot water, and wind power.

Indoor Air Quality

+ Provide good natural and mechanical ventilation. In newer homes that are tightly built for energy efficiency, install a mechanical ventilation system to introduce fresh outdoor air into the home. Also consider installing a heat-recovery system to avoid wasting energy when introducing fresh air.

+ Use effective, high-quality filters on air handlers.

+ Control pollutants and moisture by installing kitchen and bathroom exhaust fans that vent air to the outdoors.

+ Install sealed-combustion appliances and equipment to prevent carbon monoxide and other combustion gases from polluting the home.

+ If you have combustion appliances in the home, install a carbon monoxide alarm on each floor.

+ Retrofit existing wood-burning fireplaces with EPA-certified fireplace inserts. If a new fireplace will be installed, choose a direct-vent, sealed-combustion model that burns gas or propane.

+ Test for radon. Install a radon-mitigation system if radon is a problem.

+ For new construction or major remodels, consider locating the garage separate from the house to avoid polluting the home with car exhaust gases and chemicals stored in the garage. If that's not possible, make sure the door between the garage and house seals tightly, and seal any cracks or penetrations between garage and house. Also, consider installing an exhaust fan in the garage that comes on automatically when the garage door is opened or closed.

+ Consider installing a central vacuum system that exhausts to the outdoors to improve indoor air quality.

+ Choose zero or low VOC paints, sealants, stains, adhesives, and other finishes to safeguard the health of residents as well as construction workers.

+ Don't use products such as conventional particleboard that offgas formaldehyde or other problematic chemicals.

Materials and Furnishings

+ Choose environmentally preferable materials. These include products that are FSC certified, have high post-consumer recycled content, are recyclable, or are made from rapidly renewable resources.

+ Choose materials produced or manufactured within 500 miles of the home to reduce transportation-energy-related impacts.

+ Don't use tropical hardwoods or wood from old-growth trees

This kitchen, which opens onto a large great room, features a unique circular chopping block made of FSC-certified maple. Floors are bamboo. Energy- and water-efficient appliances were selected. Whole-house green features include FSC-certified framing lumber; ceiling trusses and ceiling decking are made of salvaged timbers. The home's exterior redwood siding came from old water tanks in the region. The foundation concrete contains 30 percent recycled fly ash. A 6.3-kilowatt photovoltaic system generates electricity, and solar collectors heat water.

(unless FSC certified or salvaged).

+Avoid products made from polyvinyl chloride (PVC).

Landscaping

+Design landscaping to reduce the need for water, maintenance, and synthetic chemicals; reduce storm-water runoff from the site; and reduce yard waste.

+Design landscaping so that it needs no irrigation, or install a high-efficiency irrigation system (for example, drip irrigation, separate zones based on watering needs, timers, or moisture-sensor controllers).

+Consider water-conserving systems such as rainwater harvesting or gray water reuse.

+Plant shade trees to keep the home cooler and reduce or eliminate air-conditioning use.

+Favor native plants; typically they need little or no irrigation or synthetic chemicals, and they provide locally appropriate habitat.

+Consider a vegetated, or "living," roof to provide additional natural habitat, reduce storm-water runoff, and keep the surrounding air temperature cooler in summer.

PLANNING A GREEN KITCHEN

This book is not meant to be the last word in kitchen design.

If you are sketchy on the fundamentals of kitchen design, or are starting on your first kitchen-remodel project, I suggest you use *Good Green Kitchens* side-by-side with other resources that explain general design concepts such as layout and organization so-

Adjacent to the main kitchen (above left) is a prep kitchen with walls made of earth and cement sprayed onto formwork. The cabinets are salvaged Douglas fir. The countertops and shelves were milled from redwood and Douglas fir harvested from the property. Light fixtures are energy-efficient fluorescents.

lutions; ergonomic issues such as the work triangle and counter heights; and aesthetic considerations such as cabinet door styles, color schemes, and window treatments.

This section provides general planning concepts that will help you incorporate green design in your next kitchen project, whether it's just giving the space a cosmetic makeover, or creating a brand-new kitchen. From a green perspective, each approach presents different challenges and opportunities. But no matter where you are on the design spectrum, there are many things you can do to create a kitchen that's healthier and easier on the environment.

Redecorating and Minor Remodeling

Giving your kitchen a face-lift rather than ripping it out and replacing the whole kit-and-caboodle is likely to be your most eco-friendly option. That's because in most cases, redecorating creates vastly less waste compared to full-scale remodeling. Smaller-scale remodeling takes redecorating a few steps further, and may involve replacing cabinets, counters, or flooring, without making the types of structural changes to the building envelope that are common with full-scale remodeling.

When redecorating or doing smaller remodeling projects, pay attention to the indoor air-quality implications of any new materials you introduce: make sure paints and other finishes have zero or very low levels of VOCs and be cautious about choosing plastic or compressed-wood furnishings that may off-gas noxious chemicals.

Look for ways to minimize waste. Set up a convenient spot for collecting recyclable bottles, cans, and paper. Sort through your kitchenwares and give away what you don't use. Feel good about recycling worse-for-the-wear appliances—as long as you replace them with ones that use significantly less energy.

EASIER STEPS

+ Clean cabinets and drawers; repair broken hinges and drawer slides.
+ Upgrade knobs and handles.
+ Add convenient, space-saving organizers to cabinets and drawers, such as lazy susans, pot lid holders, and slide-out bins.
+ If there's air infiltration around windows or an exterior door, install weatherstripping.
+ Replace incandescent lightbulbs with screw-in compact fluorescents.
+ Install a water filter if you have concerns about water quality or odor (countertop or faucet-mounted filters are a snap to install; carafes require no installation at all).

+ Clean range hood filters.
+ Clean refrigerator's compressor coils.
+ Set up convenient storage for recyclables and compostable food scraps.
+ Plant herbs in a window box or in small pots in the kitchen.
+ Switch to less-toxic cleaning products.
+ Don't use pesticides in the house or yard.
+ Install a carbon monoxide alarm if you have combustion appliances.

BIGGER STRIDES

+ Give walls a fresh coat of paint, using zero or very low VOC paint.
+ If the kitchen feels cramped, de-clutter it. Take everything out of cabinets and drawers; keep only what you need or love and give the rest away. Reorganize what remains.
+ Replace old appliances with energy- and water-efficient models.
+ Reface or replace cabinet doors and drawer faces.
+ Refinish rather than replace what you've got. Sand and reseal wood floors. Replace cracked ceramic or stone tiles in countertop or floor, and repair, clean, and/or reseal grout.
+ Choose environmentally preferable products, such as FSC-certified or salvaged wood, rapidly renewable resources, recycled and/or recyclable materials, and materials that emit no or extremely low levels of problematic chemicals.

Major Remodeling and New Construction

Major remodeling, which often involves gutting the kitchen to its studs and completely rebuilding it, provides an opportunity to correct problems such as inadequate insulation or weatherproofing on perimeter walls. It's also a good time to think about redesigning windows and skylights for better daylighting, and overhauling the lighting design to make it more energy efficient, functional, and inviting. If your budget allows, consider adding solar hot-water collectors or solar-electric panels; check for state and federal tax credits or rebates that may help bring the cost down.

If you're in a position to build a brand-new home, you have an unprecedented opportunity to make not just the kitchen but the whole house green from the ground up. Whole-house green-building priorities are outlined on page 26.

With major remodeling and new construction, the two largest obstacles standing between you and having a green kitchen are construction waste and overall square footage. Not surprisingly, these two issues are closely related. It's tempting to make a new kitchen as big as you can afford, but bigger often isn't better when it comes to your enjoyment of the space and its impacts on the environment. Bigger kitchens typically cost more to build, send more construction materials to the landfill, require more energy to run, and impinge on outdoor space. Also, the larger the kitchen, the more opportunities there are to introduce finishes, furnishings, and other products that may contaminate indoor air quality.

Here are some strategies to keep in mind when planning a brand-new kitchen:

EASIER STEPS

+ Choose Energy Star appliances.
+ Avoid backdrafting by choosing a lower CFM range hood.
+ Right-size, don't super size; keep the kitchen's square footage in check and look for ways to avoid expanding the home's footprint.
+ Improve insulation in perimeter walls and below the roof.
+ Seal leaky air-distribution ducts.
+ If windows are to be replaced or added, choose energy-efficient windows appropriate for your climate.
+ Favor recycled and recyclable products.
+ Avoid products made with polyvinyl chloride (PVC).
+ Install an on-demand hot-water recirculation pump.
+ Use only zero or low VOC paints, stains, sealants, and other finishes.
+ Seal any new particleboard or interior-grade plywood with a zero or low VOC clear sealant.

BIGGER STRIDES

+ Deconstruct rather than demolish. Salvage as much of the old kitchen structure as possible for reuse; sell or donate what you can't reuse.
+ Recycle construction and demolition waste that can't be reused.
+ Save energy and increase comfort throughout the house by replacing old, inefficient heating, cooling, and water-heating equipment with more efficient systems.
+ Use only FSC-certified or salvaged woods.
+ Choose cabinets with interiors free of added urea formaldehyde.
+ Favor products manufactured within 500 miles of your home.
+ Choose reused building materials and furnishings as much as possible.
+ Design for great daylighting and electric lighting; favor fluorescent lighting.
+ Install solar water-heating and/or photovoltaic systems.

GETTING STARTED WITH GREEN DESIGN

Whether you're redecorating or designing a brand-new kitchen,

here are some overarching planning concepts to keep in mind when you embark on the kitchen-design process:

Identify your green priorities. Green building covers a daunting range of strategies and concepts. To better ensure results that you'll be happy with, you may find it helpful to think about which green issues matter most to you. For example, every kitchen should be designed to be healthy, but if there are people in your household who are particularly vulnerable to chemical or biological contaminants such as VOCs or mold, you'll likely want to pay special attention to healthy-kitchen design strategies. Similarly, energy efficiency benefits everyone, but if utility costs are a major concern or you have a particular passion for energy issues, you may want to put more of your efforts into creating a super-efficient kitchen. If the destruction of rainforests or old-growth trees gets you hot under the collar, then you may want to make an extra effort to choose FSC-certified or salvaged wood.

FINDING A GREEN ARCHITECT OR BUILDER

If you're planning to hire pros to help create your dream green kitchen, the project will likely go much smoother if the people you hire have experience with green-building practices and principles. How do you find such people? Buildingconcerns.com publishes online directories of sustainable building professionals in Northern and Southern California, Florida/Georgia, and the Mountain states. The National Association of Home Remodelers, San Francisco Bay Area chapter, offers a certification program for California builders who have completed a green-building training program; for a list of certified remodelers, go to sfbanari.com. Also check with the local chapters of the U.S. Green Building Council (usgbc.org).

Think green from the start. Your efforts to green your kitchen will be most successful if you think green from the start instead of waiting until the design is nearly complete, and then trying to tack on a few eco-friendly finishes. If you're working with professional designers or builders, communicate with them from the beginning and throughout the project what your green goals and requirements are.

Do your homework. There is a lot of deliberate greenwashing out there, as well as many well-intentioned kitchen-design pros and company representatives who aren't well-informed about green principles, methods, and materials. It can be challenging to ferret out accurate information about products, but it pays to do careful research while you're still in the planning stage.

Work with experienced green-building professionals. Whether you're a do-it-yourselfer or a decide-it-yourselfer, when it comes to redoing your kitchen, there's a vast network of pros eager to help you, from architects, kitchen designers, and remodeling contractors to cabinetry companies, kitchen-design showrooms, and home-improvement stores. Remember that green building means improving on standard practice to create homes that are healthier to live in and easier on the environment. Some kitchen-design pros have a good grasp of how to do this; in fact, many have been designing or building green for years without necessarily calling it green. However, some people in the industry are not knowledgeable about green building, and some may be resistant or even openly hostile to your green goals. If you choose to work with pros who are new to green, you may have a harder row to hoe than if you select experienced green-building professionals.

Create a Green-Kitchen Owner's Manual. Before you even get started with your kitchen redo, designate a place—whether it's a drawer, a file folder, or a binder—where you can collect information about the products and materials in your new kitchen. Keep appliance manuals, product maintenance instructions, and warranty information here. Also keep track of the sources and attributes of green materials so that you'll know which floor-finishing product to reorder, and so that you'll remember the stuff that gives you green bragging rights, like the amount of fly ash in your concrete, or the super-low energy consumption of your refrigerator. Also, future owners of your home will likely be delighted to know that the floor came out of a seventy-five-year-old gymnasium, or that the ceiling decking was fashioned from the wood of industrial-size vinegar vats. You may even want to write up a page or two of information about materials, methods, and sources to give to friends and family who are interested in going green. Or consider creating a Web site or blog to share your dream green kitchen experiences with the wider world.

SPACE AND LAYOUT

For many of us, the kitchen is the nerve center of the home, perhaps the one place where the whole family spends time together. The isolated kitchen of generations past has fallen from favor; today we tend to want our kitchens to be open to other rooms so that we can spend our at-home time enjoying the company of family and friends instead of being cut off from them.

Open-plan kitchens provide good green opportunities: daylighting and views can be shared, space can be used more efficiently by eliminating unnecessary hallways, and in some cases, unused rooms like formal dining rooms and living rooms can be done away with altogether. Open kitchens do have drawbacks, but many of these can be resolved through good design. Noise transmission through the space can be reduced by using more sound-absorbent surfaces such as cork flooring. Privacy concerns can be addressed by including nooks for relaxing with a cup of tea, chatting with a friend, or doing homework. Cooking odors can be dealt with by installing good ventilation. Kitchen messes can be hidden from view with tall bars or moveable screens.

When designing a kitchen, whether it's an open-plan or more traditional layout, many people find the work triangle concept to be helpful. The work triangle represents the lines between the kitchen's main activity zones, usually the sink, stove, and refrigerator. If this triangle is too big, the kitchen will be awkward to work in because you'll have to take too many steps. One rule of thumb is to keep each of the three lines of the triangle between four and nine feet, with the three lines adding up to no more than about twenty feet total.

The work triangle is a good general planning concept, but there's no need to adhere to it too rigidly. For example, a much smaller triangle can be more comfortable, more inviting, and easier to work in than a super-sized kitchen, especially if there's just one cook in the household. Think of diminutive restaurant kitchens where the chef doesn't have to waste a single movement; everything is within reach and perfectly organized, like a ship's galley. Rather than piling on the square footage, aim for a well-organized space, with thoughtfully planned zones for cooking, eating, storing, and relaxing.

A great kitchen, whether it has an open plan or is separate from the rest of the house, starts with a great layout. But great doesn't have to mean gigantic. Here are some design strategies for designing a smaller kitchen that works well.

Design Strategies for Smaller Kitchens

+ Careful planning can help make the most of every square inch.
+ Reducing clutter and giving away stuff you don't use can free up a remarkable amount of space.
+ Creative storage solutions, such as linen storage under built-in benches, and space-saving organizers in cabinets and drawers, help keep the kitchen uncluttered.

This kitchen is in a nine-unit complex of ecologically responsible condominiums. The small but very functional and attractive kitchen features a compact gas range and recycled glass counters.

+ White or very light colors on walls and the ceiling reflect light, making the space feel larger.
+ Monochromatic color schemes and consistency in counter-top and cabinet materials will keep the space from feeling chopped up.
+ Views into other rooms, views of the outside, and daylighting from windows and skylights create a more spacious feel.
+ If you don't need a lot of storage, do away with wall cabinets to make the kitchen feel more open. Alternatively, if you need a lot of storage, go vertical and design your cabinets or shelves with usable space all the way to the ceiling.
+ Wall cabinets with glass panels make the kitchen feel brighter and more spacious.
+ Compact appliances save space and make good sense if your household isn't large or you don't cook often.

What Does a Green Kitchen Cost?

Redoing a kitchen can be expensive; in fact, for many people it's the costliest home-related expense, apart from the initial purchase of the home. It's worth taking time to plan well and make sure you're getting your money's worth.

Does going green drive that already-high cost even higher? It doesn't have to if you plan well. Many key green-building strategies cost little or nothing extra, and some even save money. Right-sizing rather than super-sizing is one example of a cost-saving green strategy: not only does it usually cost less to build a smaller kitchen, but it also costs less to furnish, heat, cool, and maintain.

The most cost-effective type of green upgrade—energy efficiency—is actually an investment that will produce a good return. Certain energy-related improvements cost a little more up front but pay for themselves quickly. These include energy- and water-efficient appliances, and good insulation and weatherproofing on exterior walls. Certain other energy-related investments may require a substantial payment up front but eventually pay for themselves over the years. These tend to be whole-house rather than kitchen-specific strategies such as high-performance windows and solar hot-water and photo-voltaic systems.

You don't have to have a luxurious kitchen with all the latest pro-style appliances to have a green kitchen. Even the simplest of homes, such as a studio apartment with two electric burners and a mini-fridge in one corner, can be designed and built in an environmentally responsible way, as affordable-housing developers from coast to coast are beginning to demonstrate.

Certain green strategies do tend to cost more but provide nonfinancial benefits that can be quite compelling. FSC-certified wood, for example, sometimes costs 5 to 10 percent more than uncertified wood, but for many people it's a small price to pay for the assurance that the wood came from well-managed forestry operations.

If you have cabinets custom made from materials that have no added formaldehyde, this will almost certainly cost more than if you were to buy stock cabinets from a home-improvement center. But the benefits will be twofold: you'll keep air pollutants out of your kitchen, and the custom cabinets will give you more design flexibility. Don't despair if you can't afford custom cabinets. Budget options range from giving your existing cabinets a makeover to sealing exposed particleboard on new cabinets to encapsulate formaldehyde.

And then there are indulgences—those pricier green products we sometimes choose just because they look fabulous. Sure, there's an eco benefit to luminescent recycled glass tiles or well-worn hickory floorboards from a deconstructed barn. But sometimes we pick something because we love it. And from a green perspective, that's a good thing, because if you love it, you're likely to take care of it and keep it around for a long time.

Six Tips for Keeping Costs in Check

1. **Redecorate rather than remodel.** Reorganize the contents of all the cabinets and drawers. Donate or sell the stuff you never use. Spiff up the room with a fresh coat of paint, new cabinet hardware, and attractive window coverings. Improve the lighting.
2. **Reuse what you've got.** Minimize structural changes. Reuse cabinets, counters, and flooring. Reuse appliances and windows unless they are energy hogs.
3. **Right-size, don't super-size.** Smaller kitchens cost less to build, furnish, heat, and cool. They're also often more efficient and enjoyable to work in.
4. **Standardize rather than customize.** Use off-the-shelf products and standard sizes rather than specifying custom designs and finishes.
5. **Use less energy.** Purchase energy-efficient appliances—especially the refrigerator. Skip the super-sized appliances.

Every home can be built to be healthier and eco friendly. This kitchen is in a housing community that helps homeless, poor, and disabled people achieve self-sufficiency. Green features include triple-pane windows with a low-e coating; fluorescent lighting; an energy-efficient refrigerator; low VOC paint; range hoods that vent to the outside to improve indoor air quality and remove moisture; and an on-demand hot-water circulation pump to quickly deliver hot water to faucets.

Design for good daylighting so you can keep electric lights off. Improve wall and ceiling insulation to keep cooling and heating costs down.

6. **Plan well and communicate clearly.** If you'll be working with an architect, kitchen designer, or contractor, communicate your specific green goals before signing a contract. If you are vague about what you mean by green, the professionals are going to have a hard time discerning your needs and sticking to a budget. For example, if you tell your contractor that you want FSC-certified wood after he's already started work on your kitchen, don't be surprised to see a change order with additional costs. Minimize change orders and unpleasant surprises by planning, planning, and more planning.

The counters facing the living area are thick slabs from an old oak tree that fell on a client's property. The slabs are notched to fit flush against the cabinet and post, while retaining the natural edge of the tree.

▼

A cabinet no wider than the doorway casing provides handy storage for spices.

▶

The kitchen is tiny, but the cook won't feel hemmed in because the room shares space, views, and daylight with the adjacent dining and living rooms. A closet on the other side of the wood counter serves as a pantry.

In Focus: Small Kitchens
A GOOD GREEN KITCHEN IN A SMALL PACKAGE

Creating a tiny but top-notch kitchen demands not just clever design solutions, but a willingness to rethink old-school design rules that were established for larger spaces.

Tweaking rules is something architect/builders Karl Wanaselja and Cate Leger never balk at: their buildings often incorporate unconventional elements such as glass awnings made from Porsche windows, a motorized driveway gate built from junked Volvo hatchbacks, and exterior siding fashioned from salvaged highway signs.

Leger and Wanaselja approached the renovation of this 850-square-foot, down-at-the-heels 1910 cottage with all the creativity and eco awareness they bring to their larger projects. They teased out the home's modest charm, tucking the new kitchen into what was once a tiny (and not to code) thirty-nine-square-foot bedroom. New FSC-certified cherry cabinets complement the original Craftsman-era wood columns and beams and original Douglas fir flooring. The diminutive kitchen manages not to feel cramped because it's now open to the adjacent dining and living rooms, and is bathed in daylight from a new skylight.

Space-saving features include a narrower-than-average twenty-four-inch gas range and a slender refrigerator. One of the counters is only twelve inches deep. Kitchen designers usually insist on twenty-four-inch counters, but a slimmer counter can be quite serviceable as long as there is no overhead cabinet or shelf to impede access. A closet near the kitchen serves as the pantry, while the original built-in china cabinet in the dining room holds tableware.

Cabinet exteriors are FSC-certified cherry; the interiors have no added formaldehyde. Glass fronts on the upper cabinets help the small room feel lighter and more spacious. The kitchen measures six feet by six and a half feet, taking up the space once occupied by a tiny bedroom.

Counters fashioned from thick slabs of salvaged oak provide warmth and luxury. Recycled glass counters and a plate-glass backsplash animate the space, sparkling in the sunlight from the new skylight overhead. This kitchen may be small, but it doesn't skimp on style.

Green Details

+ Appealing, highly functional kitchen in a very small space
+ Renovation retains the cottage's original footprint and character
+ Compact range and refrigerator are fully functional while saving space
+ Counters are made from recycled glass
+ Oak-slab counters were cut from an old tree that fell on a client's property (counters and other furnishings cut from this same tree also appear in the kitchen on page 122)
+ A new operable skylight lets in daylight and provides natural ventilation
+ FSC-certified cherry cabinets made by Silver Walker Studios have interiors with no added formaldehyde
+ Walls and ceiling are painted with AFM's low VOC Safecoat paint

Project Credits

+ Architect/Builder: Leger Wanaselja Architecture, Berkeley, California, lwarc.com.
+ Photographer: Linda Svendsen.

AN IN-LAW HOUSE

When Raymond and Patricia Buck set out to build a house for her parents next door to the couple's own residence, it was important to them that the home be green as well as gracious. At 1,000 square feet, the new house isn't large, but it offers all the comforts and beauty of a much grander residence. In and of themselves, in-law or granny units, as we often call them, are a good green strategy because they locate additional housing on a lot that's already developed instead of breaking ground on a new lot.

Architect and builder Timothy Mueller's passive solar design keeps the home comfortable while reducing reliance on energy-consuming heating and air-conditioning systems. As part of this strategy, the home's exterior walls are constructed of a three-and-a-half-inch-thick layer of clay earth. This construction method, known as pisé, or pneumatically impacted stabilized earth, involves using a high-pressure hose to spray a damp mix of earth and a small amount of cement against the wall's formwork. The result is a thick building envelope with good thermal mass that helps moderate indoor temperatures.

The Bucks designed the kitchen without high wall cabinets so as to keep kitchenwares within easy reach. The custom bamboo cabinets make the most of every inch of space in the kitchen. The cabinet exteriors are made of Plyboo, a brand of bamboo panels, fin-

▼
An open-plan kitchen, dining, and living area helps the small home feel spacious.

▲
Windows were carefully placed to allow in plenty of daylight without introducing excess heat. Cabinets were kept low to keep kitchenwares accessible. Pull-out cutting boards at the far end of the kitchen provide extra work surfaces.

ished with a linseed oil–based finish. The cabinet boxes are FSC-certified maple plywood. Mueller designed the cabinets to reduce material use; instead of each cabinet having its own box, which leads to a doubling-up of plywood where the cabinets abut, Mueller eliminated every other box. He cautions that while this strategy uses less wood, it requires more labor.

Mueller and the Bucks sourced the countertops from the "boneyard" of a local stone company, picking through odd lots and seconds to find pieces of granite that complement each other even though they don't perfectly match. For the floor, clay tiles were chosen for their good looks and low environmental impact.

The tiles provide thermal mass, which works well with the home's passive solar design and the radiant floor heating system.

Green Details

+Design for daylighting and passive solar heating
+Pisé exterior walls
+3.2-kilowatt photovoltaic system
+Tankless water heater for domestic hot-water and radiant floor heating
+Energy Star dishwasher
+Bamboo cabinets with FSC-certified maple plywood interiors
+FSC-certified framing lumber
+Exterior redwood trim from a salvaged water tank
+25 to 50 percent recycled fly ash in concrete
+Cellulose wall insulation made from recycled newspapers
+Clay plaster finish on interior walls
+Zero VOC wood finishes and stains

Project Credits

+Architect/Builder: Timothy Mueller Architecture and Building, Berkeley, California.
+ Photographer: Linda Svendsen.

▲
The owner and architect picked through odd lots and seconds at a local stone company's boneyard, choosing pieces of granite that don't exactly match but work well together.

▼
The custom-built cabinets have bamboo exteriors and FSC-certified maple plywood interiors.

◄
Interior walls are finished with clay plaster instead of paint.

In this earthen-walled, passive solar home, the south-facing great room has a concrete floor for thermal mass. In the kitchen, cork provides a more comfortable floor surface for cooks who are on their feet for long stretches. See more of this home on page 70.

This strand-woven bamboo floor is a newer entry to the bamboo flooring market. It is made from shredded bamboo strands that are glued together and processed into planks.

2 floors

Let's talk about what's underfoot. Whether it's antique chestnut planks in a farmhouse kitchen, cool ceramic tiles in a bungalow by the beach, or artfully stained concrete in a downtown loft, the right floor can make a kitchen.

With so many beautiful flooring options available, how do you choose what's right for your kitchen? Start by becoming aware of what you want and expect from your floor: style, feel, cost, durability, maintenance, and other general characteristics. Once you have a handle on your preferences, turn to the descriptions of flooring materials to learn more about what's best for your kitchen.

GENERAL CONSIDERATIONS

Look and Feel

A flooring material doesn't just provide a surface to walk on; it plays a leading role in creating the character and style of a kitchen. Think about what types of kitchen floors appeal to you. Linger with memories of homes you loved. Can you recall what was on the floor? Was it colorful, homey linoleum in your grandparents' bungalow? Scuffed parquet in your first apartment? Polished terrazzo embedded with chips of marble in the dining room of that Tuscan palazzo-turned-B&B where you spent your honeymoon?

Next time you're visiting friends' or relatives' homes, notice the kitchen floor and think about whether it appeals to you (it's probably a good idea to keep your opinions to yourself if they're not flattering!). Does the floor show every speck of dirt, and if it does, would that be a problem for you? Do high heels catch on the grout lines between tiles or make pockmarks in the wood? Does the floor exude elegance or is it a surface

WHAT'S GREEN

Reused or salvaged

FSC certified

Rapidly renewable

Zero or low emissions

Produced locally

Long lasting

Refinishable

WHAT'S NOT

Uncertified old-growth
 or tropical wood

Vinyl

Noxious adhesives used
 during installation or
 finishing in the home

High VOC emissions

Urea formaldehyde

Products shipped thou-
 sands of miles

that welcomes toddlers and their exuberant messes? Does it look like the kitchen floor of a cook who can whip up paella for twelve without breaking a sweat? Which of these styles is right for you?

Also pay attention to the feel of floors. Is the texture smooth or rough? How does it feel on bare feet or stocking feet? In my teens, my family lived in a house where the main living spaces, kitchen included, were tiled with large hexagonal Mexican pavers joined with wide grout lines—impossible for sock sliding, though ideal for providing thermal mass to soak up the sun's warmth in the winter (this was in the 1970s, when passive solar design was experiencing one of its periodic resurgences in popularity).

Consider the temperature of the floor surface too. Concrete, stone, and ceramic tile will be cool underfoot, and can make your whole body feel chilly in the winter even if you crank up the thermostat. If you live in a climate that's warm year-round, or if you have under-floor heat or a kitchen that faces south for passive solar gain, then a concrete, stone, or ceramic tile floor may be ideal. But if you live in a northerly climate, or your kitchen isn't touched by winter sun, or you just plain have cold feet, you might be more comfortable with a warmer, more insulating material such as hardwood, linoleum, or cork.

Cost

It's tough to generalize about flooring costs because there are so many options at every budget tier, whether modest or generous. Flooring prices are usually given in dollars per square foot; when evaluating costs, clarify whether the estimates are for the product alone or if they include installation, including any demolition of the existing flooring, or prep of the subflooring.

Some products are relatively easy and inexpensive to install, such as a prefinished, engineered-wood floating floor, which can even be done as a DIY project. Others are more labor intensive or require careful preparation of the subfloor—a material such as genuine linoleum (not to be confused with vinyl), for example, requires a flat, smooth subfloor because any bumps, voids, or imperfections will telegraph through the material.

When considering flooring costs, take into account not just the first cost but the long-term cost. First costs are what you pay up front for the product and installation. Long-term costs include maintenance, refinishing, and even replacement. Vinyl may seem like a bargain today, but if you wind up replacing it in ten years because it looks shabby, it may not pan out as a good investment. A hardwood floor is pricier up front but it can be refinished and with proper care can last the life of the

home. Even if you don't envision staying in your current home for decades, the hardwood floor may be a good investment if it increases your property's resale value.

Environmental Costs

There's another type of cost that's rarely mentioned in the context of kitchen design: the costs to society and the environment of using natural resources irresponsibly. When we install flooring made of an endangered tropical hardwood, we may be unintentionally contributing to the extinction of a tree species, to the destruction of habitat for creatures that depend on that species for food or shelter, to the silting of streams and harm to fisheries resulting from careless logging practices, to the loss of uncounted economic, cultural, and spiritual benefits that indigenous people received from their forests.

Who bears the burdens of these costs?

In the global sense, we all do because the environment and everyone's well-being is ultimately interconnected. But in our day-to-day lives, as we make seemingly harmless design decisions about our kitchens, it can feel like a stretch to connect the collapse of a fishery thousands of miles away to our choice of a flooring material.

What's a person who wants a nice kitchen to do? In my view, there's no need to feel guilty or to sacrifice the pleasures of a beautiful kitchen. Instead, start by recognizing that our choices do have repercussions around the globe. Many of our home-improvement projects have negative consequences for the environment, but it is possible to make choices that put us on the path to environmental sustainability. Choosing an eco-friendly flooring material may not save the world, but it's a step in the right direction.

Durability and Maintenance

Kitchen floors take a lot of abuse: besides day-to-day foot traffic across the space, spilled food and liquids, heat, humidity, and grime, the floor may also have to withstand pets' nails and kids' high-spirited activities. Durability, a key factor when it comes to selecting any green product, is especially important for kitchen floors. Replacing a floor after six or seven years because it's worn, cracked, or warped is terribly wasteful and takes its toll on the environment. Look for long-lasting products, materials that can be refinished rather than replaced after they become worn, and styles that won't look outdated in a few years.

A floor that holds up well should be a priority, but tolerance for wear-and-tear does vary and no two people will have exactly the same expectations. Some people prefer a kitchen with a lived-in, well-loved look, while others favor surfaces that will appear as pristine five years from now as on the day they were installed.

Also, if your household has just one or two people, you may not need as hard wearing a floor as a larger family. If you have a penchant for throwing raucous parties, choose a material that can take the abuse. If you have pets, you may want a floor that doesn't show muddy tracks and that doesn't scratch easily.

Before purchasing any flooring material, find out about the supplier's maintenance and cleaning recommendations. Favor flooring materials that can be easily cleaned and maintained using nontoxic products such as mild, biodegradable soaps and zero VOC sealants. If the manufacturer recommends specific cleansers, polishes, or refinishing products, obtain the material safety data sheet (MSDS). It is usually available from the manufacturer's Web site; if not, call the company to request it. Review the MSDS for any chemicals that might be troublesome to you, your family, or pets.

HEALTH CONSIDERATIONS

Floors cover a relatively large surface area, so they can affect the healthfulness of the kitchen and adjacent rooms. Health issues to keep in mind include indoor air quality and toxic chemicals; noise; comfort, safety, and accessibility; and cleanliness.

INDOOR AIR QUALITY AND TOXIC CHEMICALS

There are three main avenues by which a flooring material can pollute a kitchen. First, the material itself may give off chemical vapors, a process commonly known as offgassing or outgassing. Offgassing decreases over time, but it can take years for some substances, such as pressed-wood products made with urea formaldehyde binders, to fully offgas. Second, adhesives used to attach some flooring products to the subfloor may offgas harmful or irritating vapors. Third, some substances applied to the floor's top surface, such as sealants, polishes, and cleaning products, may contain objectionable chemicals.

How concerned should you be about chemicals offgassing from your flooring materials? There's no pat answer. Some people are highly sensitive to exposure to certain chemicals at very low levels, while others may not experience or notice any ill effects when exposed to high levels of the same substances.

Personally, I subscribe to the adage "an ounce of prevention is worth a pound of cure." In scientific and political circles this is known as "the precautionary principle," a commonsense concept meaning that when there is a reasonable body of evi-

dence suggesting that a particular substance can cause harm, we should take steps now to avoid risks to human health and the environment, even if we don't yet have definitive scientific evidence proving causation.

In the United States, more than 85,000 synthetic chemicals are registered for use, and every year more than 1,000 new chemicals are registered. Too often we assume that if a substance is used in consumer products, it must have been tested for safety. But unfortunately, fewer than 10 percent of those 85,000 substances have been tested for their effects on human health, much less for their impacts on the environment.

How close is each one of us to the threshold of not being able to bear the burden of the synthetic substances we are exposed to? We don't know. The dose makes the poison, as they say, but unfortunately, scientists don't know the dose that might lead to cancer from breathing in formaldehyde released by glues in engineered flooring products. They don't know the dose that might cause a child to have reproductive problems years in the future because of exposure to plasticizers from vinyl products.

We can't even say with 100 percent certainty that choosing a low VOC floor finish rather than one that emits high levels of VOCs will protect your health. We're exposed to so many synthetic chemicals every day, in so many combinations, that changing one thing in your home may not have any effect on the burden of chemicals your body must bear.

Some days, a simple act like choosing a kitchen flooring material can feel like a devil's bargain. In the face of this uncertainty, it's easy to feel paralyzed—but it's important not to. We have work to do, lives to enjoy, families and friends to love and cherish. So when it comes to choosing a flooring material that's healthful for your household and the planet, take some time to learn about the options, make what feels like a reasonable choice, and then enjoy.

Also, when shopping for flooring or other products for your kitchen-improvement project, take the time to tell retailers and manufacturers that you want eco-friendly, healthy products. It makes a difference. The path to a more sustainable future starts with us asking for greener, healthier products, and supporting those manufacturers that are already taking steps in this direction.

NOISE

Kitchens tend to be noisy rooms. Some of these sounds are (usually) happy ones: children's voices, friends' laughter, a tabby yowling for a bit of love or tuna. But the clatter of dishwashers, food processors, ice makers, blenders, TVs, and all the other accoutrements of the modern kitchen can grate on the nerves and add stress to our lives.

When choosing your kitchen floor, think about how important peace and quiet is to you. Hard surfaces such as tile, concrete, and stone will exacerbate noise, causing the sounds of footsteps, voices, and banging pots to reverberate. Some people love the hubbub of a boisterous home, but if you prefer more serenity, choose resilient flooring such as cork and linoleum that muffle sounds rather than reflect them. If your kitchen is open to the family room or other parts of your home, pay particular attention to how noise will travel through the air and bounce off surfaces.

Many cities as well as some homeowners' associations regulate minimum levels of acoustical privacy between floors and walls of adjoining apartment and condominium units. If you plan to change the flooring in your apartment or condo, be sure to comply with applicable regulations for both airborne noise (sound traveling through the air, such as voices or music) as well as impact noise (sound caused by one object striking another, such as footfall or a book dropped on the floor).

If you are embarking on a major kitchen remodel in your house or are building a new house, consider sound-dampening measures, such as sound-deadening boards, or foam or cork underlayment. Some of these products are designed to dampen sound transmission between floors (say between a kitchen and a bedroom below it), but may not do as much to attenuate noise within the kitchen itself.

COMFORT, SAFETY, AND ACCESSIBILITY

If you love to cook, chances are you spend a lot of time on your feet in the kitchen, chopping vegetables, stirring simmering pots, carrying heavy dishes from the oven to the counter. If your back and knees give you trouble after extended periods on your feet, consider a resilient flooring surface in the work zone to provide a bit of cushioning for your joints. Resilient flooring refers to floor coverings that give slightly under pressure but resume their shape. Good choices are linoleum or cork. If you don't want to use resilient flooring throughout the entire kitchen, you can mix and match materials: cork in the work zone, for example, and hardwood or tile in the bar or dining areas.

Avoid products that are slippery when wet, such as smooth glazed ceramic tiles; instead, choose flooring tiles with a slightly textured surface. Some highly polished floors are so shiny that it's hard to tell when liquid has been spilled on them; you might want to consider choosing a material that allows spills to be easily seen and wiped up before they become a hazard.

If people with limited mobility or visibility will use your kitchen, avoid flooring materials that might present a tripping hazard, such as rough bricks or tiles with very large grout lines. Also consider designing your kitchen, as well as the spaces it connects to, to be on one level so that less-mobile people don't have to struggle with steps.

CLEANLINESS

Floors have a way of attracting grime, dust, pet dander, and a host of other problems. For people with allergies, chemical sensitivities, or respiratory problems, keeping the floor clean is more than a matter of good hygiene; it may also be a question of breathing easier.

For those people, it's particularly important to choose flooring products that are easier to clean. Consider tongue-and-groove wood floors that fit together tightly rather than rustic planks that may have dirt-trapping gaps between the boards. Smooth surfaces such as hardwood, concrete, linoleum, bamboo, and cork may be easier to keep free of dirt than floors that have rougher texture, such as brick or some natural stone materials. Grout should always be sealed when it is first installed, and may need to be resealed periodically so that it repels moisture and doesn't trap dirt.

It's rare to see carpet in kitchens, but I have come upon it occasionally in rental apartments, as it is often cheaper for the landlord to throw down a new synthetic carpet than to replace tatty flooring with a more appropriate material. Carpet in the kitchen is a bad idea. It's a nightmare to keep clean and it acts like a magnet for dust mites and other allergens. These days, some indoor-air-quality experts advise against wall-to-wall carpet in any room of the home if household members have respiratory problems such as asthma or allergies, because of concerns that indoor air contaminants cling to carpet fibers. If you want some carpeted surface in the kitchen, such as in front of the sink or the stove, use small, machine-washable throw rugs or mats with nonslip pads beneath them. (If any members of your household have mobility problems, keep in mind that throw rugs, even when used with nonslip pads, may hinder maneuverability.)

REUSING OR SALVAGING AN EXISTING FLOOR

It's usually gentler on the planet if you maintain or restore the floor you already have rather than install a brand-new floor.

If your kitchen floor is in decent condition, another benefit to restoration is that you'll usually—although not always—save money by fixing it up rather than replacing it.

The luster of a stone floor can be restored with professional polishing. Cracked ceramic tiles can be chiseled out and replaced. Solid wood, as well as some engineered-wood floors with real wood veneers (not laminates), can be sanded, stained if you wish, and resealed. You can also paint or stencil a wood floor to give it a new look.

If you decide to replace the floor, try to salvage the material for use on another home-improvement project, or donate it to a building-materials reuse store. Solid wood floors can usually be saved, as can some engineered-wood floors. In general, wood flooring that is nailed down or is part of a floating floor assembly will be easier to take up. Floor coverings adhered to the subfloor with glues, thinset, mastic, or other adhesives are devilishly difficult to salvage and may only be worth the effort if the material has unusual historic value.

Dumping an old floor in the landfill should be your last resort, but you may have no other option for old vinyl floors. If your remodeling plans involve pulling out an old concrete slab, check with your town's recycling department or garbage hauler to see if concrete recycling is an option in your area; if it isn't, look for ways to use the broken-up concrete as backfill or in a landscaping project. In my city garden, I've used hunks of concrete slab as an urban variant on flagstone stepping-stones.

Lead and Asbestos

Some old floors contain potentially hazardous substances such as lead or asbestos. While painted floors aren't common, they do exist; if your home was built before 1978, be aware that surfaces painted with oil-based paint may contain lead. Inhalation of lead-containing dust or ingestion of lead-based paint chips can cause a range of serious health effects, including developmental disabilities in children.

If you suspect lead-based paint on an old floor or any other surface that you're planning to sand, cut into, or remove, have a sample tested before proceeding with your remodeling plans. Home lead-testing kits are available from home-improvement stores, but the results are not always accurate, so to be safe, I recommend using an accredited testing lab. Locate labs in your region in the phone book under "Laboratories—Testing" or ask your architect or builder for a recommendation.

If the test results show evidence of lead, check with the testing lab for information on local requirements for safe re-moval and disposal. For more information, contact the National Lead Information Center (epa.gov/lead/nlic.htm or call 800.424.LEAD).

Another potential hazard is asbestos, a mineral fiber that has been used for thousands of years in building products, fabrics, and countless other materials to increase strength and provide resistance to heat and fire. It's a versatile, useful mineral, but unfortunately, very high levels of exposure to airborne asbestos fibers over long periods of time can cause lung cancer, mesothelioma (a cancer in the cavity lining of the abdomen and chest), or a noncancerous but fatal disease called asbestosis. Health risks increase with the number of fibers inhaled; asbestos-related diseases have primarily been an occupational hazard for workers regularly exposed to the fibers on the job. Nevertheless, it's a good idea to avoid exposure to airborne asbestos fibers during home-remodeling projects.

Asbestos was recognized as a carcinogen as early as the 1930s, but the U.S. federal government didn't start regulating asbestos until the 1970s, by which time manufacturers had begun voluntarily eliminating it from most commercially available products. Tens of millions of homes contain asbestos products, including floor and ceiling tiles, pipe insulation, wallboard and joint compound, electrical insulation, and more. If you have resilient kitchen flooring (vinyl, asphalt or rubber tiles, or vinyl sheet flooring) that was installed before 1986, it may contain asbestos. Asbestos was also a component of some floor-tile adhesives used with genuine linoleum, vinyl, and other glued-down floors. If the flooring is in stable condition, leaving it in place shouldn't be a problem. Asbestos, whether it's in flooring or ceiling tile, duct insulation, or elsewhere in the home, is a concern only if the product is friable, allowing the asbestos fibers to become airborne. This can happen if the product is cut into, damaged, or removed during remodeling or demolition.

There is no way to tell by looking at a material if it contains asbestos; it has to be analyzed under a special microscope by a qualified professional. If you suspect that your older vinyl tiles, vinyl sheet flooring, or flooring adhesive might contain asbestos, and you're planning a remodeling project that will disturb the material, contact an accredited testing company in your region; look in the phone book under "Laboratories—Testing."

Keep in mind that even if your resilient floor covering was installed more recently, it may have been laid down on top of an older asbestos-containing flooring. As with lead, proper precautions must be taken if you plan to disturb any asbestos-containing materials.

In this renovated kitchen, the original Douglas fir subfloor was exposed, sanded lightly, and sealed. The builder took care not to disguise the old floor's character. The dark line in the center of the room marks where a wall once separated the small original kitchen from a laundry room.

LOSE THE SHOES

As much as two-thirds of the dust and dirt inside homes is tracked in on people's shoes. That dirt can contain a nasty mix of pesticides, road oil, combustion by-products from vehicles, bacteria, fungus, soil, and a host of other things I'd rather not mention. Two of the most effective ways of keeping your home pollution-free are to use doormats outside and inside all the exterior doors—including the kitchen door, if you have one—and to take off your shoes as soon as you come inside. A mudroom off the kitchen, if you have the space, is the perfect place to leave shoes. But even something as simple as a bench or stool just inside the door, and an attractive basket or box for storing shoes, can go a long way toward encouraging family members and visitors to slip off their shoes when coming inside.

For more information about asbestos hazards and abatement, visit the Web sites of the EPA (epa.gov/asbestos/ashome.html) or the American Lung Association (lungusa.org).

GREEN FLOORING MATERIALS

Virtually any building material you can dream up can be used for a finish floor—glass, metal, plastic, wood, leather, paper, fabric, rubber, concrete, stone, even earth. This chapter focuses on the kitchen-flooring materials that are most popular and that have eco-friendly attributes—wood, bamboo, laminate, linoleum, rubber, cork, concrete, tile, brick, stone, and terrazzo. But you needn't be limited by the choices described here. Want a painted plywood floor, for example? Go for it, but don't forget to look for ways to make it greener, such as choosing exterior-grade plywood that won't offgas urea formaldehyde and selecting less-polluting paint.

PROS AND CONS OF GREEN FLOORING MATERIALS

TYPE	PROS	CONS	GREEN TIPS
BAMBOO (p. 54)	Rapidly renewable resource High fiber yield per acre Requires little, if any, irrigation, pesticides, or fertilizers, according to suppliers Higher-quality products are hard and durable Solid bamboo flooring can be sanded and refinished multiple times	Many low-quality products on market Only grown in Asia; environmental and labor conditions a question Typically made with urea formaldehyde glues	Choose prefinished bamboo or use zero/low VOC or plant-based sealants Buy high-quality products Buy products with low or no formaldehyde emissions
BRICK (p. 67)	Salvaged or locally produced bricks may be available Can last generations Inert, healthful Easy to maintain Relatively low embodied energy compared to other building products	Hard surface: tough on knees and back and on dropped kitchenware Heavy; high energy costs to transport Uneven surface or grout lines may be tripping hazard for some people and may trap debris Quarrying activities damage habitats and scar landscapes	Choose locally made bricks Choose salvaged bricks Seal brick with a low or no VOC sealer
CONCRETE (p. 61)	For slab-on-grade construction, slab serves as finish floor, reducing material use Recycled fly ash can replace some portland cement content Compatible with under-floor radiant heating systems and passive solar design Long lasting Inert Easy to clean and maintain	Portland cement is energy intensive to manu-facture, contributing to global warming and air pollution Can crack Hard on the cook's knees and back and on dropped dishes Kitchen noises reverberate; particularly a problem in open-plan home Final color somewhat unpredictable Acid-based stains noxious when installed (inert when dry)	Use structural slab as finish flooring Use water-based, low or no VOC sealants Use high volume of fly ash Combine with passive solar design
CORK (p. 58)	Rapidly renewable Sound absorbent	Transported from Europe Cork granules may be bound with urea formaldehyde glue	Use low/no VOC adhesives and sealants, or plant-based sealants

TYPE	PROS	CONS	GREEN TIPS
CORK (continued)	Moisture, stain, and fire resistant Warm underfoot and easy on the back and on dropped dishes Long lasting Click-together floating floor product is good DIY option Can be installed with zero/low VOC adhesives Can be finished with water-based polyurethane or plant-based penetrating oil	Engineered plank floors may have urea formaldehyde glue in core layer Some products are actually vinyl laminates (vinyl top layer with cork underlayment) Not ideal for under-floor radiant heating systems Mild odor	Consider prefinished cork floors to protect indoor air quality Don't buy products with a vinyl wear layer
LINOLEUM (p. 56)	Made primarily from renewable resources Durable; long lasting (forty+ years) Antibacterial, antistatic Easy to maintain and keep clean Warm underfoot Many color choices Available in rolls, tiles, or tongue-and-groove panels Installed with low VOC adhesives	Offgasses VOCs Slight odor of linseed oil Made only in Europe Higher initial cost than other resilient flooring options, but life-cycle costs may be lower because it is long lasting	Install with low VOC adhesives Don't choose vinyl flooring (many people incorrectly use the word *linoleum* to refer to vinyl flooring)
STONE (p. 63)	Regionally quarried or salvaged stone often available Lasts for generations Inert, healthful Minimally processed	Hard surface: tough on knees and back and on dropped dishes Heavy; high energy costs to transport Quarrying activities damage habitats and scar landscapes Some stones prone to staining	Choose stone that is quarried and finished locally Choose salvaged stone Seal stone with a zero/low VOC sealer
TERRAZZO (p. 68)	Some products contain recycled content Durable, long lasting Easy to clean Poured-in-place floors have no seams to trap dirt	Expensive Some products made with epoxy resin matrix May be heavy; ensure adequate structural support Hard on back and joints and on dropped dishes	Choose products with high post-consumer recycled content For tile installation, avoid epoxy mortar or grout; epoxy gives off noxious fumes until cured

TYPE	PROS	CONS	GREEN TIPS
TILE—Ceramic, Porcelain and Glass (p. 65)	Ceramic and porcelain tile made from clay, a natural and abundant resource Some tiles include recycled content Durable; resists moisture and abrasion Low toxicity, inert Easy to clean if grout is sealed Provides thermal mass for passive solar design and under-floor heating systems Low VOC tile-setting adhesives available Locally or regionally manufactured tiles may be available Vast range of colors, textures, and patterns at every budget level Broken tiles can be chiseled out and replaced	Hard on back and joints and on dropped dishes Manufacturing ceramic and porcelain tile is energy intensive Some mortars and grouts contain additives that can offgas noxious chemicals Grout stains, traps dirt, and harbors mold; seal grout and use larger tiles that require fewer grout lines	Choose tiles with recycled content Choose locally or regionally manufactured tiles Use low or no VOC adhesives and sealants Choose products with lead-free glazes
WOOD— FSC-certified solid or engineered wood; reclaimed wood (p. 48)	FSC certification ensures harvesting from well-managed forests and plantations Solid wood can be sanded and refinished many times and can last a lifetime; engineered hardwood flooring can also be refinished, though not as many times May add value to home With engineered flooring, thin veneer conserves valuable hardwoods; sublayers made from fast-growing young trees Floating floors easy to install; good DIY option Wide range of milled, ready-to-install reclaimed flooring products available Some building-reuse centers carry old floorboards at discount prices (beware of labor required to install and refinish)	Certified products may be more expensive and less readily available than uncertified products Solid wood requires greater volume of high-quality wood than engineered products In engineered products, sublayers may contain urea formaldehyde binders Difficult for consumers to verify suppliers' claims about source of reclaimed wood; important to deal with reputable suppliers Reclaimed wood may cost more than new wood flooring if source is unusual, species is rare, or if added labor was required to reclaim wood	Buy FSC-certified or reclaimed wood floors Buy factory-finished products or use zero/low VOC sealants or plant-based penetrating oils Buy products that can be sanded and refinished many times Avoid engineered floors made with urea formaldehyde–based binders Avoid vinyl-based faux-wood laminates Avoid tropical or old-growth woods or woods from ecologically sensitive areas, unless FSC certified or reclaimed

Wood and Bamboo

You can't beat wood floors for their beauty, natural look, and good feel underfoot. There's a wood floor to complement every style of kitchen, whether it's blond maple in a contemporary townhouse, warm cherry in a suburban colonial, or hickory planks in a country farmhouse.

Wood floors are available to suit a wide range of budgets, although the greenest options—such as antique floorboards or FSC-certified products—generally cost more than the low-price products available from home-improvement centers and conventional flooring retailers. Be aware of potential hidden costs of some of the less-expensive options, such as urea formaldehyde glues that will offgas into your home, or environmental damage resulting from unsustainable or even illegal logging activities.

MAKE SURE IT'S FSC

Just because a company is FSC certified doesn't mean that all the products they sell are. Verify that the actual product you are buying is FSC certified, not just the company. For packaged products, check that the package has the FSC logo or certification code. Unpackaged products such as lumber may have an FSC logo stamped on one end. If the product doesn't bear the FSC mark, ask the retailer to show you the original invoice from the manufacturer; the product description should include an FSC code number.

If your budget is limited and you can't afford an FSC product or refinished antique planks, don't despair. Check under your existing floor covering: many owners of older homes are pleasantly surprised to find beautiful old fir or pine floorboards hidden beneath their existing kitchen floors. Assuming the wood isn't badly deteriorated, it can be sanded and finished. Also check local building-reuse centers; many sell bargain-price floorboards that were removed from deconstructed old homes, gymnasiums, and warehouses. Although the labor to refinish and install the old wood may be considerable, if you're a well-seasoned DIYer, it could be an economical option.

Wood floors tend to be more sound absorbent and comfortable underfoot than ceramic tile or concrete. Many wood flooring products can be used with under-floor heating systems, but always check with the supplier and installer to be sure. If wood floors have one Achilles heel in the kitchen, it's that they are susceptible to water damage, so wipe up any spills immediately.

Solid Wood

Solid hardwood flooring can last 100 years or more with relatively moderate maintenance. As the term implies, solid wood flooring is milled from whole pieces of wood. Products sold today are typically 3/4 inches thick, available in narrow strips (2 1/4 inches is a common size) as well as wide planks. Hardwood holds up well to wear and tear, and when the surface finish wears down, it can be re-coated, or sanded and refinished.

Solid wood flooring isn't recommended for installation below grade because it is subject to expansion and contraction as humidity levels rise and fall. A better option for kitchens that are below or partially below grade is a more dimensionally stable engineered flooring (see page 51). Solid wood flooring is either nailed or glued to the subfloor; unlike floating floors, installing solid wood flooring takes considerable skill and is best left to pros.

When shopping for solid wood flooring, always consider the origin of the wood. The U.S. flooring industry is one of the top users of imported tropical woods such as teak, ipé (also known as Brazilian walnut), jatoba (Brazilian cherry), mahogany, and more. Our hunger for gorgeous woods from the tropics has resulted in overharvesting and illegal logging in regions of the world where environmental regulations and enforcement are lax. Don't buy imported tropical wood flooring unless it is FSC certified, or unless it is reclaimed wood from a reputable retailer who can provide documentation of its origin. If you can't find suitable FSC or reclaimed wood flooring, choose a domestically grown species or a species harvested in a region where environmental regulations are reasonably well enforced, such as northern Europe.

While FSC certification gives you a high degree of certainty that the wood came from a well-managed source, there are other sustainably harvested sources of wood products, such as trees selectively harvested from forests to reduce the risk of wildfires, which are sometimes marketed as "suppressed" or "restoration" wood. Another option is trees removed from a property because of storm damage; these are sometimes referred to as storm-felled or selective-cut. Yet another option is urban trees cut down in developed areas because of age or hazards to properties; urban loggers who spare these trees from the chipper refer to the wood as "urban salvage" or "rescued wood."

Another very eco-friendly source of wood flooring is reclaimed wood from homes, warehouses, gymnasiums, and other

If it's true that imitation is the sincerest form of flattery, vinyl wins top honors for simulated style. You can find vinyl floor coverings that mimic just about every imaginable flooring surface—granite, marble, slate, terra-cotta, mosaic, ceramic tile, maple, cherry, genuine linoleum—all at a fraction of the cost of the real thing. Some of these vinyl products are remarkably realistic on first glance, but closer scrutiny usually reveals their true plastic nature.

Vinyl remains popular for kitchen floors because it's inexpensive and available in a mind-boggling array of colors, patterns, and styles. It's also easy to install, moisture and stain resistant, and relatively hard-wearing. It's hard to knock those traits.

Still, controversy rages about the environmental and health impacts of polyvinyl chloride, commonly known as vinyl, or PVC. The PVC industry stands behind the safety of its products, but there's heated debate in many circles about the potential hazards of vinyl from cradle to grave—in other words, from manufacturing to use to eventual disposal. The environmental group Greenpeace calls vinyl "the poison plastic," noting that "the production of PVC creates and releases one of the most toxic chemicals—dioxin" (greenpeace.org).

The Healthy Building Network (healthybuilding.net/pvc), one of the louder anti-PVC voices in the United States, claims that "PVC has contributed a significant portion of the world's burden of persistent toxic pollutants and endocrine-disrupting chemicals—including dioxin and phthalates—that are now universally present in the environment and the human population. When its entire life cycle is taken into account, it becomes apparent that this seemingly innocuous plastic is one of the most environmentally hazardous consumer materials produced."

However, even within the eco-building movement there's no unanimity about the dangers of PVC. A draft report by the U.S. Green Building Council, a nonprofit coalition working to advance environmentally responsible buildings, compared the health and environmental impacts of PVC-based building materials to PVC-free alternatives. Although the Council's final report had not yet been issued as of this writing, the draft report concluded that "the available evidence does not support a conclusion that PVC is consistently worse than alternative materials on a life-cycle environmental and health basis."

Some environmental and health advocates dispute the findings of the USGBC's draft report, and the debate continues. In the meantime, a number of major organizations have decided to play it safe and are moving toward eliminating PVC from their products or facilities. According to the Healthy Building Network, these companies include shoe and apparel makers Nike and Adidas, home furnishings giant Ikea, Apple Computer, Kaiser Permanente (the nation's largest health-maintenance organization), and toy maker Mattel.

In the face of uncertainty about the safety of PVC, I try to avoid bringing it into my home. This isn't always easy, because vinyl is ubiquitous in building materials and consumer products. Also, it's often hard to know if a product is made with vinyl, because few are labeled as such. Fortunately, in the case of kitchen flooring, there's a wide world of beautiful PVC-free alternatives.

EcoTimber offers flooring made from many types of FSC-certified wood, including the quartersawn red oak pictured here.

structures that have been torn down. Building-materials salvage yards often sell old floorboards that have been pried out intact from buildings. For salvage yards near you, check the phone book under "Salvage Merchandise"; "Building Materials—Architectural, Antique & Used"; "Lumber—Used"; and "Junk Dealers."

Also, many companies sell solid wood flooring that's been newly milled from large beams and posts taken out of old buildings. The wood is well aged and often of very fine quality. Find reclaimed wood specialists online by searching for "reclaimed wood floor" or "salvaged wood floor."

If you're considering buying solid wood flooring that is not FSC certified, the key is to deal with a reputable supplier who knows specifically where the wood came from and the conditions under which it was harvested or salvaged. Keep in mind that in the retail world the term *sustainable* is bandied around so much as to be virtually meaningless. Be skeptical of any claims unless they're backed up by the FSC logo.

Engineered Wood

Solid wood floors are beautiful, long lasting, and one of the most traditional of flooring materials in North America, where wood remains much more abundant than in other parts of the world. Solid wood flooring is a good green choice if it's from a reclaimed or FSC-certified source. But from a resource conservation standpoint, solid wood flooring is problematic because each board is a thick strip of top-quality wood, usually harvested from older, larger, more valuable trees. So even if the wood was sustainably harvested, you're using a lot of it when it's in the form of solid wood flooring.

If you're keen on protecting forests and older trees, a better choice is an engineered-wood floor that doesn't squander high-quality woods because it uses only thin hardwood veneers as the top wear layer. The veneer is glued to layers of plywood or pine in a cross-ply arrangement that provides greater stability than solid wood typically does. While the veneer may come from a large old tree, the underlayers are made from faster-growing, smaller-diameter trees and are manufactured very efficiently, with little of the tree going to waste.

Typically, engineered flooring comes in planks three to five inches wide with tongue-and-groove edges; the pieces are either edge glued during installation or, increasingly common these days, they click together without glue. Some engineered floors are designed to be nailed to a wood substrate or glued to concrete, but more commonly today they are fabricated as a floating floor that can be installed on top of a subfloor or even existing ceramic tile, concrete, or vinyl. No nailing or gluing is required. It's called a floating floor because it isn't attached to the subfloor or baseboards; the installer leaves a small gap at the perimeter of the rooms so that the floor floats freely and can expand and contract as all wood does. The floor is held in place by the weight of the wood and furniture. Engineered floors install quickly and relatively easily, and floating floors are an excellent option for skilled DIYers.

Wood tiles are another engineered-flooring option. These usually consist of thin strips of hardwood arranged in a pattern to mimic old-style parquet, and glued to a square of medium-density fiberboard. The tiles are then glued to the subfloor.

Depending on the thickness of the hardwood veneer, engineered-wood floors can be sanded and refinished two to three times. (When engineered floors first came on the market, the veneers were quite thin and difficult or impossible to sand; when shopping around, look for products with a thicker, sandable veneer.) Be aware that some products are made with adhesives that may offgas formaldehyde into your home. On the plus side, engineered floors usually come prefinished with a very durable factory-applied urethane topcoat that obviates the need for using noxious sealants in your home.

The greenest engineered-wood flooring products are those that are FSC certified and manufactured with zero or very low levels of urea formaldehyde–based glues. These products aren't readily available everywhere, although companies like EcoTimber are doing their part to make them available through local and Internet retailers (see the Resources list at the end of this section).

Do not buy an engineered floor made with tropical hardwoods or old-growth wood unless it is FSC certified. Be wary of retailers who market products as FSC when only the core is certified, not the hardwood top layer. Verify that the topmost layer is also FSC certified, especially if it is a tropical species.

Laminate

Don't confuse a solid wood or engineered-wood floor with a laminate floor. Laminates are made with a printed image of wood (or stone, terra-cotta, or any number of other materials) that is glued to a fiberboard substrate (ground-up wood particles bound with an adhesive). The material is topped with a plastic wear coat for protection, and fabricated into planks that click together. Laminates can readily be installed by pros and handy amateurs.

Laminate floors are inexpensive and hugely popular. But are they green? On the negative side, they're short lived compared to solid wood and engineered-wood floors because they can't be sanded and refinished. Their fiberboard cores are typically made with urea formaldehyde binders that can offgas into your home. They tend to be colder underfoot than natural wood, and can be noisier, although an acoustical underlayment can help dampen the hollow-footstep sound so characteristic of laminate floors.

On the plus side, a handful of laminate manufacturers have begun using FSC-certified fiberboard cores. There's vigorous competition among laminate flooring retailers, and an awful lot of greenwashing going on, so if a salesperson claims their laminate is FSC certified, ask to see the product packaging: if it's the real thing, there will be an FSC logo and certification code on the package.

My verdict? Personally, I'm not keen on laminates' faux style. In my view, a photographic reproduction of wood will never look, smell, or feel like the real thing. Aesthetics aside,

The dining room floor is salvaged red gum eucalyptus from local urban trees removed to control the risk of fire. The kitchen floor is cork.

most laminate floors are not green. But those with FSC certification and zero or very low urea formaldehyde emissions are reasonably easy on the environment. An even greener option, if your budget allows, is an engineered-wood product made with real wood veneer that will add beauty and value to your home for decades after a laminate has been relegated to the landfill.

FSC FLOORING COMPETES ON COST

Green doesn't have to cost more. FSC-certified solid wood flooring does tend to be pricier than its noncertified counterpart. But FSC-certified engineered-wood flooring is very cost-competitive with comparable quality noncertified engineered floors.

Seven Dos and Don'ts for Choosing an Eco-Friendly Wood Floor

1. Do reuse old floorboards or buy flooring milled from salvaged timbers.
2. Do buy FSC-certified engineered or solid wood flooring.
3. Don't buy tropical hardwoods unless FSC certified or reclaimed and sold by a reputable source.
4. Do buy flooring with a factory-applied finish; if you buy unfinished flooring, use a low VOC finish.
5. Do ask for engineered-wood flooring products with no or very low levels of urea formaldehyde glues (ask to see the MSDS or emissions testing results).
6. Don't take a salesperson's word that the wood is from a sustainably managed source. Ask to see the FSC label.
7. Don't confuse laminates (products topped with a photographic reproduction of wood or other materials) with solid wood or engineered-wood floors.

Wood Flooring Resources

FSC-certified wood flooring is becoming increasingly available from flooring distributors. Also, there are scores of suppliers of reclaimed wood floor in North America; search online under "salvaged wood flooring" or "reclaimed wood flooring." Here is a smattering of resources to get you started:

- **Big Timberworks**. Flooring, lumber, and other products made from reclaimed timbers. Gallatin Gateway, Montana, 406.763.4639, bttimberworks.com.
- **Building for Health Materials Center**. FSC-certified and reclaimed flooring. Carbondale, Colorado, 800.292.4838, buildingforhealth.com.
- **CitiLogs.** Flooring made from urban salvage trees. Pittstown, New Jersey, 877.CITY LOG, citilogs.com.
- **Eco Design Resources**. Distributor of EcoTimber and other eco-friendly flooring products. San Carlos, California, 650.591.1123, ecodesignresources.com.
- **Eco Friendly Flooring**. Reclaimed wood and other flooring products. Madison, Wisconsin, 866.250.3273, ecofriendlyflooring.com.
- **EcoTimber**. A leading wholesaler of FSC-certified and reclaimed wood flooring; their products are sold through distributors nationwide. San Rafael, California, 415.258.8454, ecotimber.com.
- **Environmental Building Supplies**. FSC-certified and reclaimed wood flooring. Portland, Oregon, 503.222.3881, ecohaus.com.
- **Environmental Home Center**. Solid wood floors from reclaimed, FSC-certified, and underutilized wood sources; they also offer FSC-certified engineered-wood flooring. Seattle, Washington, 800.281.9785, environmentalhomecenter.com.
- **Forest Stewardship Council (FSC)**. A nonprofit organization that sets standards to ensure that forestry is practiced in an environmentally responsible, socially beneficial, and economically viable way. Their Web site has a searchable database of FSC-certified products. Washington, D.C., 202.342.0413, fscus.org.
- **Goodwin Heart Pine Co.** Antique heart pine and cypress flooring from logs recovered from river bottoms. Micanopy, Florida, 800.336.3118, www.heartpine.com.
- **Green Fusion Design Center.** Distributor of EcoTimber and other brands of FSC-certified and reclaimed flooring. San Anselmo, California, 415.454.0174, greenfusiondesigncenter.com.
- **TerraMai.** Sells reclaimed flooring made from reclaimed tropical and domestic woods. McCloud, California, 800.220.9062, terramai.com.
- **Trestlewood**. Reclaimed wood flooring from railroad trestles and other sources. Blackfoot, Idaho, 208.785.1152, trestlewood.com.
- **The Woods Company.** Antique barn wood and heartwood flooring, Chambersburg, Pennsylvania, 888.548.7609, thewoodscompany.com.

Wood Floor Finishes

Wood floors, whether solid wood or engineered, need to be

sealed to protect them from moisture and the wear and tear of foot traffic. Most wood floors in the United States, whether they are factory finished or finished at the job site, are sealed with a barrier-type sealer such as urethane, acrylic, or a combination of the two. This coats the surface of the floor with a plastic film that is durable, relatively waterproof, and resistant to abrasion.

Selecting factory-finished floors that don't require any final finishing in your home may be the best option if you are concerned about floor-finishing fumes. Factory-applied sealants, which are applied in multiple coats and baked to a hard finish, typically last longer than sealants applied at home.

If the existing or new floor does need to be finished in your home, select either barrier sealants with low VOC content, or penetrating-oil sealers made from plant-based oils. Both of these options are discussed below.

Barrier Sealants. If the floors will be finished in your kitchen (as opposed to prefinished at the factory), request a low VOC water-based product. Avoid solvent-based finishes (also called oil-modified).

The U.S. national standard for VOC emissions from clear wood sealers is 400 grams per liter (gpl) and 680 gpl for lacquers; however, products are available with significantly lower VOC levels, such as Bona's Eon 70 (70 gpl) and AFM's Safecoat Polyureseal BP (114 gpl).

I have encountered a number of homeowners who let flooring installers talk them into using a solvent-based urethane on their wood floors, and later regretted it. Many installers prefer solvent-based finishes because they are highly durable; however, this argument isn't as valid as it once was because many of today's water-based finishes offer comparable durability. The powerful fumes of solvent-based finishes linger for as long as a week, and may take up to sixty days to fully cure. Installers applying solvent-based finishes typically require their clients, as well as pets and sometimes even plants, to stay out of the home during application and a day or two afterward. Some people with chemical sensitivities may be affected by the offgassing for much longer periods. Very young children may be particularly susceptible to ill effects from offgassing because they spend so much of their time down at floor level where the concentration of chemicals is highest.

Floors are one of the last things to be finished in a new or remodeled home, so chemicals offgassing from a solvent-based floor finish can readily be taken up by absorbent materials, including drywall, furniture, carpets, drapes, and bedding. These materials can act like sponges, soaking up the fumes and continuing to re-release the volatile chemicals long after the flooring installer has moved on to other projects.

Be particularly leery of acid-cured floor finishes, sometimes referred to as Swedish finishes. These products, used only by professional installers, provide a highly durable finish on the floor, but at the cost of very high VOC emissions. A 1999 study of formaldehyde levels in homes found exceedingly high levels of formaldehyde emissions from acid-cured floor finishes.

Penetrating Oils. Barrier sealants such as polyurethane are very durable but can make a beautiful, natural wood floor look like it has been encased in plastic.

Although penetrating-oil finishes aren't nearly as common as barrier sealants, they can produce a lustrous hard-wearing finish. Most of these products are made from linseed or tung oil. Instead of forming a plastic film on the surface of the wood, these oils penetrate into the wood, making it water resistant while maintaining the beauty and feel of real wood.

A major advantage of penetrating oil is that worn areas can be easily spot-repaired by rubbing on more oil. With conventional urethane/acrylic sealers, on the other hand, it's tough to get a good match with spot repairs; repairing a worn area often requires stripping and refinishing the entire room.

If you choose a plant-based oil finish, be aware that many products do emit a strong odor upon installation; some chemically sensitive people cannot tolerate the odor.

WHAT ABOUT TREE FARMS?

Are plantation-grown trees considered environmentally responsible? Some are, some aren't. Tree farming and logging practices vary from company to company and from country to country. The only way to know for sure that you are buying wood from well-managed plantations or forests is to make sure it's FSC certified.

Wood Finish Resources

+**AFM Safecoat.** Very low VOC finishes, 619.239.0321, afmsafecoat.com.

+**BioShield.** Linseed oil–based penetrating-oil finishes and hardwax products made from beeswax, linseed oil, and carnauba wax, 800.621.2591, bioshieldpaint.com.

- **Bona Eon 70.** Very low VOC urethane finish for professional use, 800.574.4674, www.bona.com.
- **Osmo Hardwax Oil.** A penetrating oil made from vegetable oils and waxes, available from environmentalhomecenter.com and other eco-products retailers.
- **Tried & True Wood Finishes.** Penetrating-oil finishes made from linseed oil, 607.387.9280, triedandtruewoodfinish.com.

Bamboo

Since its introduction to U.S. markets fifteen or so years ago, bamboo flooring has crossed over from the green-building ghetto into mainstream home design. And for good reason: it's beautiful, it holds up as well as hardwood, it's reasonably priced, and it's got some impressive eco credentials.

Although it looks and feels much like wood, bamboo is actually a giant grass—it's sometimes called timber bamboo—that can reach heights of 100 feet. More than a thousand varieties of bamboo exist, but few are suitable for flooring (the types used for flooring, by the way, aren't the same as the ones that pandas feed on). Harvesting bamboo doesn't kill it; the root system remains alive and the plant quickly regenerates and can be harvested again in three to five years. This speedy replenishment qualifies bamboo as a rapidly renewable resource, which are agricultural products that can be harvested on a ten-year or shorter cycle. Contrast this to many slow-growing hardwoods that can take twenty-five to fifty years to reach marketable quality for flooring. Another environmental plus, according to suppliers, is that bamboo needs little, if any, irrigation, pesticides, or fertilizers.

After harvesting, the hollow bamboo stalks are sliced into thin strips, pressed flat, dried, and laminated into solid boards. These boards are then milled into tongue-and-groove strip flooring or planks. The lamination process helps provide the finished flooring with good strength and dimensional stability. A typical dimension for bamboo strip flooring is 5/8 inches thick by 3 5/8 inches wide, with a length of three or six feet. Some suppliers also offer a six-inch-wide plank floor.

Bamboo flooring is installed just like hardwood, by either nailing or gluing it to the subfloor. In addition to solid bamboo flooring, many suppliers offer an engineered product made of a veneer of bamboo adhered to a core of pine, rubberwood, or other non-bamboo materials. Many engineered flooring products are installed as floating floors; the planks are glued together at their edges but not nailed or glued to the subfloor or the room's perimeter. From a resource-conservation perspective, solid bamboo is preferable to an engineered product because the bamboo grass is much more rapidly renewable than the pine that's typically used as the core in engineered products. (The reverse is true of hardwood flooring, where engineered-hardwood floors are more resource efficient than solid wood floors.)

Bamboo is generally available with two distinct grain patterns: horizontal (flat) grain, which shows the nodes or "knuckles" so characteristic of the plant; and vertical grain, a cleaner look created by gluing together multiple narrow strips. Some suppliers have also begun offering a third style called strand-woven bamboo, made from shredded bamboo strands that are glued together and processed into planks; since this product is quite new to the U.S. market, I'm not prepared to recommend it.

All wood and bamboo flooring expands and contracts in reaction to ambient moisture conditions. Vertical-grain bamboo, however, is more stable than horizontal-grain bamboo, making it more suitable for kitchens, which tend to be a high moisture environment. Both are available in a natural blond hue, or in a caramel color—called carbonized—achieved by steaming the bamboo before drying it. Bamboo does not take stain readily, so its color palette is generally limited to these two hues.

Bamboo flooring can be used anywhere you would install hardwood flooring. The hardness of high-quality natural bamboo flooring (the blond color) compares favorably to red oak, one of the most popular species used for hardwood floors in the United States. Bamboo's hardness gives it excellent durability, another good green quality. Be aware that carbonized bamboo (the caramel-colored product) is as much as 20 percent softer than natural bamboo, according to EcoTimber, one of the leading U.S. suppliers of bamboo and other ecologically responsible flooring products, so it may be less suitable to high-traffic areas such as kitchens.

As with wood flooring, bamboo products are available unfinished and prefinished. High-quality prefinished bamboo often has a UV-cured acrylic urethane finish, with aluminum oxide for added scratch resistance. Solid bamboo flooring can be sanded and refinished just like hardwood flooring; vertical-grain bamboo can reportedly withstand more sanding/refinishing cycles than can the flat grain. If the bamboo flooring is to be finished in your home rather than in the factory, ask the installer to use a low VOC sealant; check with the supplier for recommendations.

EcoTimber recommends sealing bamboo flooring in kitchens even if the original product is factory finished. This extra topcoat helps protect the floor from liquid spills, such as dogs that exuberantly slosh water out of their bowls.

As with hardwood, bamboo flooring can usually be used

Natural horizontal-grain bamboo.

Carbonized horizontal-grain bamboo.

Natural vertical-grain bamboo.

Carbonized vertical-grain bamboo.

Another drawback is chemical emissions. Most bamboo floors, both solid and engineered, are made with urea formaldehyde–based adhesives. Ask the retailer about formaldehyde emissions, and if you're particularly concerned about formaldehyde and VOC emissions, ask to see emissions test results from an accredited U.S. testing lab. Recently, some suppliers have begun experimenting with glues that don't contain formaldehyde. Consumer support for formaldehyde-free products may help accelerate this trend.

Most bamboo flooring comes from China or Vietnam, so if you prefer buying products that originate or are manufactured locally, you'll have to rule out bamboo. Also, there is little documented information available to consumers about the environmental conditions under which bamboo is harvested, or the labor, health, and safety conditions in the factories where it is processed. Until there is a credible, independent certification system for bamboo on par with FSC certification for sustainably harvested wood, I recommend only buying bamboo from reputable, well-established companies you can trust are providing you with accurate information.

That said, it's important to balance these drawbacks with bamboo's many advantages—including durability, longevity, rapid renewability, and not least of all, good looks. If you choose bamboo flooring for your kitchen, make sure you buy a quality product that will last a lifetime, and buy only from reputable retailers who answer your questions forthrightly and have documentation to back up their claims.

Bamboo Resources

There's an abundance of bamboo flooring suppliers in North America, including major home-improvement centers and

over radiant floor heating systems. It's critical, however, that you confirm this with the flooring supplier before purchasing, and that your installer be experienced with the special conditions imposed by under-floor heating.

What's Not to Like? With so many advantages, what's not to like about bamboo flooring? Its biggest drawback may be a direct result of its trendiness: in recent years, U.S. markets have been flooded with bamboo flooring products, some of which are of substandard quality. If you see an advertised price that's unbelievably low, remember the adage, "You get what you pay for." Seek out suppliers of high-quality products.

Unfortunately, low-quality products are giving bamboo flooring a bad rap. One of the misconceptions circulating is that bamboo is susceptible to excessive moisture-related movement. While this may be the case with the cheap stuff, top-quality products are properly kiln-dried down to 6 percent moisture content (compared to 9 to 10 percent in lesser-quality products) and properly sealed.

flooring discounters. Keep in mind that with bargain-basement prices, you may get what you pay for. Here is a sampling of bamboo-flooring suppliers; also check with local green-building supply companies and quality flooring retailers.

+ **Bamboo Hardwoods.** Seattle, Washington, 800.783.0557, bamboohardwoods.com.
+ **Bamboo Mountain.** San Leandro, California, 877.700.1772, bamboomountain.com.
+ **EcoTimber.** A wholesaler of FSC-certified and reclaimed wood flooring; also offers bamboo through its national network of authorized dealers. San Rafael, California, 415.258.8454, ecotimber.com.
+ **Smith & Fong.** One of the pioneers of bamboo flooring, plywood, paneling, and veneer in the United States; sold under the trade name Plyboo. South San Francisco, California, 866.835.9859, plyboo.com.
+ **Teragren.** Offers bamboo flooring panels and veneer. Bainbridge Island, Washington, 800.929.6333, teragren.com.

Resilient Floors

Linoleum

When people say linoleum, more often than not they're actually talking about vinyl. Genuine linoleum, which has been around since the late nineteenth century, has no vinyl in it. Its main ingredient is linseed oil; in fact, the word *linoleum* comes from the Latin *linum*, meaning flax (linseed is the seed of the flax plant), and *oleum*, meaning oil.

To make linoleum flooring, boiled linseed oil is mixed with renewable raw materials including powdered cork, finely ground sawdust, and pine resins. Mineral components include ground limestone, zinc (to hasten the oxidation of the linseed oil), and pigments. Under high heat and pressure the mixture solidifies and is formed into sheets. A burlap base is affixed to the back, and an acrylic finish applied to the top.

Today's linoleum comes in dozens of colors, from neutral to vibrant hues, in solids and marbleized patterns. Some manufacturers also offer patterned borders. It's primarily sold in sheets, for professional installation, or in tiles, which can be installed by pros or skilled amateurs. Some manufacturers also offer easy-to-install interlocking panels of linoleum glued to a substrate of high-density fiberboard (HDF) with a cork underlayment. These panels require no glue to install, making them a good option for DIYers.

In the early decades of the twentieth century, genuine linoleum was used in rooms throughout the house, but it faded from fashion after World War II as inexpensive vinyl flooring started making inroads in residential interiors. The advent of no-wax vinyl spelled the end of an era for the linoleum industry, since traditional linoleum required laborious and frequent waxing. By 1975, when the last U.S.-based manufacturer of linoleum shut down, vinyl had largely supplanted linoleum.

Fortunately, some linoleum manufacturers remained in business in Europe, continuing to supply commercial customers such as hospitals, which prize linoleum for its antibacterial properties. After years of being dismissed as hopelessly old-fashioned, linoleum is now back in style. Much of this renewed interest can be credited to the eco-building movement, which has touted genuine linoleum as a more environmentally responsible alternative to vinyl flooring.

Vinyl building products tend to raise the hackles of environmental and health professionals. While there are concerns about emissions of VOCs and phthalates from vinyl products, many experts have even graver concerns about toxins introduced into the environment when PVC is manufactured and ultimately disposed of. A number of major organizations, such as Kaiser Permanente, the largest nonprofit health-care organization in the United States, are actively exploring alternatives to using vinyl-based building materials in their facilities. While the vinyl industry stands behind the safety of its products, many environmental and consumer advocacy groups are campaigning to get the building industry to transition away from PVC and toward safer and more healthful building products.

Linoleum is generally considered to be a greener flooring material than vinyl, thanks to the primarily renewable raw materials used to make it. It's also very durable, biodegradable, and antibacterial, and the environmental impacts of manufacturing it are relatively benign.

But linoleum does have downsides. As the linseed oil in linoleum oxidizes over time, it offgasses VOCs, which accounts for the unique odor of linoleum—a smell that doesn't bother everyone but that some people find objectionable. VOC emission levels and odor do decrease significantly over time, but individuals who are chemically sensitive may not be able to tolerate linoleum in their homes.

The upside of this ongoing oxidization process is that it strengthens the linoleum over time, which contributes to the product's durability. Life spans of thirty or forty years or even longer can be expected if the floor is properly maintained. Linoleum also has antibacterial properties; it appears that the ongoing oxidation of the linseed oil kills bacteria or interferes with bacteria's ability to multiply on the surface.

Currently, all linoleum is made in Europe. For North Amer-

Today's natural linoleum floors can be traditional or bold, playful or serene—linoleum is a green material that can be customized.

ican consumers concerned about the transportation-related environmental impacts of products (depletion of fossil fuel reserves, air pollution, and global warming, to name a few), the distance linoleum is transported can be a negative. But linoleum is long-lasting, so the one-time transportation impacts are relatively insignificant when considered within the context of the product's lifetime. Still, if locally made materials are a priority for you, you may decide to cross linoleum off your list.

Installation. Linoleum manufacturers generally recommend professional installation. Linoleum sheets and tiles are glued to either the subfloor or an above-grade concrete slab using the manufacturer's recommended low VOC adhesive. If glued directly to the slab, it's crucial that the installer test the slab to make sure that moisture levels in the concrete are no higher than the manufacturer's specifications.

The subfloor must be even, smooth, and free of voids, because any imperfections will telegraph through the linoleum. Professional installers can create a nearly invisible seam using a heat-welding process.

Maintenance. Linoleum has antistatic properties, so it doesn't attract dirt and dust the way that some plastics do. However, it's important to sweep or vacuum a linoleum floor frequently to remove grit that can dull the finish. Dirt and spills can be damp-mopped.

New linoleum has a thin coat of factory-applied acrylic sealer. Typically, additional layers of this acrylic polish will be applied by the installer to provide protection against dirt, moisture, and wear. This polish needs to be reapplied once a year or so, depending on traffic in the kitchen, but it's an easy mop-on process.

Linoleum is a solid material with its color running all the way through to the backing, so minor scratches can be gently buffed out with a nylon cleaning pad.

Vintage Linoleum. If you're an aficionado of vintage linoleum, take a look at Jane Powell's book *Linoleum*. She provides an entertaining history of the material, along with advice for restoring worn or damaged old linoleum in your home. In spots where the pattern has

worn down, Powell notes that acrylic paint can be used to reproduce the original pattern. She recommends filling gouges in old linoleum with a mix of glue and shavings from a piece of linoleum taken up from somewhere unobtrusive,

Marmoleum, made by Forbo, is a leading brand of genuine linoleum.

such as underneath an appliance, and then, if necessary, touching up the filled-in spot with acrylic paint.

Powell notes that old "linoleum rarely contained asbestos, but the adhesives, and sometimes the felt underlayment, could contain asbestos." This is true of old vinyl flooring as well. If you plan to do remodeling work involving old vinyl or linoleum flooring, send it to an accredited lab to have it tested (see page 43).

Linoleum Resources

+**Marmoleum.** Linoleum sheets, tiles, and borders, and Marmoleum Click interlocking panels, made by Forbo, 866.MARMOLEUM, www.themarmoleumstore.com.

+**Marmorette.** Sheet linoleum from Armstrong, 800.233.3823, armstrong.com.

+**NovaLinoleum.** Interlocking planks of linoleum with an HDF core and cork underlayment, made in Switzerland, 866.576.2458, novafloorings.com.

Cork

Like genuine linoleum, cork is once again having its moment. With cork-flooring manufacturers now offering tiles and click-together planks in an appealing range of shades and patterns, cork is turning up—and turning heads—in all manner of homes.

Cork is an excellent choice for kitchen floors. It's fairly durable; in fact, some old churches and schools still have their original cork floors that have held up for fifty years or more. However, cork is susceptible to scratching, so it should be cleaned regularly to keep it free of grit, and it should be resealed periodically. Cork doesn't require any more maintenance than hardwood, and is naturally stain and moisture resistant, although you should never flood it with water or leave liquid standing on it. It also has good fire-resistant properties. The price of cork flooring varies greatly, depending on style and quality. In general, it's a mid-priced floor.

An inch of cork contains tens of millions of air-filled cells that provide thermal insulation, making cork feel warm underfoot. Those air-filled cells also provide acoustical insulation, resulting in a flooring surface that dampens sound transmission. In fact, cork is much better at deadening sound than wood or other resilient flooring materials, an especially important consideration for kitchens that are open to other living areas in the home.

Cork also provides a nice bit of cushioning for cooks who are on their feet for long stretches. This cushioning effect also means fewer broken plates and glasses. And because it's resilient, it springs back after being compressed, so it's less likely to dent if you drop a heavy pot on it.

In the kitchen, a cork floor provides an attractive and comfortable surface. See more of this kitchen on page 70.

Cork is naturally insulating, so it's not ideal for use over radiant floor heating; insulating materials such as cork and carpet slow the transfer of heat, hampering the performance of the heating system. If you want to use cork with a heated floor, choose thinner tiles rather than a thicker floating floor.

How and Where It's Made. From an environmental perspective, cork production is relatively benign. Cork is the dead outer bark of the cork oak—the species *Quercus suber*, a tree indigenous to the Mediterranean region. Virtually all cork sold in the United States comes from Portugal or Spain. Manually stripping off the thick outer bark doesn't harm the tree. The tree regenerates the bark, which can be harvested again in about ten years; this qualifies cork, in the world of green building, as a rapidly renewable resource. Many cork oaks have been continuously harvested for 150 years or more.

Cork flooring is made from the scrap left over after wine-bottle stoppers, cork's main commercial product, are drilled out of the bark that's been peeled from the tree. The remaining cork is ground, and the granules are bound with an adhesive

to form blocks that are then cut into tiles. Urea formaldehyde adhesives are commonly used; to reduce formaldehyde levels in your home, look for brands made with binders free of urea formaldehyde, such as polyurethane, phenol formaldehyde, or urea melamine.

Most cork flooring sold today comes in the form of glue-down tiles or tongue-and-groove engineered flooring. Lower-density cork is often used as a sound-absorbing underlayment beneath other finish-flooring products such as hardwood.

Some products are singleply, with the patterning going all the way through the tile; others are made with a decorative cork veneer laminated to a plainer cork base. Because the tiles are fairly thin and flexible, they will telegraph any imperfections in the subfloor. It's important to carefully prepare the subfloor so that you have a smooth even base on which to glue the tiles. Professional installation is recommended unless you're a highly skilled DIYer. Tiles should be installed above grade; below-grade installations are possible if the subfloor is within the range of the manufacturer's maximum-recommended moisture levels. For installation, use a low or zero VOC, water-based, solvent-free adhesive suitable for the type of subfloor over which the cork is being applied; check with the retailer or manufacturer for recommendations.

An easier DIY option is an engineered floating floor consisting of a cork top layer, a fiberboard core, and a cork cushion on the bottom. The material is fashioned into planks with tongue-and-groove edges. As with a wood floating floor, the planks are installed by gluing their edges together; they are not adhered to the subfloor or perimeter of the room (hence the term *floating floor*). Some newer products are even simpler to install—they snap tightly together, requiring no glue at their joints. Floating floors can be laid down over most types of existing floor, including a concrete slab. One potential drawback of engineered-cork floors is that the fiberboard core may off-gas formaldehyde even if the cork itself is free of urea formaldehyde binders.

Cork floors come in a spectrum of natural shades, from

In this renovated kitchen in a Victorian home, tongue-and-groove cork floorboards were used. They snap together and install easily without glue. Cork gives a bit underfoot, making it easier on a cook's back and knees. See more of this kitchen on page 145.

light tans to nearly black browns (a result of how long the cork has been baked). Granule sizes and patterns range from subdued to wild; these days, manufacturers are also getting creative with colorful pigments and blends of colored rubber and cork. If you're installing tiles, think about mixing and matching to create checkerboards, distinctive borders, or other unique effects.

Tiles and planks are available either prefinished or unfinished. Prefinished floors usually have an acrylic, polyurethane (oil- or water-based), or carnauba wax finish. Even with prefinished floors, you may wish to apply an additional sealant to help protect the floor from spills; check with the installer or retailer about appropriate low VOC sealants.

Avoid vinyl laminates that consist of a PVC top layer over a cork base; although these may be hard-wearing, questions linger about the health and environmental effects of vinyl production and disposal.

Unfinished tiles and planks are also available. If you plan to have the floor finished in your home, choose a solvent-free, water-based polyurethane or a plant-based penetrating-oil finish. Expect polyurethane finishes to last eight to ten years if properly maintained. After that time, the coating can be stripped and refinished. For a plant-based oil, Seattle's Environmental Home Center recommends Osmo Hardwax Oil. Unlike polyurethane finishes, penetrating-oil finishes allow for easy spot repairing of worn sections. Maintenance of cork floors is easy. Regularly vacuum, dust mop, or damp mop with a mild soap. Don't flood with water. With appropriate maintenance and refinishing, a cork floor can last fifty years or more.

What to Look for in a Cork Floor
+No urea formaldehyde added to cork or core
+Warranties of ten years or longer
+Zero or very low VOC adhesives and finishes
+No vinyl (PVC) wear layer
+High-density cork (34 pounds per cubic foot or greater) for the wear layer

Cork Resources
Cork is readily available from scores of green-building stores as well as home-improvement centers and flooring distributors. Here are a handful of resources to get you started.

+**Expanko.** Manufactures a wide variety of cork and rubber products, sold through dealers nationwide, 800.345.6202, expanko.com.

+**Globus Cork.** Offers bold colors, glue-down tiles, and floating floors with water-based, solvent-free finishes, 718.742.7264, corkfloor.com.

+**Natural Cork.** Offers tiles and floating floor planks, sold through dealers nationwide, 800.404.2675, naturalcork.com.

+**Nova Cork.** Swiss-made cork and linoleum flooring products, including a glueless floating floor, 866.576.2458, novafloorings.com.

+**WE Cork.** Tiles and planks sold nationally through dealers, 800.666.CORK, wecork.com.

+**Wicanders.** Portuguese manufacturer with international distribution, 410.553.6062, www.wicanders.com.

Rubber
Rubber is a warm, quiet, resilient floor covering that's mostly

used in industrial and commercial settings. Available as sheets or tiles, most rubber flooring is made from synthetic, non-renewable petrochemical-based ingredients; as such, I don't consider it a green flooring material. Natural rubber isn't common for flooring because it's less durable than the synthetic variety.

A number of companies now make recycled rubber flooring tiles and mats; these are an eco-friendly alternative to synthetic rubber, but many of these products are made from shredded tires and give off a strong odor that makes them inappropriate for residential interiors. They're better used outdoors or in commercial or recreational settings that have appropriate ventilation.

If you do choose a rubber floor for your kitchen, keep in mind that a textured surface will provide slip resistance but may also serve to trap grime and grease.

Hard Floors
Concrete

Not that many years ago, concrete floors were mostly seen in commercial buildings and renovated warehouse lofts. But today decorative concrete floors are cropping up in even the most traditional kitchens, thanks to the wide range of coloring and patterning techniques employed by concrete flooring specialists. For homes or additions built with slab-on-grade construction, exposed concrete is a practical and attractive choice for flooring.

Exposed concrete floors are a welcome addition to healthy homes because they're easy to keep clean and free of dust and other allergens—just sweep, vacuum, or damp-mop them. Once cured, concrete is inert, so it doesn't offgas VOCs or other indoor air pollutants. Another advantage is that concrete

In homes built with slab-on-grade construction, the structural slab can serve as the finish floor.

is durable; a skillfully finished concrete floor has the potential to outlast any other flooring material, and could conceivably outlast the house itself.

Concrete floors are cold underfoot, which can be a plus in hot climates. But in northerly climates, many people will find concrete uncomfortable unless used in conjunction with passive solar design, under-floor radiant heating, or strategically placed area rugs or natural-fiber mats.

Although concrete has the reputation of being a utilitarian material, a decorative concrete floor won't necessarily be cheap—there's considerable labor required to achieve a quality finish. An experienced artisan can transform concrete from a boring gray surface to a stunning work of art; some concrete finishers specialize in mimicking granite, marble, slate, or even leather at a substantially lower cost than the real thing.

A concrete floor isn't for everyone, especially in a room as visible and oft-used as the kitchen. Keep in mind that all concrete cracks. If you think of cracks as signs of character, it's a good bet that you'll be happy with a concrete floor. But if you see cracks as defects, don't choose concrete for your finish floor.

Also, if you want a floor that's perfectly monochromatic or if you want to be guaranteed certain color results, don't choose concrete. It's an inherent characteristic of concrete—and in fact part of its beauty—that stains and dyes aren't absorbed uniformly.

Keep in mind that concrete is hard—hard on the back and joints of a cook spending long hours on her feet, hard on toddlers when they stumble, hard on dishes and glasses when they're dropped. And concrete floors can be loud, which can be a particular problem for open-plan homes where the kitchen isn't separate from the main living and dining areas.

How Green Is Concrete? As with all the flooring materials described in this chapter, from a green point of view, concrete has its pluses and minuses. On the thumbs-up side, it's durable, strong, fire resistant, versatile, and made from raw materials that are abundant. The main component is aggregate—sand, gravel, or crushed rock, depending on the strength, weight, and other required characteristics of the particular application. Portland cement, a fine gray powder created by firing limestone, sand, and clay at temperatures of over 2,000 degrees Fahrenheit, binds the aggregate. Water is added to make the concrete mix workable.

Concrete production is hardly benign, however. Besides quarrying and transportation impacts, a major concern is the intense heat required to produce portland cement. The cement industry's high energy consumption, combined with the colossal quantity of cement produced worldwide, add up to significant emissions of carbon dioxide (CO_2) as well as nitrogen oxides, sulfur dioxide, carbon monoxide, and particulates.

Worldwide, in fact, cement production has been estimated to account for between 5 and 8 percent of all carbon dioxide emissions produced by human sources. As most reputable scientists have concluded, increasing levels of carbon dioxide in our atmosphere are contributing to global warming. *Environmental Building News*, one of the leading U.S. publications about green building, reports that "more than most other building materials, the manufacture of cement is contributing to global warming."

One way to reduce concrete's contribution to global warming is to substitute fly ash for some of the portland cement content. Fly ash is a waste by-product of power plants that generate electricity by burning coal. It's the fine residue removed from the flue gas by the power plant's pollution-control devices, and has traditionally been dumped in landfills. Substituting recycled fly ash for some of the portland cement in concrete puts a waste product to good use and reduces CO_2 emissions to the atmosphere. According to the American Coal Ash Association, each ton of fly ash used in concrete reduces CO_2 emissions by roughly one ton, the equivalent of about two months' emissions from a car. In the United States alone, thirteen million tons of carbon dioxide are avoided annually, thanks to the use of fly ash in concrete.

Other benefits of fly ash in concrete, in addition to avoiding landfill disposal, are reduced permeability of the concrete as well as increased strength and durability. While it is increasingly common for some concrete ready mixes to contain 15 or 20 percent fly ash (as a percentage of the portland cement content), many experienced engineers and contractors are using mixes with as much as 30 to 50 percent fly ash with superior results.

A high volume of fly ash may slow the concrete's curing time, so if you plan to use it, be sure to work with a contractor or supplier who is familiar with its properties. Fly ash concrete is typically priced the same as ordinary concrete without fly ash.

How Healthy Is Concrete? Once concrete has hardened, it's considered to be quite safe and inert. Be aware that admixtures are usually added to the concrete mix to give it desired qualities, such as providing resistance to freeze/thaw cycles, slowing down or speeding up curing time, reducing the amount of water required in the mixture, or making it more workable at colder temperatures. These chemicals are added in very small quantities, and wouldn't be expected to pose indoor-air-quality problems after the concrete has cured. But if you're concerned, ask your concrete contractor or supplier about which admixtures will be added to the concrete used for your floor, and ask to see the MSDSs for the products.

Technique. If you are building a new home or a kitchen addition with slab-on-grade construction, it's very practical to use the concrete slab as the finish floor. Your builder will have to take extra care to protect the slab during construction, because any drops of oil or other stains, scratches, or dents will affect the appearance of the final floor.

If you are remodeling an existing kitchen that's built on a slab, you may be able to expose the existing slab and add a two- to three-inch concrete topping slab for the finish floor. In typical single-family homes, it used to be rare to see exposed concrete on floors above the ground level because concrete is heavy. But these days, some concrete specialists will install thin concrete finish floors even on upper floors, on top of existing wood subfloors, if there is adequate structural support.

Some homeowners with solid DIY skills undertake concrete floor finishing themselves, but when dealing with high-visibility areas like the kitchen, most people choose to hire an experienced concrete floor finisher. Mistakes made during the final finishing process may be difficult or impossible to reverse, so you may rest easier leaving the job in the hands of professionals.

Colors. For an industrial look, concrete can be left in its natural gray state, with a clear finish added to make the porous concrete moisture-resistant. More often than not, though, decorative concrete floors are colored and may also be imprinted with patterns or textures.

When pouring new concrete floors, pigments can be either integral to the wet concrete or applied to its surface. Integral color provides a more predictable and uniform end result, but raises the cost of the concrete.

A popular option for both new and existing concrete is to stain the concrete after it hardens; acid stains are most common, though water- or oil-based stains are also available.

Acid staining, also known as acid etching, is used to create a variegated, marbleized, or weathered-looking surface. A diluted hydrochloric acid solution combined with metallic salts is applied to the cured, unsealed concrete. The acid and salts react with the limestone in the cement, penetrating the surface and creating permanent coloration. It provides a more durable finish color than surface-applied water- or oil-based stains. Colors possible with acid staining are mostly darker earth tones, including browns, coppers, ambers, and blue-greens. The process often involves multiple separate applications, sometimes with different colors.

The finished effects of acid staining can be subtle or dramatic, and each floor is unique. You can't predict exactly how the floor will turn out, so it's important to find an experienced installer whom you trust. During application, the fumes from the hydrochloric acid solution are noxious and the acid itself is caustic so installers must use proper ventilation and safety techniques. Another concern is the metallic salt pigments. Fu-Tung Cheng, a designer who creates stunning countertops and other finishes with concrete, notes in his book *Concrete at Home*, "Acid stains contain heavy metals, which are extremely toxic. Clean up with a wet-dry vac and dispose of residue at your local hazardous waste facility. Do not wash out into the soil."

Other ways to introduce color include sprinkling powdered dye on freshly poured concrete and troweling it in, or applying a pigmented sealer. The best option depends on the type of effect you are trying to achieve. Ask to see your installer's portfolio of finished floors, and explore the options with him or her (remember, though, that no two concrete floors are alike).

Sealers. Concrete is porous, so the floor should always be sealed. To reduce indoor air pollution, choose water-based, solvent-free sealants or plant-based oil sealers such as linseed oil products. Many concrete flooring installers use solvent-based sealers because they're very durable, but they offgas high levels of VOCs; some people who are chemically sensitive cannot tolerate them.

Wax is yet another option for sealing concrete, but it is less durable and will require more frequent refinishing than a water-based sealer. Wax finishes are probably better in locations that get less foot traffic than the kitchen.

Patterns. Concrete can be stamped to create a variety of unique patterns and textures or to mimic the look of ceramic tile, slate, brick, or other surfaces. The stamps are often plastic mats with handles on the back; the installer positions the stamp on the wet concrete and presses down with a tamping tool.

Another patterning technique involves using a circular saw with a masonry blade to score shallow lines in the hardened concrete surface. Any number of pleasing patterns can be created, from simple squares and diamonds to complex geometric patterns or curving shapes. Some homeowners choose to have a patterned border scored around the perimeter of the room while leaving the center of the room unscored.

When pouring a new concrete finish floor, installers and homeowners often get creative with inlaid strips of wood or metal, scatterings of pebbles or colorful glass cullet, or inserts of found objects or trinkets. Stamping, scoring, and other decorative finishes will add to the cost of the floor because of the labor involved.

Concrete Resources

Exposed concrete floors are custom works of art created in your home. Ask for referrals to experienced concrete floor finishers; interior designers and design centers are good sources for referrals. When interviewing installers, ask to see their portfolios and follow up on references. Here are two green products for use when finishing concrete floors. For more concrete resources, see page 102.

+**AFM Safecoat.** Makes low-odor, water-based sealers free of formaldehyde preservatives, suitable for interior concrete surfaces as well as tile, brick, and stone, 619.239.0321, afmsafecoat.com.

+**American Specialty Glass.** Makes finely ground glass powder from recycled pre- and post-consumer glass that can be used as a permanent coloring and texturing agent for decorative concrete floors. They also sell smooth glass chips for use in terrazzo counters and floors and for decorative landscaping, 801.294.4222, americanspecialtyglass.com.

Natural Stone

Quarried stone has been used for flooring since ancient times. Although these days many manufactured materials, such as ceramic tile and stamped concrete, are designed to imitate stone, nothing can match the luxury of a natural stone floor.

Natural stone flooring can be expensive, so it's not for every kitchen. However, the relatively high cost is offset by its durability: natural stone ages well, and it's reasonable to expect it to last a lifetime.

Stone is heavy, requiring adequate structural support and a strong subfloor such as a concrete slab or a suspended concrete subfloor. If you intend to install stone on a suspended wood subfloor, get professional advice to ensure the subfloor can take the weight. In addition, if the stone isn't installed on a concrete slab, usually a cement backerboard will be required to provide a rigid surface.

Stone is a good choice for high-traffic areas like the kitchen, although as with concrete and ceramic tile, comfort is an issue. stone is unforgiving on people's joints and on dropped dishes, it reflects rather than absorbs sounds, and it is cool underfoot. Be sure to choose tiles intended for flooring, since wall tiles may be too slippery, especially when wet.

Stone can be an excellent material for storing heat if it's used as part of a passive solar design. If you want your stone floor to provide thermal mass for solar heat gain, choose darker colors—they absorb heat better than lighter colors. Stone is cold, so consider installing it over an under-floor radiant heating system, especially if it is not part of a passive solar design.

From a healthy home perspective, stone is generally considered to be inert. The primary indoor-air-quality concern is the adhesives used to install the tiles. See the section on ceramic tiles for information about healthier tile installation.

Marble, granite, slate, and limestone are the most common stones used for interior floors. Marble is elegant, beautifully veined, and available in many colors. It's durable, but it can scratch. Also, it must be sealed to protect it from water and stains; be aware that acidic foods and beverages can etch the marble even if it is sealed. Because of those drawbacks and the high cost, it's rare to see marble used on kitchen floors.

Granite is well suited to high traffic; it's waterproof, re-

A limestone floor complements the FSC-certified cherry cabinets.

sistant to scratching, and requires no special maintenance besides vacuuming or damp-mopping. It's not necessary to seal a granite floor, although some people apply sealant to add luster. Keep in mind that granite's random vein patterns, which might look stunning on a single tile in the stone distributor's showroom or on a countertop slab, could be overwhelming when covering a large surface area such as a kitchen floor.

Less expensive than marble or granite, slate is a superb kitchen flooring material. It's quarried in many Eastern states, including Vermont and Virginia, and can be found in a range of colors, from black to dark gray, bluish green, beige, red, rust, and even purple. Some slate has beautiful variegations, while other slate is quite uniform in color. Slate is durable, and naturally water resistant, so it doesn't require sealing. However, some people choose to seal and wax it to protect it from scuffs and provide luster. In either case, the grout should always be sealed to protect it from stains and mold growth.

Limestone, sandstone, and travertine are also beautiful, if expensive, options for kitchen floors. The stones are porous, so require sealing; if the tiles themselves are very smooth, be sure to apply a nonslip finish. These stones tend to be quite heavy, so are typically installed over a concrete slab rather than a suspended wood floor, and are adhered with a traditional thickset mortar rather than a thinset product.

How Green Is Stone Flooring? Stone is a natural material but not a renewable resource. While the planet is hardly in danger of running out of stone, some types of stone have become difficult or impossible to obtain because of high demand from the building industry. And some highly sought-after stones are found only in very remote or mountainous places, and are extracted and brought to market with great effort and cost to the environment. Stone is heavy and bulky, so transportation-related energy costs are high for stone that is transported from overseas or across continents. And quarrying activities can have detrimental environmental impacts, including damaging habitats and scarring the landscape.

But these drawbacks need to be balanced against stone's durability and long life. Marble, granite, slate, limestone, and other stone flooring material can last for generations, never needing replacement and adding considerable beauty and value to the home.

If a house undergoes a gut remodel or is to be entirely torn down, in theory the stone flooring is reusable. In practice, however, it may be difficult to chisel out stone flooring tiles without fracturing them. Still, if it's a quality material, talk with a building salvage outfit about the possibility of salvaging the stone instead of relegating it to a landfill.

From an eco point of view, it's best to use locally or regionally quarried stone rather than stone that has been imported from another country, because of the transportation-related impacts on the environment. (The U.S. Green Building Council's LEED Green Building Rating System defines regional materials as those that have been extracted, harvested, or recovered, as well as manufactured, within 500 miles of the project site.) If a suitable stone isn't available locally or regionally, try to choose a domestically quarried and processed stone.

Salvaged stone is a great green choice. Salvaged slate roof tiles, with their lustrous patina of age, have long been sought after for kitchen floors and counters. For salvaged or scrap stone, check with building salvage yards, deconstruction sales, monument shops, and even local quarries. For remnants or off-cuts, check with local fabricators.

Maintenance. In general, stone flooring is easy to keep clean and maintain. Stone floor tiles are often installed with minimal grout lines compared to ceramic tiles, so dirt trapped in the grout is less of a concern. Porous stone should be sealed for protection against moisture and dirt. Check with the installer about how often the sealant may need to be reapplied. To avoid polluting the air in your home, use a zero or low VOC water-based sealant, not a solvent-based product.

Damaged tiles can often be repaired by chiseling them out and laying in a new tile. When installing a stone floor, save extra tiles for future repairs.

Ceramic and Glass Tile

Ceramic tile is made primarily of clay, an abundant, although finite, natural resource. Producing ceramic tile is energy intensive because of the high temperatures at which the molded clay is dried and fired in a kiln. On the whole, however, tile production has a relatively low environmental impact.

Most ceramic tile used for residential interior floors is supplied glazed. The glaze provides a hard-wearing surface and makes installation easier because you don't need to seal the tile, although you still should seal the grout. Glazed tile tends to be more water resistant than unglazed tile, but can be slippery when wet; for safety's sake, choose a tile with a nonslip surface, or choose smaller tiles so that you'll have more grout lines to provide slip resistance.

Porcelain tile, a type of ceramic tile made from white clay, is extremely dense and strong, with water absorption of less than 0.5 percent. Many porcelain tiles have the same color throughout the tile, which is known as through-body color. Some porcelain tiles are designed to look like marble, and because of their water resistance and durability, are a better option for the kitchen than marble.

Mosaic tile floors can be stunning, although small intricate patterns over a large surface area can be overwhelming. In the past, each mosaic tile would be painstakingly laid by hand. These days, small mosaic tiles, called tesserae, are typically supplied already adhered to a backing, which is then glued to the floor and grouted. Mosaics tend to be less durable than larger ceramic tiles, so aren't ideal for kitchens, but they can make a stunning statement when used as accents or trim.

Glass tiles, which can be translucent, semitranslucent, or iridescent, are impervious to water. A few companies make beautiful glass tiles from recycled glass. On the budget spectrum, glass tile, whether made from recycled or virgin glass, runs toward the high end. Many glass tiles are too slippery to be appropriate for flooring; if you intend to use it on your kitchen floor, check with the supplier to make sure the tile is appropriately slip resistant. Glass tiles can scratch, so you'll need to be vigilant about keeping them free of grit.

Ceramic and glass tile are low-toxic and inert, although the adhesives, grout, sealants, and caulking applied during installation may emit VOCs until they have fully cured. Use zero or low VOC thinsets, grout, and sealants.

Before the 1970s, lead was a common additive to ceramic tile glazes, and today, it's possible to occasionally encounter imported tile with lead-based glazes. If you are considering purchasing an imported glazed tile, confirm with the supplier that the product is lead-free; if you have doubts, ask to test a sample. Low-cost lead-testing swabs are available from home-improvement stores; testing by an accredited testing lab will cost more but provides more reliable results. Also, during home-remodeling projects, before cutting into or demolishing any ceramic tile that predates the 1970s, consider testing for lead. For more information about lead and other hazards in home-building materials, see page 43.

Ceramic tile is an excellent choice for kitchen floors. It's available in an enormous range of colors, patterns, shapes, and styles, so there's a suitable tile for just about every kitchen design. It's water resistant (assuming the tile is glazed or sealed and the grout is sealed), abrasion resistant, strong, and long lasting. Be sure you choose tiles specifically fabricated for floors, not walls or counters, and choose a tile rated for moderate to heavy foot traffic in residential interiors. Tile can be brittle, and

must be installed with care on a well-prepared substrate to prevent cracking.

Ceramic tile's high thermal mass means it will store the sun's heat, helping moderate temperatures inside the home when installed as part of a passive solar design. Darker tile will absorb the sun's heat more readily than light-colored tile.

Like other hard-surface flooring, tile can be uncomfortable if you're on your feet for long stretches, and is unforgiving on dropped dishes. Ceramic tile can feel cool underfoot unless installed over an under-floor heating system. Terra-cotta tile is a bit warmer to the touch than ceramic, but it is porous and requires regular sealing and waxing to protect it from moisture.

Tile ranges in price from moderate to very high end. If you fall in love with a brilliant glass tile or hand-painted ceramic tile that's out of your price range, consider using it sparingly for accents or trim, with a more economical tile used for the main areas of the flooring. Always factor in installation costs, because laying tile is a labor-intensive process.

Eco-Friendly Options. From an eco perspective, tile is an excellent choice—it's made from abundant raw materials, the environmental impacts of manufacturing are relatively low, and it's an inert and long-lasting flooring product.

To ratchet up the green factor, consider using tile made with recycled content. Some of these are expensive, so consider using them for accents if your budget precludes buying enough to cover your whole floor.

Another eco-friendly strategy is giving preference to tiles that are made in your local area or within a 500-mile radius of where you live.

Yet another green—and budget-friendly—option is reclaimed or surplus tile, which can often be found at salvage yards. If you come across a box of salvaged tiles that you love but there aren't enough to cover your whole kitchen floor, consider using them as accents, or mix and match them with another complementary style. When buying salvaged tile, consider using a lead-testing swab, available from home-improvement stores, to test for the presence of lead in the glazing.

Installation and Maintenance. Tile installation is a tricky process; it's doable by skilled DIYers, but if you're a novice at tile laying, consider tackling a small area such as a backsplash or small tabletop before taking on a kitchen floor.

Tile can be installed over a concrete slab or over a suspended-wood subfloor (assuming there's adequate structural support to bear the weight of the tiles). If installing over a wood subfloor, a cement backerboard must first be put down to provide a rigid and even surface. Tile is usually laid with a thinset mortar. To protect indoor air quality, avoid epoxy thinset mortars; epoxies give off nasty fumes. Use water, acrylic, or latex-based thinset mortars instead. Do not install tile over particleboard or interior-grade plywood.

Choose glazed or factory-sealed tile so that you don't have to apply sealer chemicals in your home. Many tile sealers are high in solvents and will give off noxious fumes; if you do need to seal tiles in your home, use a low or no VOC product. Depending on foot traffic, the sealant may need to be reapplied every year or so.

Terra-cotta tiles are fired at much lower temperatures than ceramic tiles, and are typically unsealed, so they can be quite porous. It's important to properly seal these tiles in a room like the kitchen where they'll be subject to spills.

Many grout products contain additives or epoxy that can continue to offgas until the grout has cured. If you're chemically sensitive, seek out additive-free grout. Grout lines in the kitchen should always be sealed to make them moisture resistant, prevent mold growth, and make the floor easier to clean. To further waterproof the kitchen floor, gaps between the tiles and walls and base of cabinets and other fixtures must be sealed with caulk.

Always keep some extra tiles on hand in case you ever need to replace cracked tiles.

If you already have tile floor in your kitchen, consider reusing it, because if you tear it out, the only practical disposal option is to send it to a landfill. If some tiles are chipped or cracked, consider chiseling out the tiles and replacing them with a complementary or contrasting tile, if an exact match can't be found.

Tile is easy to keep clean by regularly vacuuming or damp-mopping.

Tile Resources

Flooring tiles are widely available from home-improvement centers and tile distributors nationwide. Look for salvaged tiles at building-materials salvage yards. Here are a few companies that make tile with recycled content.

‣**Crossville, Inc.** Manufacturer of Eco-Cycle, Eco-Cycle Stone, and GeoStone Eco-Cycle. Makes ceramic tiles made with 50 to 100 percent unfired raw materials reclaimed from Crossville's standard porcelain tile manufacturing process. Crossville, Tennessee, 931.484.2110, crossvilleinc.com.

‣**Fire Clay Tile, Inc.** Their Debris series of handcrafted ceramic floor and wall tiles is made with 50 percent pre- and post-consumer recycled waste, including granite dust, recycled brown and green glass bottles, and windowpanes. San Jose, California, 408.275.1182, fireclaytile.com.

‣**Oceanside Glasstile.** Hand-cast, semitransparent glass tiles containing up to 85 percent recycled glass. Carlsbad, California, 760.929.4000, glasstile.com.

‣**Terra Green Ceramics.** Makes ceramic tiles containing 58 percent recycled glass. Richmond, Indiana, 765.935.4760, terragreenceramics.com.

Brick

Sleek materials like polished-granite counters and stainless-steel appliances remain hot choices for the kitchen. So it's not surprising that humble brick doesn't have the reputation as a chic flooring material. But in the right home, a brick floor can make for an uncommonly attractive, warm kitchen. While it's a very traditional flooring material, brick is versatile enough to be used to stunning effect in the most contemporary of kitchens.

Brick is a green and healthful material. Used for thousands of years for both structural and nonstructural purposes, it's produced from abundant, inexpensive raw materials—primarily clay and shale. From an eco point of view, its main drawback is the intense temperature at which it is fired—about 2,000 degrees Fahrenheit. (In regions where fuel was scarce, sun-baked bricks, or adobe, were traditional building materials, but on a commercial-production scale, hand-forming and sun-baking bricks isn't practical.) Brick's high initial energy use is offset by the material's long life cycle. Brick can take the abuse that a kitchen dishes out: bricks intended for flooring (called pavers) are hard wearing, resistant to abrasion, and very long lasting, although less durable than natural stone or ceramic tile. (Standard construction bricks will erode more quickly than pavers.) Another advantage to brick is that it is inert, with no VOC offgassing to contaminate your home. Some people tile their entire kitchen floor with brick, while others place it only in areas subject to heavy abuse, such as a mudroom or the area just inside an exterior door. Brick is warmer underfoot than natural stone or glazed ceramic tile.

Brick has high thermal mass, making it an ideal floor covering for passive solar homes. If your kitchen is designed for passive solar heating, be sure not to cover the brick with area rugs or other insulating materials that will hinder the brick's ability to absorb the sun's heat.

Brick comes in a range of colors, and an endless array of patterns are possible, including herringbone, basketweave, and various types of running bonds. Bricks used for interior floors are ideally laid on a concrete slab, either in a bed of mortar or directly on the slab without mortar. Installation on a wooden subfloor isn't advised unless there is adequate support for the bricks' weight. Brick pavers manufactured specifically for flooring are thinner than standard building bricks, but still require adequate support. In mortarless installations, the bricks are laid very close together, with fine sand or a dry mortar mix filling the slight gaps between the units.

Brick floors, whether mortared or mortarless, are typically finished with a masonry sealer to provide luster, lock in any loose granules of sand, create a moisture-resistant surface, and make cleaning easier. Avoid solvent-based sealers; low or no VOC water-based sealers specifically designed for interior masonry materials are readily available. Sealed brick floors are easily maintained by vacuuming and occasional damp mopping. As with all sealed floor surfaces, the sealant will need to be reapplied periodically, perhaps as often as once a year if traffic is heavy.

Buy locally or regionally produced brick whenever possible to reduce transportation-related energy impacts. Fortunately, this shouldn't be hard to do since brick is produced worldwide and in three-quarters of the states in the U.S. Shipping averages no more than 175 miles, according to the Brick Industry Association.

An even greener option is to pave your floor with salvaged brick. Brick reclaimed from old buildings usually isn't appropriate for structural purposes but can make a superb flooring material; older bricks with their veneer of age can lend rustic charm or an industrial edge, depending on the style of your kitchen. By the way, most reclaimed bricks found in salvage yards come from buildings that are fifty or more years old; that's because the tough portland cement–based mortar used with newer bricks makes it next to impossible to salvage them.

Brick Resources

For salvaged bricks, check with local building-materials salvage yards.

+**Brick Floor Tile, Inc.** Offers Old Chicago Flooring, made of bricks salvaged from buildings in Chicago and sliced into half-inch tile. Iowa City, Iowa, 319.631.3984, brick-floor-tile.com.

Terrazzo

Terrazzo is a sophisticated material used for floors, countertops, and other surfaces. A traditional flooring material for hundreds of years, terrazzo consists of small chips of marble or other stone mixed into a matrix of concrete. Used indoors and out, terrazzo is typically installed on-site as a seamless floor; the material is poured in place, and then ground and polished smooth. Some companies also sell terrazzo products as ready-to-install tile. The surface may be matte or polished to a high sheen.

Many people are more familiar with terrazzo in commercial buildings than in homes, but it makes for a superb—although expensive—kitchen floor. Its streamlined look is especially well suited to modern interiors. It is scratch resistant, strong, long lasting, waterproof, and easy to keep clean. One drawback, which applies to all hard-surface floors, is that, obviously, it's hard. That's something to keep in mind if you're on your feet in the kitchen for hours on end. It's also cold underfoot, so consider using it with under-floor heating.

A number of conservation-minded companies now make a terrazzo-like product using recycled glass as the aggregate instead of virgin stone. The glass, which shimmers like little gems, comes from discarded beverage bottles, building and auto windows, mirrors, and other pre- and post-consumer recycled sources.

The recycling of glass waste continues to be a challenge for our society; in 2003, Americans generated 12.5 million tons of glass waste, of which only about 22 percent was recycled. That's much lower than the recycling rates of many other materials: 44 percent of aluminum beer and soft drink cans, 60 percent of steel cans, and a whopping 82 percent of newspapers are recycled.

Clearly, with only 22 percent of all glass waste recycled, there's room for much more recycled glass to be used to manufacture new products. Companies making recycled-glass terrazzo are stepping up to the plate to help close the recycling loop.

Recycled glass terrazzo floors are quite expensive; if you love the look but don't have the budget, consider using a small amount of it in a high-visibility area where you'll get a big bang for your buck, such as a bar or island countertop. (See chapter four for more information on terrazzo counters.)

When glass is used as an aggregate in concrete, a chemical reaction between the silica in the glass and the alkali in the cement can weaken the concrete. For this reason, some companies use an epoxy resin as the matrix for the glass, or they coat the glass chips with epoxy before mixing them in the concrete. Other companies have found ways to make glass terrazzo products without epoxy. While epoxies are generally considered to be inert once hardened, they can be hazardous to use.

Terrazzo Resources
◦**EnviroGLAS Products Inc.** Makes poured-in-place flooring and tiles of recycled glass in a matrix of epoxy resin. Also sells recycled glass aggregate. Plano, Texas, 888.523.7894, enviroglasproducts.com.

◦**IceStone.** Makes terrazzo product with 75 percent recycled glass in a cement matrix for countertops, floors, and wall surfaces. Brooklyn, New York, 718.624.4900, icestone. biz.

◦**Wausau Terrazzo Tile.** Cementitious tile with recycled glass. Wausau, Wisconsin, 800.388.8728, wausautile.com.

SUBFLOORS AND UNDERLAYMENT

The subfloor is a structural component that's designed to bear loads and provide a base for the finish floor. Subfloors are usually either concrete or wood. Wood subfloors typically consist of plywood, oriented strand board (OSB), boards, or another structural sheathing material laid over the floor joists.

If your remodeling or building plans call for installing a new subfloor in the kitchen, try to avoid materials that will off-gas urea formaldehyde, such as interior-grade plywood. A better option is exterior-rated plywood, which is made using phenol formaldehyde binders that emit formaldehyde at a fraction of the level of interior-grade plywood. Or use a product with no added formaldehyde, such as an OSB made with methyl diisocyanate (MDI), a polyurethane binder.

Whenever possible, buy wood subfloor products with the FSC certification. If you can't get FSC-certified products, consider OSB rather than plywood where feasible. OSB is made from small-diameter, fast-growing trees so using it reduces market demand for large-diameter, old-growth trees.

If installing a new concrete slab, ask your builder or concrete supplier to include recycled fly ash in the mix (see page 62).

Some finish floors are installed directly on the subfloor, whereas others may need to be installed on an underlayment material. Underlayment is used to provide a smoother, more even surface between the subfloor and finish floor, or to provide acoustical insulation. Lauan plywood is one of the most commonly used materials for underlayment because it is smooth, hard, lightweight, and moisture resistant. Unfortunately, lauan is a tropical

hardwood from Southeast Asia that's being unsustainably harvested. Avoid lauan products unless they are FSC certified. Ask your floor-covering supplier for alternatives to lauan plywood.

Subfloor Resources
Cork
◦Cork underlayment products are readily available from flooring distributors and building-supply companies. Cork underlayment typically has a lower density than cork-finish flooring.

Recycled Fiber
◦**Homasote Company.** Makes underlayment and structural subfloor products from recycled paper. Available from building-supply stores nationwide. 800.257.9491, homasote.com.

◦**USG Corp.** Makes Fiberock Aqua-Tough Underlayment, made with no adhesives, resins, or solvents (unlike wood-based underlayment); contains primarily pre-consumer recycled gypsum, with about 10 percent recycled paper. Available from building-supply stores nationwide. 800.874.4968, usg.com.

Wood
◦**J. M. Huber Wood Products.** Makes AdvanTech, an OSB made with MDI and phenol-formaldehyde resin (contains no urea formaldehyde). Available from distributors nationwide. 800.933.9220, huberwood.com.

◦**ROM.** Makes an FSC-certified pine plywood. Also makes an FSC-certified OSB called Tuff-Strand; the hardwood strands and wafers are blended with phenolic resins. 800.299.5174, martco.com.

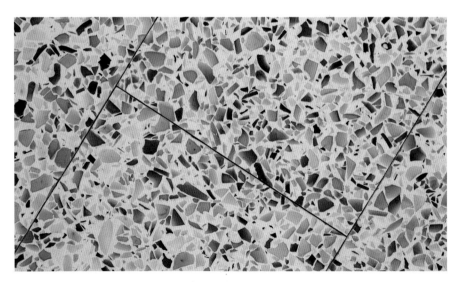

EnviroPLANK floor tiles are made with recycled glass chips in an epoxy resin base.

In Focus: New Homes

GREEN FROM THE GROUND UP

The edible organic gardens surrounding Karen Boness and Mark Feichtmeir's new home in Sonoma County's wine country produce so abundantly that the couple jokes about opening a farm stand. It's just a few steps from garden to kitchen, so their green beans, sweet corn, strawberries, eggplant, and artichokes lose none of their flavor or nutrients in the quick trip from soil to plate. Outside, the air hums with the activity of bees but inside the house is hushed, its eighteen-inch-thick earth walls dampening noise and keeping out the blaze of summer heat.

The walls are pisé, an acronym for pneumatically impacted stabilized earth, a construction method that uses a high-pressure hose to shoot a damp mix of soil, sand, and cement against framing forms. The massive walls keep the home cool without air-conditioning. Even after an extended run of days with temperatures over 100 degrees Fahrenheit, Feichtmeir says the home's interior has never climbed above 83 degrees Fahrenheit.

The home is hooked up to the municipal electricity grid, but it also boasts a 9.3-kilowatt photovoltaic system. When the solar electric panels are producing more electricity than the household requires, the excess is sold back to the utility grid. A large bank of batteries serves as a backup in case the utility's power goes down.

In the kitchen, soft-hued earthen walls offset the deeper tones of the cherry cabinets, terra-cotta tiles, and cork floor. Rustic tiles salvaged from a dismantled building in France serve as the backsplash. The cork floor, an engineered

Hefty earthen walls moderate indoor temperatures, keeping the home cool without air-conditioning despite a scorching summer climate.

The wood trim on the edges of the counters is FSC-certified Santa Maria, a tropical hardwood from Central America. It was finished with a water-resistant wood finish from Auro (aurousa.com).

tongue-and-groove product, provides a warm comfortable surface in the kitchen area; the flooring in the rest of the house is concrete. Adjacent to the Energy Star–approved refrigerator, a naturally ventilated pantry takes advantage of the wall's thermal mass to store wine and foodstuffs at a cool temperature without electricity. It's an old-fashioned concept that makes sense now more than ever (read more about "California coolers" on page 131).

During the process of building their house and planting their gardens, Feichtmeir and Boness gained valuable insights into how to create a home that's in harmony with nature. They hope to share their newfound expertise by offering sustainable design workshops at their home.

Green Details

+ Cabinet boxes made from Medite II, an MDF with no added formaldehyde
+ FSC-certified wood trim on counters with plant-based oil finish
+ Salvaged terra-cotta backsplash tiles
+ Cork floor
+ Energy Star appliances
+ Energy-efficient induction cooktop
+ Fluorescent lighting
+ Double-pane low-e windows
+ Naturally ventilated cool pantry
+ Passive solar design and thick earthen walls moderate temperature year-round
+ No air-conditioning
+ Low-slung design reduces visual impact on surroundings

- Concrete foundations, piers, and floor slabs contain 50 percent recycled fly ash content
- Geothermal heating system supplies hydronic radiant floor heat system and domestic hot water
- 9.3-kilowatt solar electric system produces 70 to 80 percent of household's electricity needs
- 50,000-gallon cistern under garage collects rainwater from house and garage roofs for irrigation
- Whole-house water purification and filtration
- Extensive native plant restoration for wildlife habitat; close to house, permaculture planting of edible gardens

Project Credits

- Architect: Todd Jersey Architecture, Berkeley, California, toddjerseyarchitecture.com.
- Builder: Beaman Construction, Napa, California, beamanconstruction.com.
- Interior design: Deborah Coburn, San Rafael, California, naturallyinspired.net.
- Photographer: Linda Svendsen.

▼

The backsplash tiles were purchased at a local tile shop but originally hailed from a building in France that was torn down.

▼

The cherry cabinets have a plant-based oil finish made by BioShield. Cabinet boxes are Medite II, a medium-density fiberboard with no added formaldehyde.

A House in the Woods

George and Karen Mandala's new home sits well below the street, at the base of a fifty-step staircase that winds its way down a wooded slope. When George Mandala bought the property a number of years ago, the existing cottage on the site was well past its prime. A 500-square-foot Sears kit house built in the 1940s, it suffered from leaks, extensive rot, and infestations of critters in the uninsulated, unweatherproofed walls.

The Mandalas decided that the cottage couldn't be saved, but rather than demolishing it, they deconstructed it, salvaging any good-quality wood for reuse. Their new home is only 1,200 square feet, with one bedroom, one and a half bathrooms, and open-plan kitchen and living areas all on one level. A lower level currently serves as a workshop but will one day be finished to provide an additional 1,100 square feet of living space.

The Mandalas worked with an architect and a builder but were closely involved in the design and construction, especially when it came to researching and sourcing eco-friendly materials. Besides salvaging wood from the original cottage, they went the extra mile to ensure that virtually all the wood they used was either reclaimed, engineered, or harvested from well-managed forests. The posts, beams, exposed ceiling trusses, and tongue-and-groove ceiling decking, for example, are FSC-certified Douglas fir.

Good woods steal the show in this new house. Exposed posts, beams, and ceiling trusses are FSC certified. Cabinets are salvaged elm and the dining table is salvaged pine.

Kitchen cabinet interiors are FSC-certified plywood, while the exteriors are from an elm tree rescued as it was en route to the dump. A friend who is a professional miller caught sight of the tree in the back of a truck, flagged down the driver, and took the tree off his hands. He milled the elm into slabs that were then air-dried on the couple's deck for over two years. When the wood was dry and stable, the Mandalas' cabinetmaker fashioned it into kitchen cabinet and drawer exteriors. The kitchen door and the main entry door were built from a dead pine from the couple's property.

In the Mandalas' kitchen, the ceiling soars, and high windows and skylights provide glimpses of blue sky and treetops, serving as a subtle reminder of why it matters that we choose wood from ecologically responsible sources.

Cabinet and drawer exteriors were fashioned from a local elm tree that was headed for the dump. Interiors are FSC-certified plywood.

The counters are Richlite, a composite of paper and resin.

The flooring is an engineered tongue-and-groove plank product with a top layer of cork.

Green Details

+ Cork floor in the kitchen
+ Bamboo floor in adjacent living areas
+ Subfloor is Medite II, an MDF with no added formaldehyde
+ Cabinet exteriors are urban-salvage elm with a low VOC, water-based clear finish
+ Cabinet interiors are FSC-certified plywood
+ Appliances are Energy Star approved
+ Kitchen and main entry door are made of wood from a dying tree cut down on the property
+ Dining table is reclaimed pine
+ Original cottage was deconstructed and much of the wood reused
+ Virtually all wood used to build the new house was FSC-certified, reclaimed, or engineered lumber
+ Interior walls are painted with low VOC AFM Safecoat paint
+ Insulation batts are made from recycled denim
+ Hydronic radiant floor heat is served by high-efficiency boiler
+ Concrete contains 40 percent recycled fly ash content
+ On-demand hot-water circulation pump reduces water and energy waste

Project Credits

+ Architect: Henry Taylor, Fairfax, California.
+ Builder: Gary Giesen Construction, San Rafael, California.
+ Photographer: Linda Svendsen.

▲
The kitchen door as well as the main entry door was built from a dying pine tree that was cut down on the property.

This modern streamlined kitchen (this page and opposite) features custom cabinets in vertical grain FSC-certified Douglas fir. Virtually all the wood used by the cabinetmaker, Woodshanti, is FSC-certified, locally salvaged, or from abundant non-commercially harvested species native to the West Coast. Woodshanti finishes their products with a hand-rubbed finish of plant-based oils.

3 kitchen storage

WHAT'S **GREEN**

Reuse of existing cabinets

Salvaged cabinets or vintage storage piece

Durable construction and hardware

Clever designs that do more with less space

FSC-certified, re-claimed, or rapidly renewable materials

Low or no VOC and formaldehyde emissions

WHAT'S **NOT**

Poor-quality cabinets that don't last

Carting old cabinets off to the landfill

Cabinets faced with PVC thermofoil

Uncertified old-growth or tropical woods

Particleboard, MDF, or plywood made with urea formaldehyde–based glues

Solvent-based finishes that offgas VOCs

Inadequate storage and dated cabinetry styles are two common reasons people embark on a kitchen rehab. Well-designed storage can turn an awkward space into a model of efficiency that's a pleasure to work and relax in. Refreshing old cabinets or replacing them altogether can transform a kitchen from frumpy to fabulous. So if your cabinets have you down, my advice is to make a change—as long as you make it green.

What's the distinction between a conventional kitchen cabinet and one that's green? Often the difference isn't apparent to the eye. The cabinets, shelves, and other storage solutions on these pages are as attractive as anything you're likely to see in kitchen-design showrooms. The difference is that green products don't pollute your home with unhealthy chemicals. And they're fabricated using materials and methods that take the environment into account—whether it's cabinet boxes made from recycled wheat straw, cabinet and drawer faces fashioned from sustainably harvested woods, or ingenious space-saving devices that maximize storage without increasing your home's square footage.

Someday, healthy eco-friendly cabinets will be the norm, but we're not there yet. Although the past decade has witnessed an explosion of interest in green-home design, the building-products industry is huge and, at times, slow to change. The information in this chapter will make it easier for you to make greener choices; be aware, though,

For these custom cabinets, Silver Walker Studios used a red birch veneer over Medite II, an MDF with no added formaldehyde.

▶

Berkeley Mills, a custom furniture and cabinetmaker, offers a luxury kitchen line of handcrafted bamboo cabinets. Many of the company's products are made with FSC-certified woods.

that going green still involves more legwork and commitment than going with the more familiar options.

Is that extra effort worth it? In my view, it's a small price to pay for a kitchen that looks great and is good for the environment.

GENERAL CONSIDERATIONS
Style

No matter which way your taste in kitchen design runs—traditional, contemporary, eclectic, industrial, Asian-influenced, Arts and Crafts, mid-century Modern, Art Deco—you can choose cabinets and other storage pieces that are healthier and gentler on the environment than the conventional options. Any style of cabinetry can be made greener—it's mostly a matter of using materials that don't pollute your home, taking care to use natural resources wisely when building the cabinets as well as designing the kitchen, and choosing durable products that will withstand the abuse a hard-working kitchen dishes out.

Although any style of cabinetry can be eco friendly, certain recent design trends mesh particularly well with the goals of a green kitchen, including the trend toward installing fewer wall cabinets and the fashion for modular or unfitted kitchens.

For the last half century, our kitchens have been dominated by banks of built-in base and wall cabinets. In the decades after World War II, manufacturers streamlined processes and standardized products to meet booming consumer demand for household goods. Whereas once a typical kitchen might have held only a few utilitarian pieces of furniture, in the postwar years, wall-to-wall cabinetry became affordable to millions of households. As economic prosperity increased, along with greater access to mass-produced goods and prepackaged foods, we found ourselves desiring more space in which to store our stuff. Banks of built-in cabinets, which excel at efficient storage, became the norm. By the 1970s, the typical American kitchen had come to resemble a cabinet manufacturer's showroom.

There are signs today that we're becoming less attached to our floor-to-ceiling, wall-to-wall built-ins. Starting in the 1990s, there was a marked trend away from wall cabinets with

CABINETS AND DAYLIGHT

Consider how your cabinet layout will affect daylighting. Try to avoid positioning wall cabinets immediately adjacent to a window where they may block daylight. For overhead cabinets that hang between the kitchen and another room, consider units with glass fronts and backs to share daylight between the spaces. Open shelves are another good option for providing storage while allowing daylight to pass through.

solid doors toward glass-faced cabinets that look lighter and less cumbersome. Taking this trend one step further, today many people are eliminating upper cabinets altogether for a cleaner look, replacing them with open shelves, windows, or even expanses of clear wall.

From a green perspective, this trend could bode well: fewer conventional cabinets mean less offgassing of formaldehyde and other VOCs into the home. In some households, fewer cabinets may also indicate a shift toward less consumption. On the other hand, it could mean that people are merely finding other places to store their kitchen gadgets and packaged foods, such as in a pantry.

I'm not knocking built-in cabinets; small kitchens in particular benefit from well-planned built-ins that take advantage of every square inch of space. But the trend over the past few decades toward massive banks of built-in cabinets in ever-larger kitchens in ever-larger houses takes its toll on the environment. Today's interest in fewer cabinets and lighter-looking styles might portend a turning away from the bigger-is-better mentality that has dominated home design in recent decades.

RETHINKING THE PANTRY

Walk-in pantries rank high on many dream-kitchen wish lists. If your kitchen is small, though, a walk-in pantry may not be the best strategy. The space required for standing and turning around in a pantry eats up valuable square footage. As an alternative, consider built-in cabinets, open shelves, and freestanding pieces with storage space for pots, cookbooks, and the like.

Another notable trend is the rising popularity of modular or unfitted kitchens. In the United States, when we buy or rent a home we expect the kitchen to come complete with built-in storage and often appliances. But in much of the world people take their kitchen storage units and appliances with them when they move. In fact, the resurgence of interest in unfitted kitchens likely originated with European manufacturers bringing their modular products to the U.S. market. The less formal look of the modular or unfitted kitchen may have also

been spurred by our current enthrallment with restaurant-style appliances and kitchens designed to be work spaces rather than showplaces.

An unfitted kitchen, which may mix and match some built-in cabinets with freestanding furniture-like pieces, offers a number of good green advantages. Modular storage units can be moved with relative ease, so if you decide to redo your kitchen, you can relocate the unit to another part of the kitchen or even another part of the house, rather than tearing it out and sending it to the dump. Freestanding pieces are also easier to resell or donate because they're not custom-fitted to one particular kitchen.

The unfitted kitchen also offers opportunities to incorporate vintage or used furniture, whether it's an eighty-year-old hutch picked up at an antiques fair or a stainless-steel workbench formerly used in a lab. Reuse is a key green-building strategy because it reduces the need to mine, harvest, or extract raw materials from the earth.

If you are concerned about the health and environmental effects of conventional cabinets, with their interiors that offgas formaldehyde and their doors made of materials that may have been unsustainably harvested, an unfitted kitchen offers an alternative. It gives you more freedom to select individual pieces made of solid or reclaimed wood rather than particleboard or plywood, or to choose alternatives such as metal or glass.

The deconstructed look can also be a good budgeting strategy, allowing you to buy pieces over time as you can afford them, rather than breaking the bank by outfitting the kitchen all at once. Keep in mind that unfitted kitchens allow for a great deal of flexibility but can be more challenging to design than conventional banks of built-in cabinets.

Cost

Cabinets account for between one-third and one-half the cost of a typical kitchen-remodeling project, according to the National Kitchen and Bath Association. Prices vary considerably depending on the materials used, the quality of construction, and whether they are stock (preassembled in standard sizes), special-order (factory made to your specifications), or custom (designed and built specifically for your kitchen, often by a small local cabinet shop).

Do green cabinets cost more? Some of the eco-friendly

strategies in this chapter do cost more. Most cabinet manufacturers are not yet using FSC-certified hardwood or formaldehyde-free substrates, so you may have to spend more to get a cabinetmaker to make semi-custom or custom cabinets using these materials.

Other green strategies cost no more, and may even save you money. Budget-conscious do-it-yourselfers can restore cabinets picked up for a song at salvaged building-materials warehouses. Another cost-cutting measure is to replace some or all of the upper cabinets with open shelves (you'll save money and use fewer natural resources to boot). As mentioned above, forgoing some built-in cabinetry for freestanding pieces—such as a restaurant-kitchen stainless worktable with shelves below, an old hutch, or a painted metal cart on casters—can cut costs, too, while providing one-of-a-kind style.

Another budget-savvy approach is to scale back on the number of cabinets in your new kitchen, and put the savings toward some custom or semi-custom construction that uses the eco-friendlier materials described later in this chapter.

DURABILITY

Durability is an important aspect of green design; frequent replacement of shoddily made products takes its toll on the environment, both in terms of natural resources needed to manufacture new products and the impact of disposing of

UNDER-SINK CABINETS AND MOISTURE

It's almost inevitable that the cabinet under your sink will be exposed to moisture, whether it's a sudden break of a pipe, a slow drip, or spills from stored trash and recyclables. Some cabinetmakers line the interior of their under-sink cabinets with sheet metal, well sealed at the seams, to prevent leaks and spills from wetting the cabinet-box material and creating conditions for mold growth.

old stuff. Whether you opt for built-in cabinets or freestanding pieces, look for products that can withstand wear and tear. Pay particular attention to the quality of base cabinets and drawers, as well as hinges, drawer glides, and other hardware. These pieces should be able to hold up to the worst your household can mete out—whether it's kids swinging on drawers; adults standing on cabinets to change a lightbulb; or the weight of heavy pots, dishes, and small appliances.

People and pets have a tendency to lean against base cabinets, so the finish should resist abrasion. Ideally the cabinets would have a surface that can be refinished so that when they do start to look worn, they can get a cosmetic makeover instead of being thrown out.

Water damage is a major source of deterioration of all manner of building materials, including cabinets. If the cabinet's finish fails, water can penetrate to the core material. Particleboard and MDF, two of the most common materials used for cabinet boxes, will degrade rapidly if allowed to get wet. Moisture plus wood fiber is a recipe for mold growth, a potentially serious indoor-air-quality contaminant. The best way to prevent moisture-related degradation is to start out with good-quality cabinets, keep the finishes in good shape, and attend to plumbing leaks immediately.

CABINETS AND THE HEALTHY KITCHEN

What's the key to healthy air quality in your home? Source control. It's much more effective to keep pollutants out of your home in the first place than to remove them once they've entered your home (the same could be said for unwanted guests).

These FSC-certified cherry cabinets have a water-based, low VOC finish.

LOW-COST WAYS TO REDUCE FORMALDEHYDE

If you can't avoid formaldehyde-containing cabinets or shelving units, take steps to limit offgassing in your kitchen. If your construction schedule allows, store the cabinets in a well-ventilated garage for a few weeks or even a month before installing them in your kitchen. Another good strategy is to seal any exposed pressed-wood surfaces with a low VOC sealant such as AFM's Safecoat Safe Seal.

New kitchen cabinets can be major indoor-air-quality offenders. Cabinet construction often uses materials that contain urea formaldehyde, a colorless, pungent industrial chemical added to more than 3,000 products. Formaldehyde vapor emitted by these products can cause burning sensations in the eyes, nose, and throat; other health effects include skin rashes, headaches, fatigue, and nausea. While some people don't seem troubled by formaldehyde, others become highly sensitized and some have strong allergic reactions to even very low levels of exposure. The U.S. EPA says that formaldehyde may cause cancer in humans.

These days, cabinet boxes are rarely made of solid wood. Instead, the boxes are constructed of interior-grade plywood or pressed wood, which may be particleboard or MDF. With a few exceptions, these materials have urea formaldehyde added as a binder to hold the wood fiber together.

Since the early 1980s, pressed-wood manufacturers have reduced formaldehyde emissions from their products by 80 to 90 percent. Still, according to the EPA, pressed wood remains the most significant source of formaldehyde in a home. Offgassing is highest when products are new; emissions drop off considerably in the first months after installation, but some products continue to emit very low levels of formaldehyde for years.

Cabinet interiors are often faced with melamine, a thin plastic resin that's thermally fused to the pressed-wood substrate. The melamine itself does not offgas, and in fact it helps prevent formaldehyde from evaporating from the pressed wood. However, unless the melamine covers the entire surface area, including all edges, undersides, and drilled holes and other openings, formaldehyde can still be emitted.

If you have pressed-wood cabinets that are a number of years old, formaldehyde emissions shouldn't worry you. But if you're in the market for new cabinets or other storage units, choose ones free of urea formaldehyde, if possible; good alternatives are described below. Also consider restoring used cabinets or purchasing good-quality stainless-steel cabinets (assuming they're entirely made of metal, and are not merely metal glued to a pressed-wood core). Cabinets constructed entirely of solid wood are another healthy option, but they will be beyond most people's budgets, even in high-end kitchen design.

REVAMPING EXISTING CABINETS

Green design requires hard-to-come-by materials, experimental building techniques, and a gargantuan budget, right? Not at all. The truth is that the greenest approaches often spare the wallet as well as sparing the planet.

When it comes to cabinets, the eco-friendliest strategy is to keep using what you've got. If the overall layout of your kitchen works well, consider a cosmetic tune-up rather than full-on replacement. A bit of advance planning and a weekend of work can bring about a remarkable transformation. Cabinets are a magnet for grease, grime, and sticky fingerprints, so roll up those sleeves and give the surfaces a thorough cleaning. Also look for hinges that need repair, scratches that can be touched up, and drawer glides that need replacement (consider upgrading to full-extension glides that allow access to the entire depth of the drawer). If you wish, change the handles and pulls for a fresh new look. While you're at it, take better advantage of the space you have by adding space-saving conveniences like lazy susans, pot lid holders, tiered racks, stemware holders, drawer organizers, and slide-out garbage bins.

METAL CABINETS

Metal cabinets offer some great green advantages. They don't offgas, the metal may contain recycled content, and they're often recyclable. Look for cabinets vintage or brand new that are 100 percent metal and not merely sheet metal glued to a fiberboard substrate.

If you have wood cabinets with a seriously worn finish, you can give them new life by sanding or stripping the surfaces (doors and drawer fronts, face frames, exposed ends, and trim) and refinishing or repainting them (using low VOC, low-toxic products, of course). Depending on the size of your kitchen, a professional-quality refinishing or paint job will take a fair amount of time and energy; if you're not a skilled DIYer, you may want to bring in an experienced painter or cabinet refinisher to ensure top-notch results.

Take a quick glance at the Saturday morning newspaper and you'll likely see ads for companies that rejuvenate cabinets by resurfacing the frames and refacing or replacing the doors and drawer fronts. Refacing is typically done with wood veneer or plastic laminate (the same sheet material used for many countertops), and works only with flat panel styles. Replacing doors is expensive but can quickly change your kitchen from dumpy to divine. Resurfacing or replacing doors is a good green strategy because it uses far fewer resources than replacing entire cabinets; one caveat is to avoid replacing old products, which finished outgassing years ago, with fresh new particleboard or plywood that might pollute your kitchen.

If you have frame-style cabinet doors, you can lighten and brighten your kitchen by taking out the panels and replacing them with inserts of old glass, wire mesh, aluminum screening, or any number of other materials (for safety's sake, don't use glass on base cabinets unless it's tempered). You can find old glass at building salvage yards and have it cut by a local glass shop. To adhere the glass to the frame, use 100 percent silicone caulk or another water-based caulking compound that's low in VOCs.

Refinishing your cabinetry or replacing the doors saves natural resources and money but may not make sense if the

HARDWARE MAGIC

Looking for a super-quick, easy-on-the-environment way to spruce up dreary cabinets? Replace dated drawer pulls and cabinet knobs with new hardware. It will be easier on your wallet—and easier on the planet—than replacing the cabinets themselves. Make sure the new hardware will work with existing screw holes.

DECONSTRUCTION

If your kitchen is going to be gutted, check into hiring a deconstruction outfit rather than a demolition contractor. Deconstruction companies manually dismantle individual rooms as well as whole buildings, and salvage materials that have resale value. Deconstruction takes more time, and therefore usually costs more money than demolition. However, many deconstruction outfits are charitable nonprofits, and homeowners sometimes can get a sizeable tax deduction for the value of the donated materials. If there's anything in your old kitchen that you intend to keep, inform the deconstruction company prior to signing the contract; these organizations depend financially on charging fees for deconstruction and on profits from reselling your old goods.

kitchen layout is sub par. If the cabinets have to go, consider ways to reuse them in your home. Depending on their condition, you might use them in a home office, bedroom, utility or laundry room, mudroom, garage, or basement. If you can't use them, evaluate whether they can be removed intact from your kitchen and donated to a building-reuse store for resale. If you're working with a builder, make sure he or she knows well in advance (before you sign the contract) that you want to salvage the cabinets. It takes the builder more time to carefully remove them intact than to yank them out and toss them in the debris box.

The flip side of all this, of course, is that if you're looking to replace cabinets, consider buying used ones from a building-materials salvage yard. Look for solidly built units that will last a long time, and be leery of cabinets stored outside that might harbor mold.

GREENER CABINET OPTIONS

There's a huge variety of options when it comes to choosing cabinets. If you're in the market for new cabinets, your budget will likely determine whether you go with stock cabinets,

▲
A bamboo cabinet from AlterECO with a recycled glass countertop by Counter Production. AlterECO's options for cabinet interiors include FSC-certified plywood, wheatboard, or solid bamboo. Cabinet exteriors are finished with plant-based oils or with a low VOC, water-based polyurethane.

which are made in standard sizes and purchased from home-improvement stores and kitchen showrooms; semi-custom cabinets, which are factory-assembled to your specifications using factory-made components; or the most expensive option, custom cabinets, which are specifically designed for your kitchen (although they also often incorporate some prefabricated elements).

Wood remains the material of choice for cabinets, according to the National Kitchen and Bath Association. Wood is a terrific building material—besides looking great, it's renewable, versatile, often recyclable or reusable, and biodegradable. Unfortunately, much of the imported wood that finds its way into our home furnishings was logged in an environmentally unsustainable and sometimes illegal manner. And the problem isn't limited to exotic woods; domestically, companies continue to clear-cut natural forests and cut down ancient trees even though more ecologically and economically sustainable options exist.

The day will come, I believe, when all cabinet manufacturers will follow the path being forged today by a few companies with leadership and vision. These companies avoid using potentially unhealthy substances such as urea formaldehyde and vinyl, and they offer FSC-certified and reclaimed woods and wood alternatives such as bamboo and wheatboard.

To get to that future, it's up to homeowners, kitchen de-

signers, architects, and builders to demonstrate to cabinet manufacturers that there is real demand for greener products.

CABINET INTERIORS

These days, more often than not, the cabinet box—also referred to as the shell or carcass—is made from plywood, particleboard, or MDF. It's not always apparent what the core material is because box interiors are often finished with melamine, a thin plastic resin that's thermally fused to the underlying core. Melamine provides a moisture- and abrasion-resistant surface. Once available mainly in white or other solid colors, melamine is now made to mimic virtually any type of wood so that the interiors match the cabinet doors. Higher-end cabinet boxes may be made with MDF or plywood instead of particleboard; the MDF or plywood is typically faced with melamine or a real wood veneer that has a petrochemical-based finish.

▼ ▶
A number of years ago, when architect Todd Jersey remodeled his house, the kitchen got a green makeover (below), with FSC-certified maple floors, plaster veneer on the walls, and a new skylight to illuminate the space. More recently, Jersey and his wife overhauled the kitchen (opposite page), upgrading the cabinets and appliances. The cabinets were made by Woodshanti of sustainably harvested maple, walnut, and madrone. Wall tiles are recycled glass.

VINYL

The jury's still out on the environmental and health hazards of polyvinyl chloride (also known as PVC, or vinyl for short). Many environmental and health advocates have called for phasing out PVC building materials because of concerns about toxic emissions of dioxin, phthalates, and other chemicals during manufacturing, use, or disposal. Significantly, furniture-giant Ikea no longer allows PVC in any of their products, with the exception of electrical cables. Steer clear of cabinets with a vinyl thermofoil finish; it's a thin decorative sheet of PVC that's heat-fused onto the cabinet surface, creating a look similar to a painted cabinet.

Some cabinetmakers have switched to using Medite II instead of conventional MDF. Manufactured by SierraPine, Medite II is a no-added-formaldehyde MDF suitable for nonstructural uses. It is certified by Scientific Certification Systems as being made with 100 percent pre-consumer recycled wood fiber.

In 2005, Columbia Forest Products, a major manufacturer of hardwood plywood, announced that it was switching to a manufacturing process that uses soy-based adhesive instead of urea formaldehyde. If your cabinetmaker uses hardwood plywood, encourage him to make the switch to products like this that have no added formaldehyde.

If you aren't able to obtain interior-grade plywood with no added formaldehyde, consider buying cabinets made with marine-grade plywood, which is made with phenol formaldehyde resin instead of urea formaldehyde. Ironically, exterior-grade plywood offgasses formaldehyde at much lower levels than conventional interior-grade plywood. Neff Kitchens constructs all their cabinet boxes and shelves with marine-grade plywood.

Wheatboard is yet another good green option for cabinet boxes. Like plywood, MDF, and particleboard, wheatboard is a compressed-fiber product available in standard four-by-eight-foot sheets. The difference is that wheatboard is made from compressed straw instead of bits of wood. Wheat straw and other agricultural residues such as rye straw and rice straw used to be burned in the field by farmers, creating significant air pollution. Building products made from agricultural residue put waste to good use. Additional good news is that these ag-waste sheet products are made without formaldehyde binders.

Cabinet Exteriors
Doors and Drawer Faces
While the cabinet shells do the

A kitchen by Neil Kelly Cabinets, a manufacturer of cabinets made with sustainably harvested woods and low VOC finishes.

work of storing our stuff, the cabinet's exterior panels, doors, and drawer faces provide the style we desire. Solid wood doors are generally the most expensive option, although attractive cabinets can be made of any number of materials, including metal and laminate. Less expensive cabinet doors may have plywood, MDF, or particleboard cores faced with wood veneer, plastic laminate, or vinyl (PVC). Avoid vinyl products and tropical hardwood veneers (unless FSC certified), and seek out manufacturers who use door cores with no added formaldehyde.

Cabinet doors and drawer faces made from FSC-certified solid wood aren't yet widely available, but this is changing as more homeowners shift their purchasing dollars to cabinet manufacturers who support sustainable forestry.

Neil Kelly Cabinets, one of the pioneers in the area of healthy, eco-friendly cabinetry, offers doors made of FSC-certified maple, cherry, red oak, pine, alder, and red birch. For Neil Kelly's cabinet boxes, melamine-laminated wheatboard cores are standard; CollinsWood FSC-certified particleboard and plywood, and SierraPine's Medite II with no added formaldehyde are other options.

If you are having semi-custom or custom cabinets made, talk to the supplier about greener options for the doors. These days many custom cabinetmakers make the boxes themselves but purchase the doors from larger manufacturers; encourage your supplier to deal with a door manufacturer that offers FSC-certified woods. If your cabinetmaker actually crafts the doors herself, you may have more flexibility in choosing FSC-certified or salvaged wood.

Sustainably Harvested Veneers

While the interiors of cabinet boxes are often faced with melamine, the exteriors are often clad with wood veneer, a very thin layer of hardwood glued to the substrate. From a resource-conservation standpoint, veneers make good sense: the particleboard or plywood cabinet box can be made from young, fast-growing, abundant trees, and then covered with a very thin veneer sliced from more mature, valuable trees. Veneer manufacturing uses the wood fiber in a log very efficiently. Unfortunately, though, demand for beautiful veneers continues to drive a large portion of the unsustainable logging practices in tropical and temperate forests around the world.

To do your part to protect environmentally vulnerable regions of the world, do not purchase any cabinets with veneers (or other components) made from exotic hardwoods or old-growth trees unless the veneers are FSC certified. Be aware that some veneered products marketed as FSC certified may have certified cores but noncertified veneers. If the salesperson doesn't know the difference, you may have to contact the manufacturer directly to get an answer. If the cabinets you want aren't available with an FSC veneer, steer clear of exotic species and choose a domestic second-growth species such as maple or oak.

Bamboo

A beautiful and increasingly popular option for cabinets is bamboo. Typically the exterior portions of the cabinet—the doors, drawer fronts, and other faces—will be solid bamboo, with the cabinet boxes themselves made of plywood or particleboard (if it's an environmentally responsible cabinetmaker, he will use box material with no added formaldehyde). As described in chapter two, bamboo is available either in its natural blond color or in

Bamboo cabinet detail.

an amber color. A rapidly renewable resource that can be grown and harvested with relatively benign environmental impacts, bamboo is equally at home in contemporary and more traditional kitchen settings.

Cabinet Resources

✦**AlterECO.** Custom bamboo cabinets. Sausalito, California, 415.331.8342, bamboocabinets.com.

✦**Berkeley Mills.** Known for its premium hardwood custom furniture, Berkeley Mills also designs and makes kitchen cabinetry with FSC-certified hardwoods and bamboo. Berkeley, California, 510.549.2854, berkeleymills.com.

CABINET KNOBS AND DRAWER PULLS

In the grand scheme of things, the cabinet knobs and drawer pulls you choose won't be the straw that breaks the environment's back. So go on, indulge yourself—select hardware that feels great in your hand and adds style to your kitchen.

If you do want to take the greening of your kitchen down to the level of cabinet hardware, keep these pointers in mind:

+Select quality hardware that will hold up for decades.

+Consider cabinet door and drawer styles with finger holes, cutouts, or lips so that no pulls are needed.

+Seek out vintage hardware or make your own from found or repurposed objects such as oversized bolts, unique pieces of cutlery, or smooth stones collected from a favorite beach.

+Buy knobs and pulls with recycled content, such as recycled glass hardware from Aurora Glass (auroraglass.org) and SpectraDécor (spectradecor.com).

+Choose hardware made by local artisans.

GET IT IN WRITING

If you ask a cabinet salesperson whether their products offgas urea formaldehyde, you won't necessarily receive an accurate answer. Ask for written literature from the manufacturer and look for a statement that their products have no added urea formaldehyde.

+**Cabinet King.** Green Leaf line of cabinets has boxes made with wheatboard. FSC-certified frames and drawers, and AFM Safecoat finishes are available. Cleveland, Ohio, 877.422.2463, cabinetking.com.

+**Columbia Forest Products.** Hardwood plywood manufactured with soy-based adhesive instead of formaldehyde. Distributed nationally, 800.237.2428, columbiaforestproducts.com.

+**Forefront Designs.** Greenline cabinets using wheatboard cores. Springfield, Oregon, 888.245.0075, forefrontdesigns.com.

+**Henrybuilt.** Modular cabinet components; sustainable materials include FSC-certified carcasses and bamboo front and side panels. Seattle, Washington, 866.624.9270, henrybuilt.com.

+**Laguna Bamboo.** Custom bamboo cabinetry and furniture. Laguna Beach, California, 888.494.0126, lagunabamboo.com.

+**Neff Kitchens.** Makes all cabinets from marine-grade plywood that is free of urea formaldehyde. Brampton, Ontario, Canada, 800.268.4527, neffweb.com.

+**Neil Kelly Cabinets.** Kitchen and bath cabinets made with sustainably harvested woods, formaldehyde-free wheatboard, and low VOC finishes. Sold nationally through distributors or direct from Portland, Oregon, headquarters, 503.288.6345, neilkellycabinets.com.

+**PrimeBoard.** Manufacturer of wheat-straw particleboard with no added formaldehyde. Wahpeton, North Dakota, 701.642.1152, primeboard.com.

+**Silver Walker Studios.** Custom cabinet shop using FSC-certified and recycled-content materials with reduced formaldehyde offgassing. Richmond, California, 510.215.1266, silverwalker.com.

+**SierraPine.** Manufacturer of Medite II, an SCS-certified, no-added formaldehyde MDF panel for nonstructural applications, including cabinets. Distributed nationally, 800.676.3339, www.sierrapine.com.

+**Smith & Fong.** Supplier of Plyboo four-by-eight-foot bamboo plywood sheets, bamboo veneer, and other bamboo products. San Francisco, California, 866.835.9859, plyboo.com.

Colorful glass cabinet hardware from SpectraDécor is made with 100 percent recycled postindustrial waste; clear-glass hardware made from 100 percent post-consumer recycled content is also available.

Woodshanti. A worker-owned cooperative making custom furniture and cabinetry using responsibly harvested lumber and natural finishes. San Francisco, California, 415. 822.8100, woodshanti.com.

WOOD CABINET FINISHES

Prefabricated wood cabinets usually have a factory-applied finish. From an indoor-air-quality perspective, factory-applied finishes are a good choice because they're applied in a controlled environment, and the finish will likely have completely cured by the time the cabinets are installed in your home.

Custom-made cabinets may have their finish applied at the cabinet shop or in your home. To protect indoor air quality, request water-based low or no VOC clear finishes such as Safecoat Acrylacq or Safecoat Polyureseal BP. If you choose painted cabinets, request a water-based low VOC paint, but verify with the cabinetmaker or paint supplier that the selected product will be durable enough for kitchen cabinets.

Synthetic paints and clear finishes, whether they are solvent-based or water-based, coat the wood with a film of plastic. To enhance the grain and texture of beautiful wood, consider instead a solvent-free, plant-based finish such as a natural oil or hard wax. Linseed oil is the primary ingredient of many of these finishes. Options include products from Tried & True, BioShield , Osmo, and Auro. Cabinets finished with penetrating oils require a reapplication of the oil every year or so to protect the wood; it's an easy process that merely involves rubbing in the oil with a cloth. And cabinets with an oil finish can be spot-refinished quite easily if the surface is worn or marred in areas; lacquered, varnished, or painted cabinets, on the other hand, are much more complicated to refinish because they have to be sanded and completely recoated.

Be cautious about using plant-based oil finishes on woodwork inside cabinets; many of these products have a strong odor that can linger for months in cabinet interiors that aren't exposed to circulating air.

Wood Finishing Resources

AFM Safecoat. Very low VOC finishes, 619.239.0321, afmsafecoat.com.

Auro. German-made finishing oils, sealers, and waxes, 888.302.0662, aurousa.com.

BioShield. Linseed oil–based penetrating-oil finishes and

Silver Walker Studios built these cabinets with Medite II faced with melamine. Exteriors are alder, a fast-growing abundant species in the Pacific Northwest. Alder has long been an undervalued wood compared to high-demand species such as cherry. Choosing abundant but lesser-known species helps forest managers maintain natural diversity in the lands they manage.

hardwax products made from beeswax, linseed oil, and carnauba wax, 800.621.2591, bioshieldpaint.com.

Osmo. Wood-finishing products made in Germany; available from various North American retailers, including Seattle's Environmental Home Center, environmentalhomecenter.com.

Tried & True Wood Finishes. Penetrating oil finishes made from linseed oil, 607.387.9280, triedandtruewoodfinish.com.

BUY LOCALLY

Support a sustainable economy in your community by buying locally made cabinets. Custom cabinets are expensive, so they're not within everyone's price range, but using a local cabinetmaker may give you more say in the style as well as materials and finish.

In Focus: Modern Style

CONTEMPORARY GREEN

Chris Parlette, an architect, transformed his home's nondescript kitchen into a light-filled space that's energy efficient, spacious, and stylish. The lot is narrow, with houses cheek-by-jowl on both sides, so Parlette added large new windows in the dining area at the front of the house to bring in much-needed daylight. The double-pane windows have a low-e-squared coating that helps keep the home cooler in summer and warmer in winter.

A shaft in the kitchen doubles as a lightwell and cooling tower. It cools and ventilates the home naturally through what's known as the "stack effect": warm air from the kitchen and other rooms on the ground floor rises and escapes through a motorized skylight at the top of the tower. The skylight also illuminates the home's core.

Eco-friendly design should never have to mean sacrificing style or function. In fact, in the right hands, green design and good design are one and the same. Many of the materials that Parlette selected—from the bamboo flooring to the salvaged

◄

Parlette designed the table, which he had built from Douglas fir salvaged from a lake bottom. He finished the wood with a beeswax-based finish.

▲

The lot is narrow, with houses close on both sides, so large new windows were added at the front of the house to introduce daylight.

fir table—are as good for the environment as they are pleasing to the eye. Throughout the project, smart energy use remained a priority, including good insulation, high-performance windows, and a rooftop photovoltaic system sized to meet 100 percent of the household's electricity needs.

The tall cabinet behind the bar stretches up into a second-story light-well, which is topped by an operable skylight for daylighting and natural ventilation.

The floor is bamboo. Parlette used scrap steel for the drawer faces and inserts between the upper cabinets.

Green Details

+ Bamboo floor
+ Energy Star refrigerator
+ Low VOC paint
+ Water-based finish on cabinets; cabinet hardware custom fabricated from scrap steel
+ Plaster veneer instead of paint over drywall
+ Locally built dining table made from lake-salvaged Douglas fir with a beeswax-based finish
+ Shaft topped with motorized skylight provides daylight and cooling
+ High-efficiency windows
+ Nearly 100 percent of the household's electricity needs are met by 3.2-kilowatt solar electric system
+ Double-pane windows with a low-e-squared coating
+ Salvaged and engineered lumber

Project Credits

+ Architect/builder: Chris Parlette, Wilson Associates, Berkeley, California, dswdesign.com.
+ Photography: David Stark Wilson.

◄

This home's greenest features are largely invisible. The previously uninsulated low-slope roof was retrofitted with rigid foam insulation. Double-pane windows with a low-e coating keep the home more comfortable and reduce energy use.

▼

One of the few overtly green statements is the five-kilowatt photovoltaic system on the roof.

thing that came out of the site was reused or recycled." And thanks to the solar panels, the Harrises' electricity meter "runs backwards at top speed," Jordan says. "We're putting a lot of green power back into the grid."

Green Details
+ Energy Star appliances
+ Bamboo flooring
+ Ninety-five percent of all new framing material is reclaimed or FSC certified
+ Exterior and interior wood trim is reclaimed from redwood wine casks
+ Five-kilowatt solar electric system
+ High-efficiency low-e windows with PVC-free interior shades
+ Hydronic radiant floor heating supplied by high-efficiency boiler
+ Recycled-cotton insulation in walls
+ Rigid foam insulation above ceiling
+ Low VOC paints and finishes used throughout
+ Recycled fly ash in concrete
+ Existing concrete pathways reused for new hardscaping at another project

MID-CENTURY MODERN REMODEL

Julie and Jordan Harris are out to prove that style and sustainability are compatible. "Our goal was to have the most energy-efficient house possible without compromising aesthetics," Jordan Harris says of their remodeled 1949 home on the San Francisco Bay.

Architect Christopher C. Deam's redesign of the house dazzles in a low-key minimalist way, paying tribute to the California ideal of the good life—rooms that casually flow into each other, walls of glass that merge indoors and out, and a sparkling lagoon just steps away from the main living spaces.

Except for the Toyota Prius in the garage and the five-kilowatt photovoltaic system on the low-slung roof, nothing about the one-story house shouts "eco friendly." The greenest features are largely unobtrusive or invisible: bamboo floors, fly ash concrete, redwood trim reclaimed from wine casks, sustainably harvested lumber certified by the Forest Stewardship Council, paints that don't emit toxic chemicals, wall insulation made from recycled denim, and high-efficiency appliances and heating systems.

Julie Harris credits their builder, Fusion Building Company, with going the extra mile to ensure that virtually "every-

- Landscaping with native grasses and other low-water vegetation
- Five-minute walk to town's retail district, and twenty-minute ferry ride to downtown San Francisco

Project Credits
- Architect: Christopher C. Deam, San Francisco, California, cdeam.com.
- Builder: Fusion Building Co., Bolinas, California, fusionbuildingcompany.com.
- Photographer: Linda Svendsen.

▲

The home has a loft-like feel, with spaces casually flowing into each other. The kitchen is the hub of the home, with easy access to a lushly landscaped courtyard on one side and stupendous views of the bay on the other. The dining table is custom crafted from a slab of locally salvaged elm.

▶

The design makes the most of spectacular views and daylighting. Deep eaves keep the sun's heat off the windows for much of the day while still letting in plenty of light. Kitchen counters are marble and Corian.

Kitchen designer Lydia Corser gave her kitchen a green makeover with the help of her husband, Brian Corser, who did the construction. The black counter is Richlite, a paper and resin composite. The bar top in the foreground is reclaimed claro walnut from a noncommercially harvested local tree. Backsplash tiles are 100 percent pre-consumer recycled glass from Sandhill Industries. The linoleum floor is Marmoleum by Forbo. The floor underlayment is SierraPine's Medite II, a medium-density fiberboard with no added formaldehyde. The cabinets, made by Neil Kelly Cabinets, have formaldehyde-free wheatboard boxes; the light-colored cabinet door panels are Dakota Burl, manufactured with sunflower seed hulls, from Environ Biocomposites. The Corsers used FSC-certified framing lumber and Ultratouch recycled cotton insulation. The Sub-Zero refrigerator and Bosch dishwasher are Energy Star approved.

This terrazzo counter is 75 percent recycled glass, including at least 30 percent post-consumer recycled content.

4 counter and wall surfaces

Here's my vision of a dream green countertop: it's sustainably produced from raw materials that are extracted, harvested, or reclaimed with relatively benign environmental impacts. It is manufactured within 500 miles of home using little energy and without petrochemical-based ingredients. It doesn't offgas formaldehyde or other chemicals that might pose a health hazard for the fabricators, installers, or household members. Highly durable, it resists scorching, scratching, staining, and moisture, and it can be refinished if it gets damaged. It is installed without noxious adhesives. It can be reused or recycled the next time the kitchen undergoes remodeling. It's affordable and gorgeous.

Nice dream, but are there actually any kitchen work surfaces that fit the bill? Not entirely, but the good news is that none of today's most popular countertop choices are egregious either.

With all the countertop options out there and no clear green winners, how do you make a choice? I recommend selecting a product within your budget that you absolutely love. Remember that you'll be looking at and touching the counters every day, so it's important that they be as pleasing to the eye as they are to the hand.

WHAT'S GREEN

Reuse of existing counters and backsplashes

FSC-certified or salvaged wood

Post-consumer recycled content (minimum 25 percent)

Excellent durability

Surfaces that can be refinished if damaged

Benign environmental impacts during extraction and manufacturing

Materials extracted, processed, and manufactured regionally (within 500 miles of your home)

Zero or very low VOC paints, stains, and other finishes

WHAT'S **NOT**

Sending reusable or recyclable counters to the dump

Adhesives or finishes that emit noxious chemicals

Substrates such as particleboard that offgas formaldehyde

Tropical or old-growth wood (unless FSC certified)

Also, choose work surfaces suited to how you use your kitchen. If you are a no-holds-barred cook who wields a mean cleaver and liberally sloshes the balsamic vinegar, then no-nonsense surfaces like stainless steel and butcher block are good bets.

If you are keen on materials that develop a patina with age—if knife marks, discolorations, and worn surfaces remind you of good times, good friends, and good meals—then you'll likely be comfortable with wood, softer stones like marble and slate, and concrete. If you can't tolerate scratches, nicks, or stains, consider one of the more impervious materials like solid-surface plastics, granite, or engineered stone.

GENERAL CONSIDERATIONS

VERSATILITY

In most households the kitchen is the hub of multiple activities and it's tricky to find a single countertop material perfectly suited to them all. Consider including two or even three surfaces tailored to the major activities in your kitchen—stainless steel around the sink for easy cleanup, a butcher-block work surface for chopping, perhaps an elegant stone or polished concrete bar top if you entertain in the kitchen. Do keep in mind that small kitchens may look chaotic if there are too many different countertop materials.

If the cooks in your household are unusually tall or short, the standard countertop height of thirty-six inches may not suit them. Consider customizing the counter heights to better suit your needs. Couples with a big height disparity sometimes include counters at different levels to provide a comfortable workstation for both people. Also, people who bake a lot appreciate having one lower counter for kneading and rolling out dough. If your kitchen is on the small side, you may not have the space for different height counters; in that case, a tall person could use an extra-thick cutting board to build up the height of the surface, and dough kneading and rolling could be done at the kitchen table. Modular base cabinets with adjustable-height legs offer flexibility to raise or lower the counter height by an inch or two without incurring extra costs.

COST

Prices for countertops span the spectrum, ranging from as low as $5 per square foot for some plastic laminates to $250 per square foot and up for the rarer granites. The greener options don't necessarily cost more, provided you do an apples-to-apples comparison with similar conventional material. For example, terrazzo-like counters made with recycled glass can be expensive, but no more so than many high-end stone surfaces such as granite. Recycled-paper composites may cost more than low-budget laminates but less than many plastic solid-surface materials.

BACKSPLASHES

Most kitchens include a vertical backsplash on the walls behind the sink, cooktop, and other food-preparation surfaces. The majority of materials suitable for a countertop also perform well as a backsplash. Although backsplashes were traditionally only a few inches high, these days many people choose to run the backsplash material farther up the wall. The wall surface between the cooktop and the range hood is an especially popular area for a tall backsplash, or "back wall."

Since backsplashes usually cover a smaller surface area than the counters, floors, or main wall surfaces, it's common for them to include bolder colors and patterns and more deluxe materials. By all means, splurge a little to add panache, but don't lose sight of the backsplash's main function: to provide a vertical surface that stands up to moisture, heat, grease splatters, and vigorous scrubbing.

The backsplash and countertop connection should be designed to keep food from falling behind the cabinets. Many solid-surface counters are fabricated with an integral backsplash, creating a seam-free surface that won't trap crumbs and grime.

Tile—whether ceramic, glass, or stone—remains one of the top choices for backsplashes despite the hassle of keeping grout clean. But there are many other serviceable and attractive options, including plate glass, stainless steel, aluminum, copper, zinc, plastic laminates, and more.

Recycled glass backsplash.

COUNTERTOP MATERIALS

This section addresses the environmental pros and cons of the most popular countertop and backsplash materials. But there are plenty of other options, so don't hesitate to be creative and make your kitchen your own. When evaluating products, favor those with eco-friendly attributes, especially ones that have relatively benign environmental impacts during harvesting, extraction, and manufacturing; are hardwearing; don't offgas VOCs or require maintenance with noxious chemicals; and can be refinished, reused, or recycled.

BUTCHER BLOCK, WOOD, AND BAMBOO

Easy on the eyes and warm to the touch, wood has been a favored counter surface for ages. But with the staggering number of countertop materials on the market these days, wood isn't

▶

This breakfast counter was once the floor of an old bowling lane.

▼

These backsplash tiles are 100 percent pre-consumer recycled glass made by Sandhill Industries.

PROS AND CONS OF GREEN COUNTERTOP MATERIALS

TYPE	PROS	CONS	GREEN TIPS
BUTCHER BLOCK, WOOD & BAMBOO (p. 97)	Butcher block is best surface for chopping Can be refinished Renewable resource Reusable; potentially recyclable Cost: low to high	Susceptible to moisture damage Not heat-proof Will show nicks, stains, and cuts	Choose wood that is FSC certified or salvaged Choose high-quality bamboo from a reputable supplier Avoid exotic hardwood unless FSC certified
CERAMIC TILE (p. 102)	Heat-proof Stain and water resistant Many colors and styles Relatively benign manufacturing process Cost: low to high	Grout can discolor and collect dirt and bacteria	Choose tiles with recycled content Choose locally made tiles
CONCRETE & FIBER-CEMENT (pp. 102 & 104)	Custom concrete counters offer vast design flexibility Long lasting Cost: high (concrete); moderate (fiber-cement)	Heavy Concrete counters may crack or chip Porous; will stain, even with regular application of wax or sealant Fiber-cement counters offered in limited colors	Seek out fabricators who use recycled materials such as fly ash or recycled aggregate
ENGINEERED STONE (STONE/ RESIN COMPOSITE) (p. 105)	Durable Scratch and stain resistant Doesn't require sealing Many colors and styles Cost: moderate to high	Synthetic look Plastic resin binder	None
GLASS & GLASS TILE (p. 105)	Relatively benign environmental impacts Doesn't stain Hygienic Good backsplash material Glass often contains recycled content Cost: moderate (plate glass) to high (glass tile)	Can chip, crack, or shatter Plate glass may show fingerprints, watermarks, or streaks	Choose glass tiles with recycled glass content (preferably post-consumer)
LAMINATES & PAPER/RESIN SLABS (p. 107)	Laminates available in many colors and patterns	Laminates can scorch, chip, or scar; can't be resurfaced	Laminates: choose FSC-certified substrates

TYPE	PROS	CONS	GREEN TIPS
LAMINATES & PAPER/RESIN SLABS (continued)	Laminates resist stains, scratches, and moisture Easy to clean Raw materials include paper, a renewable resource Cost: low (laminate); moderate (solid paper/resin slab)	Raw materials include petrochemical-based resin Paper/resin slabs available in limited colors; sunlight may fade some colors Paper/resin slabs are porous and may stain Plastic resin component doesn't appeal to some	Laminates: avoid substrates of interior-grade plywood, particleboard, or MDF made with urea formaldehyde (or completely seal the substrate with a low VOC clear sealant) Choose slabs with recycled-paper content (preferably post-consumer)
LINOLEUM (p. 108)	Made from natural ingredients including linseed oil, sawdust, ground cork, and pine resin Antistatic, antibacterial Easy to clean Wide range of colors Cost: moderate	Gives off mild odor, especially when new	Install on a substrate with no added formaldehyde
METAL—STAINLESS STEEL, COPPER, ZINC (p. 108)	Heat-proof, waterproof Stainless steel is stain resistant Hygienic Long-lasting May contain recycled content; usually recyclable Cost: high	Scratches and dents Zinc susceptible to staining May show fingerprints and water marks May be noisy Made from nonrenewable resources Energy-intensive manufacturing process	Look for salvaged metals
SOLID SURFACE (p. 110)	Material consistent all the way through so scratches can be sanded out Many colors Easy to clean Cost: moderate to high	Synthetic look doesn't appeal to some Made from petrochemical-based acrylics and polyesters	None
STONE (p. 111)	Hard-wearing Heat-proof and waterproof Natural material Minimally processed Cool surface of marble excellent for rolling out pastry dough Cost: high	Some stones will stain Can crack or chip Finite natural resource Quarrying has detrimental effects on environment	Choose stone quarried within 500 miles of your home Choose salvaged stone Use thinner stone
TERRAZZO (p. 114)	Some terrazzo products contain post-consumer recycled glass, pre-consumer recycled stone chips, or fly ash Cost: high	Not as readily available as many other counter materials Some products made with an epoxy resin matrix	Choose products with high post-consumer recycled content

The main work surfaces are durable, recyclable stainless steel. The rich-hued floor is FSC-certified solid Brazilian cherry from EcoTimber. The refrigerator and dishwasher are Energy Star approved. The skylight's deep well provides diffuse daylight and minimizes glare.

nearly as common as it once was, and the look of wood counters doesn't appeal to everyone. The no-frills persona of a scarred and stained butcher block may be out of place in more formal kitchens. That said, a counter of lustrous, richly hued hardwood could be right at home in the most elegant of kitchens.

An FSC-certified or salvaged wood counter probably comes closest to the dream green countertop I described earlier. Wood is a renewable resource. Wood-countertop manufacturing requires minimal processing. Often, wooden work surfaces are fabricated locally by woodworkers or do-it-yourselfers. Wood counters are resilient and can be refinished easily. At the end of their life as counters, the wood can potentially be reused or recycled.

Environmentally preferable wood counters are made from FSC-certified wood or salvaged wood. FSC certification pro-

vides assurance that the wood came from a sustainable forestry operation. Salvaged sources run the gamut from old wood counters rescued from another kitchen to timbers reclaimed from a dismantled building to storm-felled trees from your neighborhood that might otherwise have been burned for firewood or chipped for mulch.

Don't buy counters made with tropical hardwoods unless they have the FSC seal of approval. Keep in mind that while the manufacturer or retailer may have FSC certification, the products they sell are not necessarily all certified; this is an important point to clarify before making a purchase.

Some wood counters have such a finely finished and sealed surface that you wouldn't dream of putting a knife to them. Others are utilitarian butcher blocks that practically beg for the cleaver. While dense maple is the most common butcher-block material, a wide variety of hardwoods make suitable cutting surfaces. Even softwoods such as pine can be used, but be prepared for more scratches and dents and periodic refinishing.

Solid wood counters not intended as cutting surfaces

The bar top is a slab of salvaged black acacia.

are often finished with a plastic polyurethane-type sealant. This finish may be factory applied or applied in your home after the counters are installed; if applied in your kitchen, insist on a water-based, low VOC product to protect air quality. For a true butcher block intended for use as a cutting surface, forgo the polyurethane and apply an oil to provide resistance to heat, stains, and moisture; use mineral oil, tung oil, or linseed oil, not food-grade oil that might go rancid. Reapply the oil periodically to protect the wood.

Prices for wood counters range from low to expensive, depending on the species, thickness, edge detailing, and other factors. Wood counters are relatively easy to work with and install. They can be installed directly on cabinets without underlayment, which reduces resource use. Also, they can be mechanically fastened rather than glued down, which makes refinishing, remodeling, and even deconstruction easier in the future.

Wood countertops do come with some caveats. While some people install wood counters around their sinks, it's generally not recommended in areas where there's likely to be standing water; if exposed to excessive moisture, the wood may warp or rot. Wood counters installed over a dishwasher should have a moisture barrier on their underside.

Bamboo

Bamboo is a rapidly renewable resource that provides the warmth, natural look, and durability of wood, although it's actually a giant grass. It's an increasingly popular material for floors and cabinets. Bamboo cutting boards are readily available from housewares retailers, but bamboo counters are still relatively uncommon. Contact cabinetmakers who work with bamboo for custom bamboo counters. Keep in mind that most bamboo comes from China, so if you prefer to source local materials, a domestic wood might be a better choice. For more information about bamboo, see chapter two.

Resources

Butcher-block and solid wood counters can be custom fabricated by local woodworkers from FSC-certified or salvaged hardwood. Make sure the glue used is water resistant and FDA approved for cutting boards if you plan to use them as a cutting surface. If custom counters aren't in your budget, look to retailers who have made public commitments to supporting sustainable forestry. Global retailer Ikea, for example, tells its suppliers that they must not "use wood originating from national parks, nature reserves, intact natural forests or any areas with officially declared high conservation values, unless certified."

- **Endura Wood Products.** Butcher-block countertops made with FSC-certified Oregon white oak and Eastern hard-rock maple. Portland, Oregon, 503.233.7090, endurawood.com.
- **Spekva A/S.** Danish manufacturer of wood counters, some of which are FSC certified. Available from North American distributors, spekva.com.
- **Smith & Fong.** Manufacturer of Plyboo laminated bamboo panels used for making cabinet, counter and table tops, and furniture. South San Francisco, California, 866.835.9859, plyboo.com.
- **Windfall Lumber Products.** Butcher block from wood

Bamboo, a rapidly renewable resource, can be used to make cabinets and counters, such as in this unique kitchen by Laguna Bamboo.

reclaimed from industrial vinegar tanks and other eco-friendly sources. Olympia, Washington, 360.352.2250, windfalllumber.com.

CERAMIC TILE

With a vast range of colors, patterns, and sizes readily available, ceramic tile offers terrific design flexibility for kitchen counters and walls. Glazed ceramic tile provides a durable, heat-proof, water-resistant surface. Pricing for ceramic tile ranges from modest to steep.

The main drawback of tile is grout. Crumbs and grime catch in grout lines, and inadequately sealed grout will stain and is prone to mold growth in wet areas. If you want to use tile in your kitchen but are concerned about upkeep, install it on a vertical surface such as a backsplash where it won't collect crumbs or be exposed to standing liquids. If you have your heart set on tile counters, minimize grout lines by selecting large tiles.

As discussed in more depth in the Floors chapter, ceramic tiles are a good green option. Tile production is relatively benign in terms of environmental impacts; although it does require considerable energy to fire tile, the raw materials used to make it are abundant. Tile is highly durable, with the added advantage that damaged tiles can be chiseled out and replaced.

Apart from the potential mold concern with grout, ceramic tile is an inert, healthful material for kitchen surfaces. However, adhesives, grout, sealants, and caulking applied during installation may emit VOCs until they have fully cured. Use low or no VOC thinsets, grout, and sealants.

To ratchet up the greenness, choose tiles with recycled content. Another good green option is to choose tiles manufactured locally or regionally.

Fireclay Tile handcrafts decorative tiles on a custom-order basis. Their standard tile base is clay, but they also make a line called Debris, with 50 percent post- and pre-consumer recycled content, including granite dust, discarded brown and green glass bottles, and window glass.

Resources

Ceramic tiles are widely available from home-improvement centers and tile distributors nationwide. Look for salvaged tiles at building-materials salvage yards.

Here are two tile makers that use a recycled base:

+ **Fireclay Tile, Inc.** Fireclay's Debris series of handmade tiles contains 50 percent pre- and post-consumer recycled waste, including granite dust, brown and green glass bottles, and windowpanes. San Jose, California, 408.275.1182, fireclaytile.com.

+ **Terra Green Ceramics, Inc.** Makes ceramic tiles containing 58 percent pre-consumer recycled glass. Richmond, Indiana, 765.935.4760, terragreenceramics.com.

CONCRETE

A construction material once considered suitable mainly for utilitarian applications such as foundations, sidewalks, and bridges, these days concrete turns up in all manner of kitchens, from traditional to ultramodern. It's a versatile material that lends itself to unique shapes and edge treatments, takes color readily, and brings out the creativity of talented craftspeople. With an appealing solidity and texture, concrete counters can be made to look earthy, industrial, or even glamorous, depending on the pigments and aggregate used and the fabricator's production and finishing techniques.

While concrete counters can be poured on-site in a mold built on top of the cabinets, it's more common to have them precast to your specifications and installed by the fabricator. Part of concrete's appeal is that it can be infinitely customized, or, more accurately, customizing is limited only by your imagination and budget and the fabricator's skills. Popular features to cast into concrete counters include integral drain boards and trivets; whimsical accents such as favorite trinkets, shells, or stones; and indentations for holding a bar of soap or a handful of nuts.

To provide structural strength, concrete counters are reinforced during the pour with steel mesh or rebar. Grinding gives the top surface a smooth polish. Concrete counters need regular applications of sealant or wax; even so, concrete is porous by nature, so the counters will be prone to staining. If you can't tolerate stains or the potential for cracks, don't choose concrete counters.

In this kitchen, the work surfaces and one wall are Syndecrete, a concrete-based solid-surfacing material that contains up to 40 percent recycled content.

HOW CLEAN IS CLEAN ENOUGH?

Bacteria and dirt congregate in work-surface seams and grout. For the sake of hygiene, consider seamless materials or minimize the number of seams. If you must have tile counters, choose a style with narrow grout lines, make sure the grout is sealed when originally installed, and reseal periodically. But for most people, when it comes to counters, there's no need to go overboard with antibacterial zeal. The antibacterial products promoted today—sprays, soaps, sponges, cutting boards, and even countertops treated with bactericides—may be doing more harm than good by creating conditions for bacteria to build resistance to germ-killing chemicals. The best defense against bacteria, health experts advise, is washing one's hands often with ordinary soap.

With its newfound reputation for chic, concrete sometimes gets branded as green. Truth be told, most concrete counters are no more or less eco friendly than any other countertop material. It's likely that they've picked up their green reputation by association with concrete floors, which do have a distinct eco advantage. When a home's structural concrete slab does double duty as the finish floor, resource consumption goes down thanks to the avoidance of an additional floor covering such as wood, carpet, or tile.

With concrete counters, there is no such resource savings. In fact, concrete counters are resource intensive: they're thick and heavy, and often poured in custom-built forms that get discarded after a single use. To their credit, concrete work surfaces can last a long time. But since concrete is prone to staining, chances are good that future owners of your home won't be enamored of the patina you left behind. In a generation's time, many of today's concrete kitchen counters could be destined for the dump (or more optimistically, the local recycling center, since concrete can be crushed and reused as fill or road-bed aggregate).

That said, it's possible to ratchet up the greenness of concrete counters. Syndecrete, a concrete solid-surfacing product used for counters, vertical surfaces, furniture, and more, contains as much as 40 percent recycled content, including metal shavings, recycled glass chips, and scrap wood chips.

Another green option is concrete made with a high percentage of recycled fly ash, a waste by-product from the flues of coal-burning power plants. Traditionally fly ash has been dumped in landfills, but these days many companies add it to their concrete mixes as a substitute for some of the portland cement content. Portland cement manufacturing is very energy intensive, producing significant carbon dioxide emissions that contribute to global warming, so substituting fly ash for some of the portland cement in concrete reduces carbon dioxide emissions to the atmosphere.

For large projects such as pouring concrete slab or footings for an entire house, it's possible to replace as much as 30 to 50 percent of the portland cement content with fly ash. For small projects such as kitchen countertops, it may not be possible to get concrete with fly ash, but it's worth asking the fabricator.

If you're having custom counters made, another option is to mix in an eco-friendly aggregate such as tumbled recycled glass. Glass can sometimes react with the cement and cause cracking, so consult with an experienced fabricator. In addition to using recycled aggregates such as glass, appealing decorative effects can be achieved by inlaying found or salvaged objects along the edges or top surface of the counter.

Custom concrete counters are pricey. If your budget is tight but you have ample time and creative talent, consider casting your own counters. Practice first by making small samples before you commit to a large countertop.

Fiber-Cement Counters

An appealing alternative to custom-made concrete counters is precast fiber-cement slabs such as SlateScape, Fireslate 2, and Squak Mountain Stone. Made from a blend of cement and cellulose fiber, these prefabricated products offer the modern look of concrete at a more moderate price. Colors are limited. Some of the charcoal-black products have the look of a laboratory work surface.

Fiber-cement counters are strong and durable, but like concrete, they are porous and can stain. They need to be resealed periodically with tung oil or a manufacturer-recommended sealant or wax.

Resources

◦**Portland Cement Association** lists concrete countertop suppliers on its Web site, cement.org/homes/ch_bs_countertops.asp.

◦**Syndecrete,** made by Syndesis, Inc., is a concrete-based solid-surfacing material containing up to 40 percent recycled content. Countertop slabs are cast to your specifications. Santa Monica, California, 310.829.9932, syndesisinc.com.

These two companies are renowned for their custom concrete countertop and furnishing designs. They also offer workshops for contractors and DIYers and sell ready-made mixes, pigments, and accessories:

◦**Cheng Design.** Berkeley, California, 510.849.3272, chengdesign.com.

◦**Buddy Rhodes Studio.** San Francisco, California, 877.706.5303, buddyrhodes.com.

DEMATERIALIZATION

How can you lighten a countertop's burden on the environment? Use less of it. Of course, you can limit the overall square footage of your counters, but adequate counter space is paramount to creating a kitchen that's a joy to cook, eat, and relax in. Rather than being too miserly with the square footage, think about dematerialization. This refers to products redesigned to use less material without sacrificing performance or aesthetics. Dematerialization offers a promising path for companies interested in reducing the environmental footprint of thick-slab products such as solid surface, concrete, fiber cement, and engineered stone. German manufacturer Bulthaup (bulthaup.com) has moved in this direction with their ultrathin $2/5$-inch engineered-stone countertop, available as part of their elegant b3 kitchen line.

Fiber-cement countertop manufacturers include:

◦**Fireslate 2.** E. Wareham, Massachusetts, 800.523.5902, fireslate.com.

◦**SlateScape,** manufactured by American Fiber Cement. Littleton, Colorado, 800.688.8677, americanfibercement.com.

◦**Squak Mountain Stone** contains 3 percent post-consumer and 64 percent pre-consumer recycled content, including waste paper, fly ash, and crushed-glass dust. Available from Environmental Home Center, Seattle, Washington, 800.281.9785, environmentalhomecenter.com.

ENGINEERED STONE

Engineered-stone countertops combine many of the qualities of natural stone and solid-surface counters. Engineered-stone products, including well-known brands such as Silestone, Zodiaq, and Cambria, are made from a blend of stone aggregate (usually quartz), plastic resin, and pigments. The surface is nonporous, so it's not prone to staining the way that some natural stone is. Engineered-stone manufacturers claim that their products are heat resistant and highly durable. However, some of these products are fairly new to the countertop market and quality varies, so it pays to do your homework before purchasing.

Often priced as high as granite, engineered-stone counters are sold in a wide range of patterns and colors. Many are designed to mimic the look of real granite, but their uniform appearance usually gives away their man-made origins.

These are durable, practical products, but they don't offer any convincing green advantages over solid stone counters. If you are averse to plastic-based or highly processed synthetic surfaces in your kitchen, engineered stone may not be the best choice for you.

GLASS AND GLASS TILE

Solid glass counters aren't used much in residential kitchens, but they can be a real showstopper. From a design perspective, glass is quite versatile: it can be clear, translucent, opaque, or textured, and it can be cut to almost any size or shape. For counters, tempered glass provides

The mosaic border on the backsplash is recycled glass. Counters are limestone on top and honed granite below.

strength, but if abused it can chip, crack, or shatter. There's no repairing the glass once that happens, so don't use it as a cutting surface, and consider keeping it away from areas where heavy pots or dishes are likely to be dropped. Glass is nonporous, so it won't stain but it can scratch.

From an environmental perspective, the impacts of glass production are relatively benign. Although high heat is required to produce it, the primary raw materials—silica sand, soda ash, and limestone—are plentiful and inexpensive. Many glass manufacturers also use recycled glass cullet as a raw material.

The main drawback to glass counters is their high maintenance: untextured glass shows every fingerprint, dust speck, and water spot. From a maintenance perspective, glass backsplashes make better sense than glass counters because the vertical surface is less likely to be a magnet for fingerprints and dust. Narrow or wide panels of tempered or laminated glass can be screwed to the wall behind the counter (don't overtighten or the glass will crack) or attached with silicone glue.

Glass Tile

A deluxe option for backsplashes is glass tile, available in enticing jewel-like hues. While glass production is relatively benign from an environmental perspective, you can push the green envelope further by choosing tiles made from recycled glass (not all glass tiles contain recycled glass). Bedrock Industries, for example, makes Blazestone tiles using 100 percent recycled glass. The company reports that they keep more than 50 tons of pre- and post-consumer glass out of landfills annually.

Glass tiles can be used for counters as well as backsplashes, but as with any tiles, keeping the grout clean can be a hassle. Whether or not they contain recycled glass, glass tiles are a luxury item, especially if they're handcast and hand-finished. If you need to keep costs down, stick with more affordable ceramic tile or just use glass tile as decorative accents rather than for the entire backsplash.

For more information about recycled glass tile, see chapter two.

Resources

Contact local plate-glass suppliers for counters and backsplashes.

Keep in mind that not all glass tiles contain recycled glass.

A back wall of recycled glass tiles from Oceanside Glasstile. Some of their tile lines contain as much as 85 percent recycled glass from discarded bottles.

Here are glass tiles that do:

• **Aurora Glass.** Makes recycled glass accent tiles, liner bars, and field tiles in various colors, shapes, and patterns. Eugene, Oregon, 888.291.9311, auroraglass.org.

• **Bedrock Industries.** Makes Blazestone, a handmade tile crafted from 100 percent recycled glass (pre- and post-consumer). Seattle, Washington, 877.283.7625, bedrockindustries.com.

• **Oceanside Glasstile.** Handcast glass tiles, some of which contain up to 85 percent post-consumer recycled glass. Carlsbad, California, 760.929.4000, glasstile.com.

• **Sandhill Industries.** Glass tiles made from 100 percent pre-consumer plate glass. Boise, Idaho, 208.345.6508, sandhillind.com.

LAMINATES AND PAPER/RESIN SLABS

Laminate materials for counters and backsplashes come in an exhaustive variety of colors, finishes, and styles. While laminates don't have the cachet of deluxe surfaces like granite or marble, they actually have a lot going for them. They are inexpensive, readily available, relatively hard-wearing, easy to clean, nonporous, and stain resistant. On the downside, laminates are not heat-proof, and they are difficult, if not impossible, to repair if gouged or cracked. Better-quality laminates have the color running all the way through the material, which helps to hide nicks and scratches.

Most people are familiar with thin-sheet laminates made by major manufacturers such as Formica and Wilsonart. These consist of layers of kraft paper permeated with phenolic resin, fused under pressure, and topped with a decorative layer of melamine-impregnated paper. To create a countertop, the laminate, which is usually about 1/16 inch thick, is glued to a 3/4-inch-thick substrate such as particleboard or plywood.

If you are installing the laminate yourself, select a greener substrate such as FSC-certified plywood or particleboard. To protect indoor air quality, choose a substrate with no added urea formaldehyde such as exterior-grade plywood, plywood made with soy-based adhesives, or Medite II, a medium-density fiberboard with no added formaldehyde. If you must use a formaldehyde-containing substrate such as conventional particleboard, seal the underside and any exposed edges with a low or no VOC clear sealant to inhibit offgassing. Use a low VOC glue to attach the laminate to the substrate.

Solid Paper/Resin Slabs

Some companies make thicker paper/resin counters that bear

These bamboo cabinets made by AlterECO are topped with a Richlite counter and backsplash.

some resemblance to slate, soapstone, or a laboratory bench top. Like the thin-sheet laminates, these thicker slabs are made of layers of resin-impregnated kraft paper, but their heft, ranging anywhere from 1/4 inch to two inches thick, gives them a more deluxe presence. They are installed directly on the cabinets without a substrate.

These paper/resin composites are available in a limited color palette. Some colors may darken over time due to exposure to UV light. Paper/resin composite counters are durable although not impervious to stains or scratches. They can be finished with mineral oil, tung oil, or linseed oil; periodic reapplication of the oil helps maintain a protective surface.

How green are laminates and paper/resin slabs? They are made in large part from wood fiber, a renewable resource. However, that fiber is bound with petrochemical-based resins,

a nonrenewable resource. Laminates don't offgas, although the substrates below them might, as mentioned above. Paper/resin slabs with recycled-paper content have an eco edge over competitors. In the future, look for eco-savvy manufacturers to begin making laminates with FSC-certified paper.

Resources

Conventional laminates made by companies such as Formica and Wilsonart are widely available at home-improvement centers. Among the thicker paper/resin slab materials, consider these options:

◆**PaperStone.** Introduced in 2003, PaperStone is made from paper containing 50 percent post-consumer recycled content. The paper is bonded with a water-based resin. Hoquiam, Washington, 360.538.9815, kliptech.com.

◆**Richlite.** Richlite is made of paper treated with resin and then pressed and baked to create solid sheets. Sold as an installed product through a network of authorized dealers. Richlite also offers a countertop made with hemp instead of tree fiber. Tacoma, Washington, 888.383.5533, richlite.com.

◆**Trespa.** Based in the Netherlands, this company manufactures high-pressure laminate panels that are a blend of phenolic resin, polycarbonate resin, and kraft paper. Two of Trespa's products, Athlon and TopLab, are suitable for kitchen counters. Poway, California, 800.487.3772, www.trespa.com.

Linoleum

Linoleum is more often found underfoot than on counters, but it makes an attractive and functional work surface. It's easy to clean, naturally antistatic, and antibacterial. It comes in a rainbow of colors and patterns. Make sure you select the real McCoy: genuine linoleum is made from linseed oil, sawdust, ground cork, and pine resin, and it's a whole different animal than the vinyl products people often mistakenly refer to as linoleum.

For more information about linoleum, see chapter two.

Metal

Once associated with industrial design, metal surfaces now appear in even the most traditional kitchens. The vogue for metal took off in the 1990s with stainless-steel appliances that paid homage to restaurant kitchens. It wasn't long before stainless-steel worktables, counters, and shelving units came into favor for residential kitchens, and with good reason. Stainless steel is hygienic, strong, heat-proof, rust-proof, and virtually indestructible. It does tend to show fingerprints (a brushed finish will help hide them), and it can dent and scratch. Over time the finish burnishes slightly, making scratches less visible. On countertops, thinner-gauge products will be noisy unless installed with an underlayment; if using particleboard, MDF, or plywood underlayment, choose a brand with no added formaldehyde.

Besides being a rugged, no-nonsense performer in the kitchen, stainless steel has a powerful eco advantage over many other materials: it's 100 percent recyclable. At the end of its life as a kitchen counter, range hood, or refrigerator door panel, the metal is fully recyclable. New stainless steel typically contains recycled content, although as with glass, suppliers can't usually tell you the exact percentage. No downgrading occurs when recycling stainless steel, so new products made with recycled-content steel are as high in quality as stainless steel made entirely with virgin raw materials.

Still, metal production is far from benign. Extracting the raw materials for metal manufacturing disrupts habitats, scars landscapes, and can contaminate water, air, and soil. Although many of these raw materials are abundant, they are finite, not renewable. Processing metal creates pollution and uses vast amounts of energy. Indeed, metal has a very high embodied energy, which refers to the sum total of all the energy required to make and transport the product, from mining to manufacturing to final installation in your home. The durability and recyclability of stainless steel and other metals does, however, offset some of this high embodied energy.

Stainless steel is king in kitchens today, but metals like zinc and copper can also be used to create distinctive countertops and backsplashes. Usually these are fabricated with a thin metal sheet bonded to a rigid backing such as MDF. Zinc is a silver-colored metal that mellows to a dark bluish gray patina; it's been used for ages on bar and tabletops in Europe. It's softer than stainless steel, and prone to denting and scratching. Copper also oxidizes and will darken to a weathered brown. If you want zinc or copper to retain its original gleam, be prepared for regular polishing. But for many people the mottled, oxidized patina is a large part of the material's charm.

As with stainless steel, most metals are fully recyclable. A copper industry trade association claims that nearly all of the 700 billion pounds of copper mined globally to date are still in circulation today. So although the virgin raw materials used to manufacture metals are mined from the earth, their recyclability gives them a green advantage over nonrecyclable products like solid-surface plastics.

A butcher-block counter paired with Eleek's 100 percent recycled cast-aluminum countertop, backsplash, and sink.

RECYCLING METALS

Manufacturing metal takes its toll on the environment. Ease the burden by recycling all metal that comes out of your kitchen-construction project, including old appliances, ducts, and pipes. Metal is a valuable commodity, so most municipalities have procedures for separating usable metals from the rest of the trash; contact your garbage hauler for information. If you hire a general contractor or kitchen-remodeling company, include a requirement in the contract stating that they must recycle to the greatest extent possible; this should include setting up a system on the job site for separating and storing recyclable materials and getting them delivered to a recycling facility.

Metal countertops can be very expensive, especially if custom fabricated for your kitchen. Special finishes, edges, and other details can increase prices even further. If you want the durability and robust good looks of metal at a budget price, look for used stainless-steel worktables at flea markets, used restaurant-equipment outlets, or online auction sites.

An alternative to sheet metal is metal tile. Eleek makes pricey but gorgeous cast-metal tiles from 100 percent recycled aluminum or bronze. The tiles, which can be used for counters and backsplashes, have a nonreactive clear powder-coat finish. The 5/16-inch-thick tiles come in a variety of shapes and sizes and are adhered to a substrate with tile adhesive or mastic, as with ceramic tiles.

Crossville, a manufacturer of porcelain tile, offers porcelain tiles wrapped with one millimeter of stainless steel; available in a variety of textures and sizes, they are installed like regular ceramic tiles. Some manufacturers also make metal wall tiles molded to a plastic backing. From an environmental perspective, these hybrids would seem to defeat one of the advantages of metal: the ease with which it can be recycled.

Resources

Sheet-metal counters and backsplashes are typically custom-fabricated; check with local cabinetmakers or metalwork companies. For metal tiles, visit local tile showrooms.

Freestanding stainless-steel worktables are readily available from restaurant supply companies—for bargain prices, and to do a good turn for the environment, track down used pieces. Consider adding industrial chic with unconventional items such as metal lockers and lab cabinets. If you're a DIYer, check junkyards for scrap sheet metal that you can transform into backsplashes or countertops; use low-toxic glues to adhere the sheet metal to the substrate, or even better, attach with screws for easier recycling in the future.

◆**Crossville, Inc.** Porcelain tile wrapped with stainless steel.

Crossville, Tennessee, 931.484.2110, www.crossvilleinc.com.
◆**Eleek, Inc.** Cast-aluminum tiles for counters and walls made from 100 percent recycled aluminum (minimum 70 percent post-consumer content). Portland, Oregon, 503.232.5526, eleekinc.com.

Solid Surface

Solid-surface countertops, introduced more than three decades ago, are familiar to consumers as brands such as Corian, Avonite, Swanstone, and Gibraltar. These products are solid slabs of plastic, typically 1/2 to 3/4 inches thick. They're made from either acrylic or polyester resin blended with mineral fillers and pigments.

Often installed directly on cabinets without a supporting substrate of plywood or particleboard, these synthetic products offer attractive, highly practical surfaces that are scratch and stain resistant. The color runs all the way through the material, so scratches that do occur can be removed with fine sandpaper. Solid-surface counters come in many colors and patterns, some of which mimic the look of granite or marble. From a design perspective, these materials are highly versatile; they can be fabricated with integral backsplashes, sinks, and drain boards, and can be cut, carved, drilled, routed, and shaped to accommodate just about any design concept.

Prices vary depending on the brand and the specific features you choose, but in general, solid-surface counters are quite expensive. They are installed by professional fabricators.

From a healthy home perspective, solid-surface countertops are a reasonable choice because they don't offgas noxious chemicals (as long as they're not mounted on a formaldehyde-emitting substrate like particleboard). Also, because they're nonporous, they don't invite mold growth and are easy to clean.

What are the downsides? A solid-surface counter is a big hunk of plastic, which isn't to everyone's taste. It's made from nonrenewable petrochemical-based raw materials. It is not recyclable or biodegradable, so after your countertops have ended their service life in your kitchen, they may be destined to spend eons buried in a landfill.

What's the green bottom line? Solid surfacing does not offer any ecological advantages over other countertop materials.

If you desire the durability and practicality of plastic but want to reduce consumption of nonrenewable resources, a better choice might be a thin laminate installed over a substrate of plywood, particleboard, or MDF. Chose substrate brands with no added urea formaldehyde, and if possible, FSC-certified fiber content.

> ## NOT ALL RECYCLED CONTENT IS CREATED EQUAL
>
> Some manufacturers boast of recycled content in their products when in fact they're merely putting their manufacturing scrap back into their product mix. This does not make it a green product. Smart, profitable companies find ways to reduce waste—whether by not creating it in the first place or by reusing it. Reusing their own scrap helps the company's bottom line but doesn't address society's environmental ills. When it comes to recycled content, a good green rule of thumb is to favor products that contain at least 25 percent post-consumer recycled content—discarded beverage containers, newspapers, used tires, and the like.

A RECYCLED ALTERNATIVE TO SOLID SURFACES

If you are hankering after a playful plastic with high recycled content, check out Origins from Yemm and Hart (yemmhart.com). A high-density polyethylene sheet available in thicknesses from 1/8 inch to two inches, some colorful Origins patterns have as much as 100 percent post-consumer recycled content. The thinner sheets can be treated like a laminate and glued to a substrate, while the thicker versions can be used like a solid-surface material without a substrate. Origins is softer than conventional solid-surface and laminate products though, so it may be better suited to surfaces not subject to heavy-duty wear and tear such as backsplashes. Find out more at yemmhart.com.

Resources

Conventional solid-surface countertops are widely available through home-improvement stores, kitchen-design centers, and local cabinet/counter fabricators.

STONE

There's no doubt about it, stone counters are gorgeous. With the exception of wood, there isn't a more natural countertop material than solid stone. Much of the beauty of stone comes from the fact that every piece is one of a kind, with veining and variegated colorations that are endlessly pleasing to the eye.

I've met some eco-minded designers who won't use quarried stone in their projects. But in my opinion, stone is not out of place in an eco-friendly kitchen: it's as natural as you can get, minimally processed, extremely durable, and potentially reusable. Stone is not a renewable resource, of course, but the stones most often used for counters and backsplashes—granite, marble, slate, and soapstone—are relatively abundant.

Stone counters have the potential to last forever, which could be a powerful eco benefit if it weren't for the fact that kitchens get remodeled more frequently than any other room in the house. The elegant black granite slab that seems so timeless today may be the first thing that the next owner of your house decides to tear out.

The Achilles heel of natural stone is the environmental impacts of quarrying. Stone is cut out of mountainsides in huge blocks, leaving permanent gashes on the landscape. While some quarrying is done responsibly, as a consumer it's very difficult to assess whether the stone you've fallen in love with was responsibly quarried without damage to nearby habitats and waterways. Unfortunately there is no environmental certification program for stone that's the equivalent of FSC certification for the forest products industry.

Your best bet is to choose stone quarried close to home, or within no more than 500 miles of your home. This makes sense for three reasons: first, it's reasonable to assume that domestic quarrying activities would be subject to more stringent environmental regulations than quarrying in certain other parts of the world, especially developing countries; second, using materials extracted from our own region increases our awareness of the value of natural resources and the environmental and social impacts that occur when we consume them; third, using locally or regionally sourced stone uses less transportation fuel than transporting heavy, bulky stone from mountaintops a half a world away.

Besides choosing stone quarried in your region, how else can you ratchet up the greenness of stone countertops and backsplashes? Continue using any stone counters you already have rather than tossing them in the debris box. If they truly have to go, have them removed intact if possible. Arrange for delivery to a local building-materials reuse yard, or put the counters up for sale on an online classifieds site such as eBay or Craigslist.

STONE SEALANTS

Stone counters are often factory finished with chemicals called penetrating or impregnating sealers. Ask the supplier whether your counter will require periodic resealing. Many conventional stone-sealing products contain toxic petroleum distillates and high levels of VOCs that you may not want to use in your home. Get the brand name of the recommended product and download the Material Safety Data Sheet (MSDS) from the manufacturer's Web site. If the list of chemicals and precautions gives you pause, ask the supplier for a safer water-based sealant or consider going with unsealed stone. Many people actually prefer their stone counters to have a worn, lived-in patina.

The countertop is honed granite, with a glass tile backsplash.

Instead of buying newly quarried stone, scour local junk-yards, flea markets, online auction sites, and antiques stores for salvaged stone counters, slabs, or tiles.

Another green option is to use less stone: scale back on the square footage of your counters, choose thinner slabs, or both. Thin slabs must be installed over a substrate such as plywood; choose a brand that's FSC certified and that has no added urea formaldehyde.

Finally, ask the installer to use mechanical means rather than glue to fasten the counter to the cabinets; this will make it easier in the future to remove the slab intact and reuse it elsewhere.

For more information about using stone in kitchens, see chapter two.

Granite

Notwithstanding their high price, granite counters remain wildly popular. Quarried all over the world, granite slabs are sold in a stunning array of colors and patterns. Typically fabricated as 3/4- to 1 1/4-inch-thick slabs or as tiles, this igneous stone is hard, dense, heat resistant, and difficult to chip or scratch. But it is not impervious to staining: while it is relatively resistant to acids like lemon juice and wine, it is susceptible to stains from oils.

Granite slabs sold for counters come from all over the world, including Brazil, China, India, and African nations. But gorgeous granite is quarried closer to home too. If you're passionate about granite counters but concerned about environmental impacts, choose granite quarried within 500 miles of your home. If that's not available, select granite sourced from countries with strong environmental and worker health and safety protections.

Marble

Some kitchen designers don't recommend marble counters because they scratch easily and can be etched by acids such as lemon juice, or by alcohol. But there's an old-world look to marble that makes for gorgeous counters. And bakers adore its cold, smooth surface for rolling out pastry dough. (Granite is also cold and smooth, but butter and oil can stain it.) If you want your counters to look pristine forever, don't choose marble, or install a marble inset that's just large enough for pastry-making. For a more eco-friendly alternative to newly quarried marble, look for salvaged marble slabs at building salvage yards and antiques stores.

Limestone

Limestone is a beautiful stone that comes in a range of colors, but is most often seen in light tones with subtle veining. A sedimentary rock, it is quite porous, so not usually recommended for counters. If you've fallen in love with limestone and must have it in your kitchen, consider it for a backsplash instead.

Jesse Cool has been dedicated to using local, seasonal, and organically grown foods throughout her thirty-year career as a chef, caterer, and restaurateur. Her Northern California–based company, CoolEatz, includes three restaurants and a catering company. Cool's own home kitchen recently underwent a dramatic transformation from a cramped, dark galley to a roomy space ideal for cooking, entertaining, and teaching cooking classes. Cool chose granite counters for their good looks, durability, and cool-to-the-touch surface that helps keep produce fresh. Wall tiles are Fireclay Tile's Debris series made from 50 percent pre- and post-consumer recycled waste.

Slate

A metamorphic rock with a smooth, velvety feel, slate slabs for counters come in luscious blacks, deep reds, greens, and grays. Choose domestically quarried slate, or even better, if you live in a region where slate roofs are common, track down salvaged slate roofing tiles for your kitchen counters. Check with building salvage yards and roofing companies that remove old roofs.

Soapstone

Soapstone is a blue-gray stone that oxidizes over time to a dark charcoal. Soapstone is dense, heat-proof, and stain resistant, but it is soft and will scratch. It is also more likely to chip or crack than granite. To reduce environmental impacts, choose domestically quarried soapstone. Periodic applications of mineral or linseed oil enhance the deep luster of soapstone.

Volcanic Stone

A relatively new entry to the stone countertop market is glazed lava stone. Quarried volcanic rock is sliced into slabs, coated with a pigmented glaze, and kiln-fired. The final result is a glassy, heat-resistant, nonporous surface. The look is deluxe but the cost is extremely high. Also, the glazing process offsets one key eco advantage of natural stone: that it is minimally processed.

Brands of glazed lava rock include Pyrolave from France and Vulcanite from Fireclay Tile in San Jose, California.

Resources

Natural stone counters and tiles are widely available from stone distributors, kitchen-design centers, and major home-improvement stores.

For salvaged stone, check with building-materials salvage yards, companies that deconstruct existing buildings, and online classifieds ads.

Terrazzo

Terrazzo counters are thick slabs made of chips of marble, granite, glass, or other aggregates embedded in a binder of cement. These days, a number of companies make terrazzo-like products using a plastic resin binder instead of cement.

For the greenest terrazzo, choose products with a high post-consumer recycled content (at least 25 percent of the product's weight) or choose locally made products. Counter Production makes its Vetrazzo counters with 80 percent or higher post-consumer recycled glass in a cement-based binder.

Some companies use mostly pre-consumer aggregate such as granite or marble chips left over from quarrying or stone-cutting activities or scrap glass from plate-glass-, mirror-, or auto-glass-making activities. Some products also have a small amount of recycled fly ash in the cement binder. If you don't want a plastic-based countertop, avoid those made with epoxy resin.

For more information about terrazzo, see chapter two.

RADON AND STONE

Radon is a colorless, odorless, radioactive gas derived from the natural decay of uranium in soil, rocks, and water. According to the U.S. Surgeon General, radon is the second leading cause of lung cancer in the United States.

Radon is virtually always present at very low levels in outside air; it's really only considered a health problem if it accumulates at high levels inside buildings. Although it is more prevalent in some regions than others, the U.S. EPA recommends that all homes below the third floor be tested for radon.

Can granite counters or other natural-stone materials used inside buildings emit enough radon to cause concern? It seems unlikely. The EPA states that "building materials rarely cause radon problems by themselves. In the United States, radon gas in soils is the principal source of elevated radon levels in homes."

If you are concerned that stone materials in your kitchen might be producing radon, you can have your home tested for radon; inexpensive, easy-to-use short-term testing kits are available online and from hardware stores. If the results show elevated radon levels, have an independent radon-testing laboratory conduct a more accurate, longer-term test. Make sure the lab is certified by your state and not affiliated with a radon-services company that sells or installs mitigation equipment. If the lab's results also indicate high levels of radon, work with them to pinpoint the source. Chances are it will be the soil, not your home's building materials or furnishings.

Homes found to have high levels of radon can be retrofitted with radon mitigation systems installed by experienced contractors. The EPA says the cost of reducing radon in a house ranges from about $800 to $2,500, depending on how the home was built and the extent of the radon problem.

For more information, go to epa.gov/radon, or call the National Radon Information Line at 800.SOS.RADON.

Resources

+**Counter Production.** Makes Vetrazzo from 80 to 90 percent post-consumer recycled glass in a cementitious binder. Berkeley, California, 510.843.6916, counterproduction.com.

+**Coverings, Etc.** Distributes Italian terrazzo products, including Eco-Tek tiles made with pre-consumer recycled stone chips (remnants of marble and granite slabs) in a cement binder that contains 5 percent fly ash. Also offers Eco-Terr tiles and slabs; Eco-Terr with glass chips contains 70 percent post-consumer and 10 percent pre-consumer recycled content, while Eco-Terr with marble or granite chips contains 80 percent pre-consumer recycled content. Miami, Florida, and New York, New York, 800.720.7814, www.coveringsetc.com.

+**EnviroGLAS Products Inc.** Offers EnviroSLAB, a one-inch-thick counter made from as much as 75 percent recycled glass by volume (the percentage of post- versus pre-consumer recycled glass depends on specific color mix chosen). The matrix is an epoxy resin. Plano, Texas, 888.523.7894, enviroglasproducts.com.

+**IceStone.** Makes terrazzo counters from 75 percent recycled glass in a cementitious binder. Post-consumer and pre-consumer content varies depending on color; products average at least 30 percent post-consumer recycled material. Brooklyn, New York, 718.624.4900, icestone.biz.

WALL FINISHES

One of the fastest and least expensive ways to dress up a kitchen is to give it a new coat of paint. When choosing primers and paints, do yourself and your household (not to mention

▲
Eco-Tek tiles are made with remnants of marble-and-granite slabs in a cement binder.

▼
Eco-Terr tiles and slabs contain marble, granite, and glass chips in a cement binder.

your painter) a favor by selecting zero or very low VOC products. VOC, as described on page 24, stands for volatile organic compound, a class of organic chemicals that readily evaporate at room temperature. VOCs occur naturally in many materials, and are added to an array of building products, including paints, primers, sealants, adhesives, and wood finishes.

Exposure to VOCs can cause symptoms ranging from nausea, eye irritation, and headaches to more severe, longer-lasting effects. The VOCs in paint also contribute to the formation of smog outside. Fortunately, there are many products formulated to have very low or zero levels of VOCs. A good rule of thumb is to choose interior flat paint with a VOC level of 50 grams per liter or less, and interior non-flat paint with 150 grams per liter or less. The VOC content should be labeled on the product packaging; you can also download the material safety data sheet (MSDS) from the manufacturer's Web site.

Keep in mind that paints labeled "VOC compliant" are not necessarily low VOC; VOC compliant merely means that the product complies with federal or state regulations for VOC content; it's usually possible to buy a product with much lower or zero VOC levels.

Also be aware that "low odor" is not the same thing as low VOC. Some companies add fragrance to mask odor rather than reformulating the product to remove the harmful volatile chemicals.

Paints and other finishes deemed "natural" are usually made largely from plant- and mineral-based ingredients rather than synthetic chemicals. With any alternative paint, verify with the supplier that it is appropriate for high-moisture, high-wear applications such as kitchens. If you are chemically

▲ ▶
EnviroGLAS counters (above and opposite page) contain as much as 75 percent recycled glass.

sensitive, be aware that plant-based finishes can have strong odors that take time to dissipate. Be particularly cautious about using a high-odor plant-based finish on the inside of cabinets, drawers, or closets; in areas where the finish is not exposed to frequent air changes, it will take even longer to fully cure.

Resources

Most major paint manufacturers offer low VOC interior paints, including Benjamin Moore's EcoSpec and Kelly-Moore's Enviro-Cote. Other companies go one step better, offering zero VOC paints or products without biocides, fungicides, or other potentially problematic chemicals. Consider these products for your next interior painting project:

◆**AFM Safecoat.** Offers an extensive line of low and zero VOC paints and finishes. Distributed nationally, 619.239.0321, afmsafecoat.com.

◆**Aglaia.** German-made paints derived from plants and minerals, aglaiapaint.com. Sold by a limited number of U.S. retailers, including Environmental Building Supplies, Portland Oregon, 503.222.3881, ecohaus.com.

WALLPAPER

Think twice about using wallpaper in the kitchen. Some wall coverings, such as many vinyl-coated wallpapers or paper-backed vinyl wallpapers, are impermeable and can act as a moisture barrier on the wall. If water or water vapor gets behind the paper, it can remain trapped there and cause mold to grow. Since the mold will be invisible behind the paper, it may grow to cover extensive areas of the wall before it is noticed, creating unhealthy conditions in the home and potentially causing structural damage to the wall.

+**American Clay.** Premixed earth plasters for finishing interior walls. Distributed nationally, 866.404.1634, americanclay.com.

+**American Pride Paints.** Zero and low VOC interior paints available nationally from green building supply stores and traditional paint stores 601.271.2588, southerndiversifiedproducts.com.

+**Anna Sova.** High-end milk-based paint. Distributed nationally, 877.326.7682, annasova.com.

+**Auro USA.** Plant-based paints, stains, oils, and other finishes. Petaluma, California, 888.302.9352, aurousa.com.

+**Best Paint.** Low and zero VOC, biocide-free paints and clear coats. Seattle, Washington, 206.783.9938, bestpaintco.com.

+**BioShield Paint Co.** Extensive line of zero and low VOC paints, sealers, wood preservatives, and other finishes, including milk-based and plant-based products. Online sales, 800.621.2591, bioshieldpaint.com.

+**Dulux Lifemaster 2000.** Solvent-free, zero VOC interior paint. Sold nationally by ICI Paints stores, 800.984.5444, iciduluxpaints.com.

+**Livos.** German-made zero and low VOC plant-based paints and wood finishes. Portland, Oregon, 503.257.9663, livos.us.

+**Old-Fashioned Milk Paint Co.** Paints made with casein (milk protein), lime, clay, and earth pigments, sold in powdered form. Distributed nationally, 978.448.6336, milkpaint.com.

+**Osmo Wood Stains and Finishes.** German-made plant-based wood finishes. Sold by Environmental Home Center (environmentalhomecenter.com) and other green-building retailers.

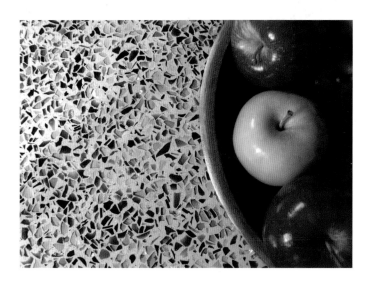

+**Pittsburgh Paints Pure Performance.** Zero VOC interior paint. Sold in paint stores nationwide, 800.441.9695, voiceofcolor.com.

+**Rodda Horizon Interior.** Ultra-low VOC interior paint and low VOC exterior paint. Available from Rodda's online store and select paint stores in the northwestern United States, roddapaint.com.

+**Sherwin-Williams Harmony.** Zero VOC interior paint. Sold nationally by Sherwin Williams paint stores, sherwinwilliams.com.

+**Tried & True Wood Finishes.** Made from polymerized linseed oil, zero VOC, no heavy-metal driers. See Web site for regional retailers, 607.387.9280, triedandtruewoodfinish.com.

+**YOLO Colorhouse.** Zero VOC interior paints in forty colors. Portland, Oregon, and local distributors, 503.493.8275, yolocolorhouse.com.

ECO-FRIENDLY WINDOW TREATMENTS

Eco-friendly options for window treatments include organically grown cotton, silk, or hemp curtains, or shades made from natural reeds, bamboo, or other grasses. If you live in a cold-winter climate, consider insulated curtains or shades to keep the kitchen cozier at night, especially near seating areas. If you are chemically sensitive, you may want to avoid fabrics treated with stain-resistant or anti-wrinkle chemicals such as formaldehyde. Avoid window coverings made from PVC (polyvinyl chloride, or vinyl for short); many eco-advocacy groups have raised concerns about the environmental and human-health hazards related to PVC's manufacturing, use, and disposal.

RECYCLED PAINT

Some paint companies take leftover paint from municipal paint-collection programs and recycle it into new paint. It's a good way to keep paint out of the waste stream, but I recommend recycled paint only for exterior purposes because of its higher VOC content (often in the range of 250 grams per liter). For healthy interiors, choose paints with zero or very low levels of VOCs.

REMODELING A 1940s HOUSE

When Barbara Peterson and Tom Beach bought their house, they knew it was a fixer-upper. Built in the 1940s, the 2,100-square-foot house cried out for a thorough overhaul of its interior spaces, not to mention a new roof, windows, and exterior siding. Although the house sits on a double lot that affords plenty of room for expansion, the couple chose to keep the building compact, preserving space for gardens, protecting mature oaks on the property, and providing a yard where their two boys could play.

Kathryn Rogers of Sogno Design Group worked with the couple to come up with a plan for reconfiguring the kitchen, living room, and dining room to improve the flow and provide a better connection to the large yard. The new kitchen remains modest in size yet serves as the hub of the house. Dutch doors open onto a colorful garden and the street, making it easy to chat with neighbors walking by. One corner of the kitchen has large windows over the sink that look out on the yard where the boys play, while another window faces west, affording views of the deck. On the north wall there is a small window with a view of the front door. A bar with a top

◄ Although the kitchen isn't large, peaked ceilings and good connections to the great room and the outdoors help it feel spacious.

▲ The counters are burgundy-hued Richlite, a paper and resin composite.

The Dutch door was made locally from salvaged Douglas fir. The woodworker didn't try to disguise the old nail holes, also known as "beauty marks."

The ceilings in the great room and kitchen were raised, providing a sense of loftiness. The exposed ceiling trusses, posts, and beams are reclaimed timbers purchased at a local salvage yard.

The refrigerator, an extremely energy-efficient Sun Frost model, is in a hallway just off the main kitchen space.

fashioned from an old bowling lane separates the kitchen from the open dining and living areas.

Peterson and Beach decided against upper cabinets, which freed up wall space for the large windows and Dutch door. A hall that leads from the kitchen to the front door serves as a pantry, with base and wall cabinets along one wall providing plenty of storage. The kitchen is airy, bright, and comfortable, yet the compact floor plan means that it is never more than a few steps from stove to sink to refrigerator.

Green Details

+ Dutch door locally made of salvaged Douglas fir
+ Breakfast counter fashioned from a piece of an old bowling alley
+ Very energy-efficient Sun Frost RF-16 refrigerator

- Good daylighting, with natural light entering the kitchen from all four sides
- Compact floor plan
- Tall peaked ceiling with trusses of salvaged Douglas fir purchased at a local salvage yard
- Exterior trellises built from salvaged railroad trestles dredged from Utah's Great Salt Lake
- Tankless on-demand water heater
- Compact fluorescent lights widely used
- Blown-in cellulose insulation (recycled newspaper) above ceiling and in walls; recycled cotton-batt insulation below kitchen floor
- A 2.4-kilowatt solar electric system

Project Credits

- Architect: Sogno Design Group, Albany, California.
- Builder: Cerami Builders, Berkeley, California.
- Photographer: Linda Svendsen.

The trellis outside the kitchen is fashioned from a railroad trestle dredged from the Great Salt Lake. Beach and Peterson said that when the trestle wood was cut, they could smell the salty brine of the Great Salt Lake.

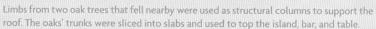

Limbs from two oak trees that fell nearby were used as structural columns to support the roof. The oaks' trunks were sliced into slabs and used to top the island, bar, and table.

REMODELING A 1970S HOUSE

Few of the principles behind green building are new: improve dwellings rather than knock them down; make the most of salvaged materials; build with local resources.

Nothing could be more local than the two giant Coast Live Oaks that toppled near Suzanne Jones and Rob Elia's house in a semirural suburb forty minutes from San Francisco. Fallen trees are usually chopped for firewood or chipped for mulch, but Jones devised a more noble fate for hers. With guidance from Leger Wanaselja Architecture, she salvaged the trees, putting massive limbs into service as structural posts supporting the roof of her newly renovated mid-1970s house. Jones and her remodeling crew chiseled off the thickest bark by hand, and then ground and sanded the limbs to a sensuous sheen. Limbs destined for interior posts were treated with a linseed oil–based finish, while limbs used outside to support the roof over the main entry were weatherproofed with polyurethane.

Huge slabs from the trees' trunks were sliced lengthwise into one-and-a-half- to two-and-a-half-inch-thick slabs, and air-dried for two years. Jones treated the slabs repeatedly with a boric acid solution to get rid of bugs. Eventually the trunk slabs were fashioned into tops for the kitchen island, as well as the bar and a table that separate the kitchen from the dining area. The organic forms provide a surpris-

An oak counter and bamboo drawer detail.

Custom kitchen cabinets made by Serge Bouyssou have bamboo exteriors finished with a linseed-based oil. Cabinet interiors are FSC-certified maple plywood.

The breakfast nook table and benches were also fashioned from the salvaged oaks.

ingly elegant counterpoint to the home's sleek bamboo cabinetry and mid-century Modern furnishings.

Jones marvels that the tree "was literally 200 yards from the house. It fell there as an acorn probably 350 years ago and fell over at the end of its life. It was all milled here on-site. And now it's being used here. It never left the site."

Green Details

+ Bamboo cabinet exteriors with FSC-certified maple plywood interiors
+ Cabinet doors and oak countertops finished with lead-free linseed-based oils from BioShield
+ Energy Star refrigerator and dishwasher
+ Electric convection oven and magnetic induction cooktop
+ Vermont slate kitchen floor
+ Maple flooring in dining and living areas salvaged from a 1920s post office
+ Fallen oaks salvaged for interior and exterior posts, counters, furniture, stairs, and railing
+ Extensive use of salvaged wood for exterior siding, fences, deck, interior trim, and built-in shelves and cabinets in office
+ Three-kilowatt solar-electric system
+ Rooftop solar collectors for water heating
+ Single-pane windows replaced with low-e double-pane windows
+ Insulation improved in walls and ceilings
+ Ten-thousand-gallon tank on property stores rainwater runoff from roof for irrigation

Project Credits

+ Architect: Leger Wanaselja Architecture, Berkeley, California, lwarc.com.
+ Builder: Owners.
+ Photographer: Linda Svendsen.

▲

In this newly renovated mid-1970s home, the formerly isolated kitchen was opened up to the living and dining areas.

▶

Countertops fashioned from the oaks' trunk nestle against large limbs that serve as structural posts. Slabs from the same trees were used for counters in the kitchen on page 34.

The Equator Conserv refrigerator is one of the most energy-efficient refrigerators available, and its tall, slender design makes it a good fit for smaller kitchens.

Clutter-busting features like a tilt-out sponge drawer in front of the sink are particularly important in very small kitchens. The backsplash is laminated glass attached to the wall with silicone glue. See more of this kitchen on page 34.

5 energy, water, and cleaning up

They don't make appliances like they used to—they make them better. Compared to kitchen equipment manufactured just a generation ago, today's appliances use less energy and water and are quieter and more convenient to use. So whether you are building a new house, remodeling, or just planning to replace a worn-out dishwasher, there's a wide range of first-rate appliances to choose from.

There are important differences between models, however, so if you hope to wind up with an appliance that meets your performance and style expectations and is among the greenest of its class, expect to do some homework. Major appliances remain in service for years, so a little research upfront will be well worth the trouble.

ENERGY

Kitchens are more than the hub of household activity; they are also a major hub of household energy use. Apart from a home's heating and air-conditioning systems, the kitchen accounts for the biggest chunk of a typical home's energy bills. Fortunately there are many options for energy-efficient appliances that work great, save money, and are better for the environment.

125

ENERGY EFFICIENCY

Paying attention to energy efficiency is one of the smartest things you can do when planning your new kitchen or shopping for new appliances. Before you start looking, it helps to understand what energy efficiency actually means. The term is often used interchangeably with "energy conservation," but they're not the same. Energy conservation means doing without—driving your car less, putting on a sweater instead of turning up the heat, turning off the lights when you leave a room. Conservation makes good sense but it rubs some people the wrong way because it smacks of deprivation.

For many, energy efficiency provides a more appealing path to a sustainable future. Energy-efficient products and technologies do more with less. An energy-efficient refrigerator wrings more cooling out of each watt of electricity consumed, just as an energy-efficient car goes farther on a gallon of gas. With energy efficiency, you get better performance, spend less money, and give the environment a break.

Giving the environment a break isn't a "feel good" abstraction. Smarter energy use—whether through conservation, efficiency, or a combination of the two—reduces the production of heat-trapping greenhouse gases that contribute to global warming.

What's more, global warming is only one of many energy-related concerns: respiratory disease, cancer, mercury contamination of waterways, and acid rain have all been linked to pollutants emitted by electric power plants, especially older plants fueled by coal. Air pollution resulting from electricity generation affects us all, but it can be particularly harmful, and sometimes deadly, for children and the elderly, as well as asthmatics and people with other respiratory conditions.

Reducing energy consumption is the most essential step you take to protect the environment—and the kitchen is one of the best places to start.

EnergyGuide and Energy Star

Much of the improvement in appliance performance over the past fifteen years can be attributed to standards established by federal agencies, as well as certain states that take a leadership position on energy issues, such as California and New York. At the federal level, three entities are charged with helping consumers purchase more energy-efficient products: Department of Energy (DOE), Federal Trade Commission (FTC), and Energy Star, a program run jointly by DOE and the Environmental Protection Agency (EPA).

DOE requires manufacturers to comply with minimum efficiency levels for certain types of home appliances. FTC requires the yellow-and-black EnergyGuide labels on refrigerators, freezers, dishwashers, and many other products. The information on the EnergyGuide label allows consumers to compare the projected energy use of various models; the data is based on tests the manufacturers conduct using Department of Energy test procedures.

Energy Star sets the energy efficiency bar even higher than the federal minimum standards, awarding the Energy Star seal of approval to products in roughly the top 25 percent of energy performance in each category. Energy Star's efforts to help consumers identify better-performing products are having results: in 2004, Energy Star–approved products helped Americans

▶

The U.S. Federal Trade Commission requires an EnergyGuide label on many types of appliances, including refrigerators, freezers, and dishwashers.

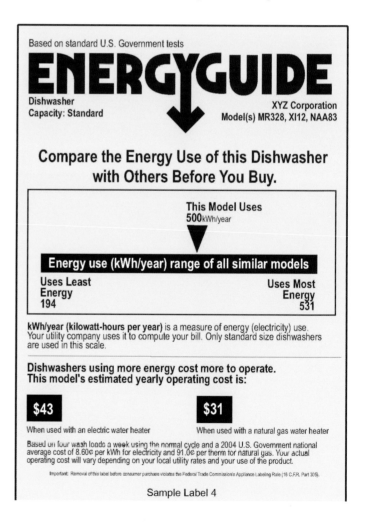

Based on standard U.S. Government tests

ENERGYGUIDE

Dishwasher
Capacity: Standard

XYZ Corporation
Model(s) MR328, XI12, NAA83

Compare the Energy Use of this Dishwasher with Others Before You Buy.

This Model Uses
500kWh/year

Energy use (kWh/year) range of all similar models

Uses Least
Energy
194

Uses Most
Energy
531

kWh/year (kilowatt-hours per year) is a measure of energy (electricity) use. Your utility company uses it to compute your bill. Only standard size dishwashers are used in this scale.

Dishwashers using more energy cost more to operate.
This model's estimated yearly operating cost is:

$43
When used with an electric water heater

$31
When used with a natural gas water heater

Based on four wash loads a week using the normal cycle and a 2004 U.S. Government national average cost of 8.60¢ per kWh for electricity and 91.0¢ per therm for natural gas. Your actual operating cost will vary depending on your local utility rates and your use of the product.

Important: Removal of this label before consumer purchase violates the Federal Trade Commission's Appliance Labeling Rule (16 C.F.R. Part 305).

Sample Label 4

slash their energy bills by approximately $10 billion while reducing greenhouse gas emissions equivalent to those produced by 20 million cars.

You can't tell by looking at an appliance how energy efficient it will be, so the EnergyGuide label, the Energy Star program, and other published sources of data about energy usage are critical to making smart buying decisions. What distinguishes an energy hog from an energy-saving appliance isn't usually visible: it's often a matter of better motors, compressors, gaskets, seals, and insulation, as well as electronic sensors with smart controls. In general, an energy-efficient appliance is a better-made appliance.

In addition to government agencies, many groups provide useful information to help people make energy-smart choices. *Consumer Reports* regularly tests most types of major appliances and is an excellent source for information about overall performance as well as energy efficiency. Also, the American Council for an Energy-Efficient Economy publishes the *Consumer Guide to Home Energy Savings*, a useful book that offers home energy-efficiency tips and lists of top-rated energy-efficient appliances.

Does Energy Efficiency Cost More?

In some cases, although certainly not all, Energy Star–approved appliances will cost roughly 10 or 15 percent more than comparable non–Energy Star products. That's a small additional price to pay for a better product that saves money and reduces pollution month after month, year after year. Keep in mind

Look for the Energy Star logo when purchasing major appliances.

that you pay the purchase price only once, but when you buy a more efficient appliance, you reap savings every day for the life of the product.

Besides the energy savings, rebates offer another way to come out ahead. Many local power and water companies offer cash incentives to customers who replace old appliances with more efficient ones. For information about available rebates, contact your local utility company, or enter your zip code into the rebate finder feature on the Energy Star Web site.

Resources

+**ACEEE.** Publishes the *Consumer Guide to Home Energy Savings*, aceee.org/consumerguide.

+**Consumer Reports.** Consumerreports.org.

+**Energy Star.** 888.STAR.YES, energystar.gov.

+**EnergyGuide.** Information about EnergyGuide labeling requirements and energy-use data for appliances, ftc.gov/bcp/conline/edcams/eande/index.html.

Refrigerators and Freezers

Refrigerators and freezers used to be real energy hogs, but in recent years, thanks to government efficiency standards and incentives, manufacturers have dramatically improved their products' performance. Refrigerators made before 1990 consumed an average of 1,250 kilowatt hours per year each, whereas today's most efficient refrigerators use less than 500 kilowatt hours annually.

RECYCLE IT

Planning to replace a kitchen appliance? Don't junk the old one—recycle it. Major appliances such as refrigerators, dishwashers, and ranges contain recyclable metal, glass, and plastic. According to the Association of Home Appliance Manufacturers, discarded appliances are second only to old automobiles as a source of recycled metals, particularly steel. Check with your town's recycling department or visit earth911.org (phone: 877. EARTH911) to find out about local recycling facilities. Also, ask your power company about recycling rebates. My power company paid me $35 for the privilege of hauling away and recycling my old energy-hog fridge.

ARE LEASED APPLIANCES IN OUR FUTURE?

It doesn't take a crystal ball to predict that energy prices will continue to climb and appliance efficiency standards continue to get more stringent. Given that scenario, wouldn't it make sense if we could lease our major kitchen appliances rather than own them outright? I recently bought a new refrigerator, one of the most energy-efficient models available, and while I'm happy with it, I would be delighted if the manufacturer would take it back in a few years for re-manufacturing or recycling, and replace it with an even more efficient model. What's the point of owning this big box of metal and plastic when all I want to pay for is the service of keeping my veggies crisp and my Ben & Jerry's frozen?

DON'T OVERDO THE DRAWER APPLIANCES

In any kitchen showroom these days you'll find drawer-style refrigerators, freezers, wine coolers, dishwashers, warming ovens, ice makers, and even temperature- and humidity-controlled humidor drawers for cigar storage. They're certainly handy since they can be located just about anywhere, from the media room to the master bedroom, from the home office to the pool side. They also can help improve accessibility for people with physical disabilities. But excessive use of drawer appliances throughout the home can drive up a household's energy consumption. What's the eco-friendliest strategy for drawer appliances? Install them instead of, not in addition to, full-sized appliances.

Still, refrigerators and freezers account for roughly 9 to 15 percent of a household's energy use. They run 24/7, year after year, so buying a more efficient model can make a sizeable dent in your utility bill and slash your contribution to air pollution and global warming.

Energy-saving models have very efficient compressors and motors, improved insulation, and better temperature controls. Energy Star–approved full-sized refrigerators use at least 15 percent less energy than refrigerators that merely meet the minimum federal standards, and they use 40 percent less energy than conventional models sold in 2001. Energy Star–approved freezers use at least 10 percent less energy than required by current federal standards, while Energy Star compact refrigerators and freezers (less than 7.75 cubic feet) do at least 20 percent better than the minimum federal standards.

With widespread consumer recognition of the Energy Star program, it's a wonder that some manufacturers bother to make inefficient products that aren't Energy Star approved. But inefficient refrigerators are for sale—at all price levels, from budget to luxury—so it pays to shop carefully.

▶

Sun Frost makes one of the most energy-efficient refrigerators. It is especially popular in off-the-grid households that generate all their own electricity and aren't connected to the municipal electric-utility grid.

MANUAL LABOR

Small electric appliances like mixers, food processors, and spice grinders save labor and time but nudge up electricity use. If you've already addressed all the big energy hogs in the kitchen—the fridge and dishwasher, the water heater, leaky windows, and uninsulated walls—you could take your quest for energy savings to the next level by using fewer electric gadgets for chopping, grinding, mixing, and grating. Full confession: this is a case of do as I say, not as I do. Don't ever try to get between me and my Cuisinart.

Choosing an Energy Star–approved refrigerator is one of the easiest steps you can take to green your kitchen. Some Energy Star models cost more than comparable non-approved units, but you'll likely recoup the added expense within a few years. And refrigerators go on sale so often that chances are good you can find an Energy Star model that meets your needs and doesn't cost any more than a similar non-approved model.

Of course, the bigger the refrigerator, the more electricity it demands, even if it is Energy Star–approved, so try not to go overboard with capacity.

Seven Tips for Choosing an Energy-Efficient Refrigerator/Freezer

1. If the refrigerator is more than about twelve years old, replace it with a new Energy Star–approved model. Don't keep your old energy-hog fridge in service; have it recycled.

2. Purchase the right size for your needs. Super-sized units use super-sized quantities of electricity. Keep in mind, however, that you'll use much less energy with one large refrigerator than multiple small ones.

3. Compare projected electricity use of the models you are interested in. Check the Energy Star Web site (energystar.gov), or look at the appliances' yellow-and-black EnergyGuide label.

4. Models with the freezer on top use the least amount of energy. Bottom-freezer models use more energy. Side-by-side models use the most.

5. Ice makers and through-the-door water/ice dispensers increase energy consumption by as much as 14 to 20 percent, according to Energy Star. Skip these features if you don't really need them.

6. Manual defrost freezers use half the energy of automatic defrosters. But if you're not likely to defrost your freezer periodically, you're better off with an automatic defroster because a thick buildup of frost makes the motor work harder, canceling out your energy savings.

7. If you need a separate freezer, choose a chest freezer rather than an upright model. Chest freezers can be as much as 10 to 25 percent more energy efficient than

The energy-efficient Sun Frost refrigerator is dressed up with cork panels. The handcrafted handles and trim were fashioned from salvaged wood. To the right of the refrigerator, the pantry door conceals a "California cooler," which draws in air from the basement to keep food cool without electricity. See more of this kitchen on page XI.

an upright model, according to the *Consumer Guide to Home Energy Savings,* because they are better insulated and cold air doesn't spill out as readily.

How to Get the Best Performance from Your Fridge or Freezer

- Don't hold the doors open longer than necessary.
- Don't position the refrigerator near the range, dishwasher, or heating vents or in direct sunlight. It will have to work harder to stay cool. If you have no choice but to locate it next to the cooktop or oven, make sure there is adequate insulation between them to prevent heat transfer to the refrigerator.
- To allow air to circulate in the condenser coils, leave space between the refrigerator and the walls or cabinets, unless the model is designed for enclosed spaces.
- Unless you have a "no-clean" condenser model (check your owner's manual), vacuum or brush dust off the condenser coils at least once a year.
- If you have a manual defrost freezer, defrost it when a quarter-inch of frost builds up.
- Keep your refrigerator between 37 and 40 degrees Fahrenheit and your freezer between 0 and 5 degrees Fahrenheit. Use an appliance thermometer intended for refrigerators and freezers—they're designed to be accurate at cold temperatures.
- If your unit has an energy-saver switch, turn it on unless you're having a problem with condensation on the fridge.
- Excess moisture increases energy use. Keep foods and liquids covered so they retain their moisture rather than releasing it into the refrigerator's interior.
- Your fridge and freezer will use less energy if they're relatively full, but not so crammed that air can't circulate inside. If it's often mostly empty, store plastic containers filled with water inside the fridge or freezer, and the next time you replace the unit, consider downsizing.

Cool Pantries

I don't predict that cool pantries are going to knock Sub-Zero out of the refrigeration game anytime soon, but I have started to see them pop up in some new kitchens. Once known as California coolers, cool pantries are typically insulated cabinets built into a perimeter wall on the cooler (usually northerly) side of the kitchen. The cabinets have two exterior vents, a screened

RETIRE YOUR OLD FRIDGE

When you buy a new refrigerator, don't move the old one down to the basement or give it away. It's better for the planet if inefficient appliances are recycled rather than kept in service. As much as 95 percent of the materials in a fridge can be recycled. If you must have an additional fridge or freezer in your house, buy a new, top-rated energy-efficient model.

REFRIGERATOR MADNESS

A current trend in home design is the proliferation of point-of-use refrigeration. Convenience is king, and as the average house size continues to increase, refrigerators seem to be multiplying like rabbits to fill up all that space.

In luxury homes today, there are often several refrigerators in the kitchen: a main unit, a smaller snack and beverage fridge for the kids, and a wine cooler. If there's a bar in the great room or living room, there's often a compact fridge underneath it. The master suite might have its own mini fridge holding milk for the morning cappuccino, or a refrigerated drawer in the bathroom for medicine and cosmetics. If there's a home theater, it often has a fridge of its own. Peek in the garage or basement and you're likely to find a full-size refrigerator or freezer running 24/7. And as the traditional patio outfitted with a simple barbecue grill has morphed into an extravagant outdoor kitchen, refrigerators have started to proliferate outside too.

At the risk of sounding like a Grinch out to deprive people of their icy-cold drinks, what are we thinking? I don't believe that people who have a multitude of refrigerators in their homes do so out of a malevolent wish to poison the air or melt the Arctic's ice fields. Most people, I suspect, just have not given much thought to the fact that these major appliances have a major impact on air quality, global warming, and ultimately our ability to thrive on this planet.

Of course most people don't have the money or inclination to fill their houses with refrigerators. But if you do, hear my plea: refrigerate responsibly!

For a healthier body and planet, choose food that is locally produced, organically grown, and minimally processed. Also, a diet that's lower on the food chain, with an emphasis on plant-based foods rather than animal products, is much gentler on the environment.

If you are planning a new kitchen, keep in mind that from an energy perspective, your refrigerator matters much more than your cooktop or oven. Refrigerators demand significant electricity and run around the clock, whereas cooking appliances use relatively little energy and are operated intermittently. Because they are not big energy users, cooking appliances are not covered by either the federal minimum efficiency standards or the Energy Star program.

That said, the cooking appliances you buy and how you use them do have an impact on the environment. Some cooking methods use less energy, for example, or create less indoor pollution. Also, cooking generates heat, which can run up summertime air-conditioning bills. If your home is air-conditioned, selecting energy-efficient cooking appliances and choosing low-energy cooking methods make particularly good sense.

vent near ground level to allow in cool air from the basement or from the outside, and another vent near the top of the cabinet that allows rising warm air to exit. This creates what's known as the stack effect, naturally pulling cooler air into the unit. The cabinet should be insulated to maintain acceptable temperatures, and the door needs to seal tightly to prevent air leakage into the kitchen. During very cold spells, the vent should be closed to prevent freezing.

Cool pantries are a great low-tech way to store wine, cheese, grains, certain fruits and vegetables, and other foods that don't need to be refrigerated but benefit from air that's cooler than the ambient temperature in the kitchen. Another low-tech, zero-energy option is the old-fashioned root cellar, which is typically dug into the ground to provide a cool, high-moisture environment for root vegetables and other foods.

Of course, a cool pantry or root cellar will only reduce your overall energy use if it means you can forgo that extra refrigerator or downsize your fridge to a smaller model.

COOKING APPLIANCES

What you eat has a much bigger impact on the environment and on your health than the type of appliance you cook with.

Cooktops

Gas or electric? That's a moot question if you don't have gas service at your home. But for people who do have a choice, gas is often favored because it's highly responsive to setting changes and the flames give immediate visual cues as to the heat level. Electric cooktops have their advantages too, the most compelling being that they don't pollute your kitchen. Read on for a summary of the pros and cons of these two cooking technologies.

Gas Cooktops. There's no doubt about it: cooking with gas is more energy efficient than cooking with electricity. Gas appliances burn the fuel right where you need it, with relatively little wasted energy. By comparison, generating and distributing electricity involves considerable waste as fuels such as coal and natural gas are first converted to electricity and then sent great distances across power lines to reach your home.

▶

In this naturally cooled pantry, wine and food are stored at a cool temperature without electricity. An air duct at the bottom of the pantry draws in cooler air from the outside, while an exhaust duct at the top allows hot air to flow out. See more of this kitchen on page 70.

However, unless you run a commercial cooking operation out of your home, the difference in energy use isn't huge. Since cooktops account for only a small portion of a household's energy use, you likely wouldn't notice a dip in your energy bills if you replaced an electric cooktop with a gas range.

The main drawback to cooking with gas is it pollutes your home. Burning gas produces undesirable, potentially unhealthy combustion by-products, including carbon monoxide, carbon dioxide, and nitrogen dioxide.

If you prefer cooking with gas, always use the range hood ventilation when cooking, and make sure the ventilation system is ducted to the outdoors (recirculating fans that send pollutants back into your kitchen are ill-advised). Also, consider installing a carbon monoxide detector in or near your kitchen in case your gas range malfunctions and produces dangerous levels of this poisonous gas.

Gas ranges used to have pilot lights that burned constantly. Today's models are required to have an electric ignition so that gas is ignited only when needed, saving energy and producing less pollution. If you have an old range with a pilot light, it might be time to upgrade to a new model. For easier clean up and to reduce indoor pollution from burnt food particles, look for gas ranges with sealed burners.

Electric Cooktops. Most electric cooktops sold in the United States have either coil elements or heat-resistant ceramic glass over radiant ribbons. Coil elements heat up faster, whereas ceramic-glass cooktops have a smooth surface that is easier to clean. These two technologies offer similar energy efficiency.

Other electric-cooktop technologies such as halogen, solid disk, and induction burners haven't made much of an inroad into the American market. Halogen units use tungsten halogen

▲
Gas burners that are working properly should have blue flames, as on this Bosch cooktop. If the flame burns yellow, have the cooktop serviced.

▼
Some people prefer electric cooking appliances because they don't produce combustion by-products. Electric range by Bosch.

bulbs under a glass surface to generate heat. They heat up and respond to adjustments in temperature settings very quickly but are not significantly more energy efficient than conventional ceramic-glass and coil cooktops.

Solid-disk cooktops, which are common in Europe but not in the United States, have cast-iron disks on top of electric resistance wires. They are less energy efficient than coil and ceramic-glass cooktops.

Induction cooktops are the most energy efficient of all the electric-cooktop technologies. Induction elements transfer electromagnetic energy directly to the pan. The cooking surface itself does not heat up, so less heat is wasted. Induction elements are very responsive to changes in temperature settings—many people consider them to be nearly as responsive as gas ranges. They are also excellent at maintaining very low temperatures. There are three main drawbacks to induction cooktops: few companies sell them in North America, they are currently very expensive, and they can only be used with ferrous metal cookware, such as stainless steel and cast iron. They will not work with aluminum pots and pans. Despite their energy efficiency, do not expect to recoup the added cost unless you use your cooktop all day long, every day.

Tips for Using Less Energy When Cooking on the Stove

+ Use the right-size pan. With electric burners, use a pan matched to the element's size; you'll waste heat if the pan is much smaller than the element. With gas burners, if the flame is reaching up the sides of the pot, turn it down.
+ Put a lid on pots to keep heat in and cook at a lower temperature.
+ Efficiently burning gas elements will produce a blue flame. If the flame is orange, the burner likely needs servicing.

◄

All-electric kitchen appliances take advantage of the large photovoltaic system that powers this house (see more of this kitchen on page 70). Next to the full-size radiant cooktop is a single-hob induction cooktop made by Cooktek. Magnetic induction elements are very energy-efficient; they work by transferring electro-magnetic energy directly to the pan.

appliances such as a microwave or toaster oven. If your range has a smaller auxiliary oven adjacent to the main compartment, use that in favor of the bigger oven whenever possible. Also, don't preheat the oven unless you're baking something that requires full heat from the start, such as pastries, bread, or homemade pizza. Besides saving energy, these strategies will keep the kitchen cooler in the summer, which helps cut air-conditioning costs.

Self-clean ovens are often made with better insulation than manual-clean ovens; the added insulation also helps save a little energy whenever you use the oven to cook. Even if you never use the self-clean feature, it might be worth buying a self-cleaning oven for the improved insulation.

Convection Ovens. Convection ovens have an internal fan that distributes hot air evenly around the food. Temperatures and cooking time can be decreased compared to a conventional oven, reducing energy use by 20 to 30 percent. Convection ovens cost more, though, so if you don't use the oven much, you likely won't notice any savings on your energy bill.

+ Keep the plates under burners clean. Blackened burners won't reflect heat well. If you can't scrub them clean, line them with aluminum foil or replace them.
+ Consider using a pressure cooker. These specialized pots use pressure and high temperatures to dramatically reduce cooking time, thereby saving energy.
+ Don't boil more water than you need. And when the water reaches boiling, turn the heat down.

Ovens

Conventional Gas and Electric Ovens. Many cooks prefer electric ovens because they maintain a more even temperature than gas ovens do. Also, with an electric oven you don't have to worry about polluting your home with combustion by-products such as carbon monoxide. If you do choose a gas oven, run the kitchen exhaust fan whenever the oven is on (and be sure the ventilation system is ducted to the outside rather than merely recirculating pollutants in your kitchen).

Whether you have a gas or electric oven, from an energy perspective it's better to use it only when cooking large dishes. When making smaller dishes, use smaller

▼
An Advantium oven by GE uses a combination of microwave and halogen light technologies. It cooks faster than a traditional oven, reducing energy use and keeping the kitchen cooler. Unlike a conventional microwave oven, it can brown and broil food. See more of this kitchen on page 70.

Microwave Ovens. Microwave ovens work by generating high-frequency radio waves. When food is exposed to microwaves, water molecules in the food vibrate, converting the microwave energy into heat that cooks the food. The microwave energy quickly penetrates deep into the food, greatly reducing cooking time and energy use. In fact, microwave ovens use roughly 75 percent less energy than a conventional electric oven. An added benefit is that they don't produce surplus heat, which saves on air-conditioning energy in the summer.

Microwave ovens are enormously popular but don't appeal

OVEN CLEANING

Whatever way you look at it, oven cleaning is nasty business. Store-brand oven cleaners contain toxic ingredients that don't belong in a healthy kitchen, such as lye and ammonia. Self-cleaning oven cycles use a lot of energy and create noxious fumes; some experts recommend only running the self-cleaning cycle when the house is not occupied, making sure the kitchen is well ventilated. A healthier alternative is a non-chlorine scouring powder or a paste of water and baking soda, accompanied by lots of elbow grease.

to everyone. Some people just don't feel the need for one, especially because many microwave ovens are not suitable for certain types of cooking, such as roasting, grilling, browning, or baking.

Others express concern that food cooked in a microwave oven loses nutritional value. I have not come across any convincing evidence to back up this claim. And contrary to popular misconceptions, food cooked in a microwave does not become radioactive, and microwaves do not remain in the oven or in the food. The microwave radiation disappears as soon as the unit shuts off, just as light disappears when a lightbulb is turned off.

Other people worry about possible health effects from microwave radiation leakage. Although manufacturers must comply with federal and international standards for microwave oven safety, radiation leakage is possible if the oven has been damaged. Do not use a unit that is malfunctioning or that has a damaged door, seals, or latch. Replace it or have it repaired by a manufacturer-approved technician. Also, keep the door and seal clean of food residue to ensure that the door closes properly.

Some health experts recommend not cooking food in plastic containers in a microwave because of the potential for chemicals to migrate from the plastic into the hot food. To be safe, cook food in ovenproof glass or ceramic containers in a microwave.

Combination Ovens. Oven technology continues to evolve to provide greater convenience, faster cooking times, and more options. From an eco perspective, faster cooking times mean that less energy is used and the kitchen remains cooler, which puts less demand on the air conditioner in the summer.

Combination ovens use conventional, convection, microwave, and halogen technologies to cook food five times faster than in a conventional oven, while producing oven-quality results. Combination ovens are considerably more expensive than conventional or microwave ovens alone; unless you use your oven constantly, it's unlikely that you'll recoup the added cost based on energy savings alone. That doesn't mean you shouldn't consider them; just have realistic expectations.

Steam Ovens. Built-in steam ovens are rare in American homes, but are more frequently found in European and Japanese kitchens. These ovens are plumbed into the water supply and cook food quickly under high pressure and temperature, similar to a stove top pressure cooker. Some manufacturers make a combination steam and convection oven. Steam ovens are very expensive; consider a stove top pressure cooker as a budget alternative.

Tips for Oven Cooking

◆ Smaller appliances use less energy. Use a toaster oven, microwave, slow cooker, or the stove top rather than a full-size oven whenever possible. Using a smaller appliance can cut energy use by as much as 50 percent.

SOLAR COOKING

If you really want to embrace eco-friendly cooking, give solar cooking a whirl—it's a simple technology designed for cooking outside under sunny skies. Solar cookers make particularly good sense in parts of the world where people are very poor and fuel is scarce. But anyone with access to sunny outdoor space can give solar cooking a try. You can make a solar cooker using little more than cardboard, aluminum foil, black paint, and a piece of glass, or buy a more elaborate model. Configurations vary; one of the simplest is a glass-topped box lined with reflective foil. The sun's heat passes through the glass, a black pot inside the cooker absorbs the heat (reaching temperatures up to 275 degrees Fahrenheit), and the food inside cooks slowly. Learn more from Solar Cookers International (solarcooking.org) or Sun Ovens International (sunoven.com).

- If you're buying a new oven, consider a model with two oven chambers: a normal-size chamber and a smaller auxiliary oven that you can use for small dishes.
- Don't preheat the oven unless necessary. Homemade pizza, bread, cookies, and cakes require preheated ovens, but most dishes do not.
- Use the oven window and light to check on food rather than frequently opening the door.
- With most dishes, you can turn off the oven a few minutes before the dish is finished cooking. The heat retained in the oven will finish cooking the dish.

RANGE HOOD VENTILATION

Range hoods today play a much larger design role than they once did. While unobtrusive under-cabinet range hoods are still the basic workhorse of kitchen ventilation, there has been a trend toward more elaborate, ornately adorned hoods that mimic the stone hearth of centuries past. Another trend is the sleek chimney-style hood with exposed metal ducting stretching to the ceiling, evoking the look of a restaurant kitchen.

Downdraft systems have also gained popularity with the advent of cooktops located on kitchen islands. Downdraft systems don't work as effectively as overhead hoods—heat rises, after all. If possible, design the kitchen with overhead exhaust.

Most people use their kitchen ventilation system to remove undesirable odors, whether it's yesterday's sautéed cabbage or this morning's burned bagel. But the range hood actually serves a higher purpose than protecting olfactory sensibilities. Its job

LESS IS MORE

Cooking meals in smaller appliances such as a microwave or toaster oven saves energy and keeps the kitchen cooler compared to a full-size oven. But I don't advocate going overboard on buying hot-dog makers, panini presses, raclette makers, popcorn poppers, and all those other limited-use cooking gadgets that manufacturers like to tempt us with. Producing all those products takes its toll on the environment in terms of natural resources extracted as well as manufacturing and transportation energy used. So while smaller appliances do use less energy, there's an argument to be made for keeping consumption in check.

INSTALL A CARBON MONOXIDE ALARM

Carbon monoxide is a colorless, odorless by-product of combustion that can be deadly if high levels accumulate in the home. If you have any fuel-burning appliances or equipment in your home—cooktops, ovens, water heater, clothes dryer, furnace, fireplace—play it safe and install a carbon monoxide alarm. They can be bought at any hardware store for $50 or less. Unfortunately, not all models are reliable. Check product reviews with a reputable independent organization such as *Consumer Reports*, and make sure the product you chose has an Underwriters Laboratories certification (UL 2034).

is to keep the kitchen healthy by removing dangerous pollutants like carbon monoxide produced by gas-burning devices. It also draws moisture out of the kitchen, making it a less hospitable place for mold.

The range hood must be vented to the outside. Recirculating, ductless fans are simply not effective at removing pollution or moisture from the kitchen. If the range is in a spot where it is too difficult to install ducted ventilation, consider installing a second kitchen exhaust system that is vented to the outside; this auxiliary system can be either ceiling or wall mounted.

Make sure the ductwork is well sealed, with no gaps at joints so that moisture and combustion by-products don't leak into the wall or ceiling cavities that the duct travels through. Also, the shorter the duct run and the fewer turns the duct takes, the more effective it will be at removing pollutants and moisture from the kitchen. The exhaust system should have a backdraft damper to prevent outside air from flowing into the kitchen when the fan is not operating.

People often don't use their range hoods because they're too noisy. Systems with exterior blowers are much quieter than interior blowers, but cost a lot more. If you choose a product with an interior blower, ask for the sone rating—that's a measure of how much noise it makes. The lower the sone, the quieter it is.

Pro-Style Ventilation: Bigger Is Definitely Not Better

Commercial-size range hoods are all the rage today in home

kitchens. These pro-style ventilators can suck upwards of 1,000 cubic feet per minute of air out of the home. Unfortunately, people who install and use these powerful fans in home kitchens often don't realize that they're creating a potentially dangerous situation.

If the system's fan or blower is overly powerful, it creates a risk of backdrafting. A high cubic-feet-per-minute (cfm) range hood will suck air not just out of the kitchen but out of other parts of the house. If the house is tightly built and no windows are open to supply make-up air to replace the air that's being sucked out, the range hood can pull air back down the flues of naturally venting gas- and wood-burning devices including fireplaces, furnaces, water heaters, and gas dryers. Noxious gases, smoke, and particulates that are meant to flow up and out of the flues can be pulled back into the home, creating unhealthy and potentially extremely hazardous conditions in the home. New houses that are tightly built for energy efficiency are particularly susceptible to backdrafting.

Building codes for restaurant kitchens regulate ventilation and require that the system provide make-up air to prevent backdrafting. Most residential building codes, on the other hand, usually assume that range hoods are small, pulling a mere 100 or 150 cfm, so they often don't require make-up air or any kind of testing to ensure safe performance.

What's the solution to backdrafting? Don't choose an overly powerful range hood. A good rule of thumb is 40 cfm per linear foot of cooktop. For a thirty-six-inch cooktop, that's only 120 cfm, a far cry from the 400-cfm and higher exhaust fans turning up in many home kitchens.

If you already have a powerful range hood, run it at low speed. Make-up air can be supplied through an open window, but with very powerful fans, even that may not be enough to counteract backdrafting. And an open window wastes energy on days when the heater or air conditioner is running.

If you are determined to have a powerful pro-style range hood, hire an experienced HVAC (heating, ventilation, and air-conditioning) contractor to design and install an effective ventilation system that will provide adequate make-up air to prevent backdrafting. Once installed, the system should be tested to ensure it is performing safely.

Range Hood Tips

+Overhead exhaust systems are more effective than downdraft systems.
+Do not vent range hoods into the attic or wall cavities. Moisture buildup can lead to problems with mold and rot.

+Choose exhaust systems that vent to the outside, not ductless models that recirculate pollutants in your home.
+Don't choose an overly powerful pro-style range hood. Strong exhaust systems can cause backdrafting, sucking dangerous fumes from fireplaces, gas dryers, and water heaters back into the home.
+Choose a range hood that is as wide as or slightly wider than the length of the cooktop to effectively capture steam and grease.
+Avoid long duct runs. The exhaust system will work more efficiently if you minimize the length of the duct runs and the number of turns the ducts take.

WATER

These days, with rising energy prices and predictions of catastrophic climate changes as a result of the accumulation of greenhouse gases in the atmosphere, we tend to focus on our use of fossil fuels. But energy isn't the only looming environmental crisis. Some experts predict that a shortage of freshwater will be the greatest global challenge our society faces in coming decades. Imagine what life would be like with chronic

SAY GOOD-BYE TO THE OPEN HEARTH

As romantic as it may seem to have an open hearth in the kitchen for roasting meat or baking bread or pizza, it's a terrible idea from a healthy-home perspective. Open hearths can pollute the home with carbon dioxide, carbon monoxide, and a host of other noxious gases and particulates. If you want to cook in a wood-burning oven, be safe and build an oven outside. If you are determined to have a wood-burning oven in your kitchen, hire a qualified HVAC contractor to provide an adequate ventilation system (see the section above on range hoods and backdrafting for more information). If you want a fireplace in the kitchen for heat or cozy ambiance, the best choice from an air-quality perspective is a sealed-combustion, direct-vent gas fireplace. Wood-burning stoves used for heating should be EPA certified; if you have an old masonry fireplace, have it retrofitted with an EPA-certified insert to reduce pollution.

COOKWARE CONTROVERSIES

After studies in the 1970s found elevated levels of aluminum in the brain cells of Alzheimer's patients, people ditched their aluminum cookware in droves. But since then the aluminum-Alzheimer's connection has been largely debunked. As the *New York Times* reported in May 2000, "sick cells tend to accumulate toxic metals because they are unable to eliminate them. Despite numerous investigations, there is no scientifically reliable evidence that aluminum is the cause, rather than the result, of a diseased brain."

Recent studies have raised concerns about another type of cookware, nonstick pots and pans coated with Teflon. Perfluorooctanoic acid (PFOA) is a synthetic chemical used to make Teflon and other products such as breathable, waterproof clothing. PFOA has been found in low levels in the environment and in the blood of people worldwide, according to the U.S. EPA. The *New York Times* reported in July 2005 that studies have shown that PFOA causes cancer and other health problems in laboratory animals.

How PFOA gets into our blood and what kinds of hazards it might present remain unknown. DuPont, the maker of Teflon, states that "consumers cannot be exposed to PFOA through cookware coated with Teflon nonstick finishes." The EPA has not yet made a determination about whether products made from PFOA pose a risk to the public. While the EPA continues its deliberations, watchdog organizations such as the Environmental Working Group keep pressure on manufacturers and regulatory agencies to get to the bottom of the issue.

Until the PFOA controversy gets resolved, there's another reason to consider avoiding nonstick cookware. The Environmental Working Group reports that empty nonstick pans that are overheated on the stove top can produce toxic vapors lethal to pet birds, a condition dubbed "Teflon toxicosis." It's unknown whether these fumes cause any adverse human health effects. If you don't want to wait to find out, skip the nonstick cookware and use a well-seasoned cast-iron pan.

Besides consuming water, dishwashers also use energy, although they account for only about 3 percent of a typical household's energy bill. More than 60 percent of the energy used by a dishwasher is for heating the water. Energy-efficient dishwashers have an internal booster heater that raises the water temperature to sanitize the dishes. This feature allows the home's water heater to be turned down to 120 degrees Fahrenheit, which can be a major energy saver. Dishwashers without booster heaters need the home's water heater to be

▲

If your household is small or you don't eat at home often, you may save water and energy with dishwasher drawers or smaller-sized appliances such as this eighteen-inch Integra dishwasher by Bosch.

water shortages—our health, prosperity, and future ability to thrive as a society are predicated on access to abundant supplies of clean water.

The kitchen isn't the largest user of water in a typical household. Outdoor watering accounts for more than half of a typical single-family home's water use; indoors, the toilets, showers, and clothes washers are the big water hogs. Still, even in the kitchen there are a number of steps we can take to use water wisely, which will help ensure adequate freshwater supplies in the future.

In addition to conservation, the safety and quality of our drinking water is a key concern. All of these issues are discussed below.

DISHWASHERS

Using a dishwasher consumes much less water and energy than hand washing the dishes. So don't feel guilty about running the dishwasher—just be sure you have an efficient model, and operate it with full loads. And don't rinse those dirty dishes before loading them; rinsing just wastes water. Scrape off any solids, and then let the dishwasher handle all that gunk and grime—that's what it's designed to do.

set at 140 degrees Fahrenheit, which is much hotter than required for other household uses, including showers, faucets, and clothes washers.

If you're in the market for a new dishwasher, purchase an Energy Star–approved model. Energy Star dishwashers are about 25 percent more energy efficient than comparable non–Energy Star models. To compare the energy use of models, check the yellow-and-black EnergyGuide labels, or review the product lists on the Energy Star Web site or in the book *Consumer Guide to Home Energy Savings*.

Consumer Reports also provides excellent performance data based on the results of their own tests of dishwashers. They report that today's dishwashers do a very good job of cleaning dishes,

ELECTROMAGNETIC FIELDS IN THE KITCHEN

Does exposure to electric and magnetic fields emanating from kitchen appliances cause cancer or other illnesses? Health advocates, scientists, policy makers, and others have studied this question since the mid-1970s. After conducting an in-depth review of the scientific literature, the World Health Organization has concluded that "current evidence does not confirm the existence of any health consequences from exposure to low level electromagnetic fields." Electromagnetic fields (EMFs) found in the home environment are low-level fields.

Electric and magnetic fields are different but related phenomena. Most health concerns about electromagnetic fields in the home are actually related to the potential biological effects of magnetic fields. In a home, electrical wiring is always emitting electric fields as long as the circuit is live, but only emits magnetic fields when current is flowing. A kitchen appliance will only emit magnetic fields when the appliance is turned on and causing current to flow.

Magnetic fields are strongest closest to their source and drop off dramatically as you move away from the source. If you're concerned about exposure to magnetic fields in your home, you can buy a gauss-meter to measure their levels or hire an electrician or home inspector to take the measurements for you.

There are some easy steps you can take if you wish to reduce exposure to magnetic fields. One step is to use energy-efficient equipment and appliances: less flowing current means less exposure to magnetic fields. Also, eliminate "phantom loads" by unplugging appliances or equipment that consume energy even when turned off (anything with a remote, a timer, or memory, such as a TV or stereo). If there's an always-on appliance like a refrigerator on the other side of the wall from your bed, you may want to reposition the appliance or the bed since magnetic fields can travel through walls.

The World Health Organization has good information about electromagnetic fields and human health on their Web site, who.int.

---

4. Use the dishwasher's energy- and water-saving settings.
5. If you have a newer dishwasher with an internal booster heater, turn your main water heater down to 120 degrees Fahrenheit.

DRINKING WATER AND FILTERS

Is your tap water safe to drink? Municipal water supplies in the United States are generally of good quality, but that doesn't mean we should take our drinking water for granted.

In 2003, the environmental advocacy group Natural Resources Defense Council (NRDC) issued a report that reviewed tap water quality in nineteen cities, rating them on a scale of excellent, good, fair, poor, and failing. For water quality, five cities rated poor: Albuquerque, Boston, Fresno, Phoenix, and San Francisco. Only one, Chicago, got an excellent grade. According to the report, high levels of rocket fuel have been measured in the water in Los Angles, Phoenix, and San Diego. Boston, Newark, and Seattle exceeded the national action level for lead. And arsenic, according to NRDC, is present at significant levels in the tap water of twenty-two million Americans.

While contaminated water is something we should all be concerned about, pregnant women, infants, young children, and people with compromised immune systems are particularly vulnerable to ill effects from polluted drinking water. The first step to understanding whether there might be contaminants in your tap water is to read your municipal water report. The federal Safe Drinking Water Act requires municipal water agencies to provide a water quality report that list levels of detected contaminants in water. These reports are sent to households in their water bills once a year; you can also obtain a copy by contacting your water company. The water report will give you a feel for the types of contaminants that may be of concern in your local water supply.

About 15 percent of the U.S. population relies on private water sources, which are not subject to EPA standards or the Safe Drinking Water Act. If you have well water, EPA recommends having it tested annually for coliform bac-

---

but that there is a noteworthy variation in how much water they use, ranging from about 3 1/2 to 12 gallons per load. Higher water use means higher energy use because of the energy required to heat the water.

Set your dishwasher's options to the lowest energy and water levels appropriate for the load. Use the option to dry without heat for all loads—this can reduce your total monthly energy bill by as much as 1 percent. Also, use the water-miser or china-light mode whenever doing a light load.

Five Tips for Water- and Energy-Efficient Dishwashing

1. Use a dishwasher rather than washing dishes by hand.
2. Scrape but do not rinse dirty dishes before loading them.
3. Run the dishwasher with full loads only. If your household doesn't generate many dirty dishes, consider installing a small-capacity dishwasher or dishwasher drawer.

teria, nitrates, total dissolved solids, and other possible contaminants.

Even if your municipal or well water supply is free of contaminants, it may pick up pollutants from the pipes in the home. Some pre–World War II houses may still have original lead-based supply water pipes; these should be replaced. Copper supply lines installed in homes before 1988 may have lead-based solder that can leach into the tap water. Be safe and have a plumber inspect the joints and solder, or have your water tested, particularly if there are children in your household. Lead can cause serious harm to the brain, nervous system, kidneys, and other vital functions, and children are especially susceptible to its effects. To have your water tested, check with your county government or local health department for a list of state-certified testing laboratories.

If lead is found, you can replace the pipes. If you're not in a position to do that, install a filter that's certified to remove lead. Running cold water from the tap for about three minutes will also flush lead from the pipes. Hot water is more prone to leaching lead out of the pipes, so if lead is suspected, never use water from the hot tap for drinking or cooking.

If you choose to install a home water-treatment system, select one designed to deal with the types of contaminants likely to be found in your water supply. No type of treatment system eliminates all contaminants; some filters are only geared to improving the taste and smell of water, while others target the removal of specific types of contaminants.

Whole-house systems, also known as point-of-entry systems, treat all the water for the entire household. These are installed where the main water line enters the house. Point-of-use filters are installed at a single fixture, either under the sink, on the counter, or attached to the faucet itself. Some filters employ more than one type of treatment technology.

For more information about drinking water safety, visit the EPA's Web site, epa.gov/safewater, or call their Safe Drinking Water Hotline at 800.426.4791.

WATER TREATMENT DEVICES

Water Treatment Devices	Description
Activated carbon filter	Improves taste and odor Some designs remove lead, copper, mercury, chlorination by-products, solvents, and pesticides Does not remove bacteria, nitrates, or dissolved minerals Carbon cartridge must be replaced periodically Easy to install, inexpensive, and available in under-counter, countertop, faucet-mounted, and carafe designs
Ion exchange	Removes minerals ("softens" water that has high calcium and magnesium levels) Some designs remove radium, barium, fluoride, or arsenate Must be regenerated periodically with salt or potassium Whole-house, point-of-use system
Reverse osmosis	Improves taste and odor Removes nitrates, sodium, other dissolved inorganics, and certain parasites Some designs reduce levels of dioxin, pesticides, chloroform, and petrochemicals Under-sink system; filters require periodic replacement Delivers water very slowly and wastes roughly five gallons of water for each gallon produced Expensive
Distillation	Removes bacteria, nitrates, sodium, hardness, dissolved solids, most organic compounds, heavy metals, and radionuclides Does not remove some VOCs, certain pesticides, and volatile solvents Available as under-counter or whole-house, point-of-use system Operates very slowly and uses a lot of electricity Expensive
Ultraviolet disinfection	Kills bacteria and parasites Under-sink unit Often used in combination with a carbon filter

Sources: U.S. Environmental Protection Agency, "Water on Tap: What You Need to Know," Oct. 2003, publication #EPA 816-K-03-007, epa.gov/safewater/wot; and Natural Resources Defense Council, "Consumer Guide to Water Filters," rev. August 16, 2005, nrdc.org.

PLUMBING

Kitchen remodels often involve considerable plumbing work, including running new potable water supply lines to the kitchen. From a green perspective, there are no perfect choices for water supply pipes.

Your choice of piping material may be constrained by local building code requirements; in some cities, for example, copper tubing is mandatory for household water supply. Copper has long been used for drinking water; it is long lasting and recyclable but expensive, and mining copper ore causes environmental damage. Also, if the pH of the local water is less than 6.5, copper may leach from the

REFRIGERATOR FILTERS

If you have a late-model refrigerator with built-in filters for the water dispenser and ice maker, replace them at the intervals suggested by the manufacturer.

supply pipes into the drinking water. In this situation, consider installing filters designed to remove copper from the water or use non-copper piping.

If you live in an older home that might have lead pipes or lead solder on copper-pipe joints, have your water tested for lead. See the Drinking Water section on pages 138 and 139.

These days, various types of plastic plumbing are sometimes used for potable water, including PVC (polyvinyl chloride), CPVC (chlorinated polyvinyl chloride), high-density polyethylene (HDPE), and cross-linked polyethylene (PEX). These tend to be inexpensive relative to copper tubing. Plastic piping for potable water must be NSF certified, indicating that they meet this independent, third-party certifier's standards for health and environmental quality. However, even if PVC piping does bear the NSF certification, many environmental and health advocates recommend against using it because of potentially harmful health effects associated with manufactur-

IS BOTTLED WATER BETTER THAN TAP WATER?

When you're away from home, reaching for a bottle of water is undeniably convenient. But if you're drinking bottled water at home because you think it's safer than tap water, you might want to reconsider. A number of years ago, NRDC tested more than 1,000 bottles of 103 brands of bottled water, and found that while most of it was of very high quality, some samples were contaminated with bacteria, arsenic, or synthetic organic chemicals. NRDC estimates that 25 percent or more of bottled water is actually just tap water in a bottle, and that it hasn't necessarily been further treated. You'll save a lot of money and create a lot less packaging waste if you drink filtered tap water at home rather than bottled water.

ing and disposing of PVC-based products. See page 49 for more information about PVC.

A relative newcomer to the North American plumbing scene is polypropylene pipe. *Environmental Building News* writes favorably of polypropylene water supply lines, calling it "one of the cleanest plastics" because it is free of potentially toxic halogenated chemicals such as chlorine or bromine. Polypropylene is also recyclable. Polypropylene piping was recently approved for addition to the International Plumbing Code (IPC) and the International Residential Code (IRC).

Sinks

From a green perspective, there's no overwhelming reason to choose one type of kitchen sink over another. Select a sink that you love and that's well made so that it will stand up to decades of hard use. Popular options include stainless steel, enameled cast iron or steel, and porcelain (fired clay with an enamel finish). Newer materials include composite surfaces that blend ground quartz and plastic, and plastic solid-surfacing materials such as those that are used for countertops.

Stainless steel does have a leg up on other sink materials because it usually contains some recycled content, and the steel can be recycled again when the sink reaches the end of its service life. It's a hard-wearing material too: it's tough and heat-proof, resists stains and rust, and it's easy to clean. Choose thicker-gauge steel (18 gauge or lower); it will be quieter and less likely to flex.

For an option that's easy on the planet and on your wallet, consider a used sink. Building-materials salvage yards, used restaurant-equipment retailers, and online classifieds such as eBay and Craigslist are good sources for old sinks.

Many new kitchens have multiple sinks, making it more enjoyable for two people to cook and clean up together. Water use probably doesn't rise significantly even if there are multiple sinks. The main eco drawback is that the more sinks there are in the kitchen, the larger the kitchen likely is. And big kitchens, as we know, mean more stuff and higher energy use.

Pot fillers are another newly popular kitchen feature. These faucets are plumbed into the wall next to the cooktop; they usually have swivel necks that swing out over pots, eliminating the need to carry a heavy, water-filled pot from sink to stove top. But it's really only half a convenience: once done cooking, you still have to carry the hot, heavy, water-filled pot back to the sink. Before being swayed by the fad, consider whether the convenience is worth the added expense and resource use of the plumbing.

Water Heating

Water heating accounts for roughly 14 to 25 percent of a typical household's energy use. Not all of that hot water is used in the kitchen, of course, but if you're planning a major kitchen remodel, that's an ideal time to take a look at your current water-heating system. You can save considerable energy by replacing an older, inefficient water heater with a high-efficiency model or by supplementing your existing system with a solar water heater. This section takes a quick glance at three common water-heating technologies: storage water heaters (by far the most widely used system in the United States), tankless heaters, and solar heaters.

All water heaters that use electricity or fuel must meet federal minimum efficiency standards, but the Energy Star program does not cover water-heating products.

Storage Water Heaters

With conventional-storage water heaters, electricity, gas, or another fuel is used to heat water, which is then stored in a large tank until needed. From an environmental perspective, there's a fairly obvious problem with this technology: the water in the tank cools off and must be continually reheated to maintain the set water temperature. Fifteen percent of a water heater's energy can be lost via this process, known as standby heat loss.

Tankless water heater made by Rinnai.

When shopping for a new water heater, compare the estimated energy use of various models by looking at the EnergyGuide label. Choose a heater with a high Energy Factor (EF). Keep in mind, however, that while electric water heaters have a higher EF than similar gas-burning heaters, electricity is expensive compared to natural gas. If you have a choice where you live between an electric or gas-fired water heater, the gas model is likely to save you more money over the years. If your water heater doesn't yet need to be replaced, you can reduce energy use by wrapping it in an insulating jacket (see tips below).

Nine Tips for Saving Water Heating Energy

1. Don't run hot water longer than necessary.
2. Fix leaks in faucets and pipes.
3. Install low-flow faucets. A new kitchen faucet will have an aerator (the faucet's screw-on tip) that limits water flow to 2.2 gallons per minute. You can reduce water and energy use by replacing the standard aerator with a low-flow aerator that limits flow to no more than 1.0 gallons per minute.
4. Lower the water heater setting to 120 degrees Fahrenheit (unless the dishwasher doesn't have an internal booster heater).
5. When going out of town for more than a few days, turn the water heater's thermostat to the lowest setting. Check the product manual for instructions.
6. Wrap the water heater in an insulating jacket. Jackets on older, less-efficient models can reduce water-heating costs by 4 to 9 percent, but they're often a good idea even on more recent models. A good rule of thumb is that if the tank feels warm to the touch, it needs a jacket. Precut jackets are inexpensive, readily available at home-improvement stores, and easy to install (carefully follow the manufacturer's directions).
7. Insulate all accessible hot-water pipes. This reduces heat loss and provides faster delivery of hot water to the faucets, which conserves water. Use pipe insulation wrap that fits snugly against the pipes.
8. Replace an inefficient older water heater with an energy-efficient storage heater or a tankless heater.
9. Take advantage of the sun's free energy—install a solar water heater.

Tankless Water Heaters

Tankless water heaters—also called demand or instantaneous water heaters—heat water only as needed instead of holding hot water in a storage tank. Although they're more expensive to purchase and install, they can save energy because they don't produce standby losses. The federal Department of Energy estimates that a household that uses forty-one gallons of hot water a day can reduce water heating energy by 24 to 34 percent by switching to a tankless water heater. A household that uses eighty-six gallons of hot water per day could reduce water heating energy by 8 to 14 percent.

Tankless water heaters are available in gas or electric

THE WAIT FOR HOT WATER IS OVER

Tired of wasting water, energy, and time while you wait for hot water to reach the kitchen faucet? Consider installing an on-demand hot-water recirculation system. This is a small pump that's typically installed under the sink located farthest from the water heater; an activation button is installed at each fixture where there is demand for hot water. When you want hot water, you push the button. Cool water that normally goes down the drain while you wait for the hot water to reach the tap is instead recirculated back to the water heater through the cold water line, and hot water is pumped to the fixture much more rapidly than normal. It's a technology that makes particularly good sense for large sprawling houses where the sinks and showers are far from the water heater. Manufacturers include Taco, Inc. (taco-hvac.com) and Advanced Conservation Technology, Inc. (gothotwater.com).

models. They provide continuous hot water, but not all units keep up with high simultaneous demand, such as when someone is showering while the dishwasher is running. To ensure adequate hot-water flow, larger homes often need two or more tankless heaters. Consult with a plumber to determine the correct capacity and configuration for your household's water use.

Solar Water Heating

Solar water heaters use the sun's free energy to heat water. Solar water heaters are a very different technology from the solar panels used to generate electricity. Solar water heaters absorb the sun's heat and transfer it to water that is then used for regular household needs, swimming pools, and spas, and sometimes for space heating too.

A typical system used for heating household water consists of one or more collectors; configurations vary, but the collector is often a glass-topped insulated box that contains a black metal panel designed to absorb heat. The collectors are typically mounted on a roof and angled to face south. Liquid circulates in tubes through the collectors, where it heats up when the sun is shining. In some systems, the liquid is potable water that's stored in a tank until needed. In other systems, the liquid is an antifreeze solution that flows through a heat exchanger to heat potable water.

Most people who have solar water heaters for household use also have a backup heater, such as a conventional storage heater or a tankless heater, to ensure that there's plenty of hot water when the sun's not shining. If your household uses a lot of hot water, and you live in a place where there's ample sunshine, solar water heating can be very cost effective.

Resources
+ "A Consumer's Guide to Energy Efficiency and Renewable Energy," U.S. DOE, www.eere.energy.gov/consumer.
+ **ACEEE.** Publishes the *Consumer Guide to Home Energy Savings*, aceee.org/consumerguide.

DON'T BE A DRIP

A faucet that's leaking thirty drips per minute will waste 130 gallons of water a month—that's 1,577 gallons a year! Do a good turn for the environment and fix that leaky faucet.

GRAY-WATER SYSTEMS

Gray water is wash water from a home's sinks, bathtubs, showers, and clothes washer; essentially, it's all the indoor wastewater a household produces, with the exception of toilet wastewater, which is dubbed black water.

In areas where freshwater is scarce, gray water has long been reused for irrigating vegetation. Gray-water reuse conserves freshwater and reduces strain on aging municipal water-treatment facilities. The lowest-tech gray-water system is a bucket placed under the showerhead; the captured water can be easily reused for flushing the toilet or watering plants.

More elaborate gray-water systems divert household wastewater (everything except toilets) into an assembly of filters, and then collect the water in a holding tank and pump it via subsurface pipes to the area that requires irrigation. With a well-designed gray-water system such as this, a family of four could capture 30,000 to 50,000 gallons of water annually for outdoor use. Contaminants such as bleach, paint, and harsh cleaning chemicals must be kept out of the gray-water system.

Gray-water systems are not legal in some cities and states; where they are permitted, they are typically limited to subsurface irrigation. Find out more at Oasis Design's Web site, graywater.net.

CLEANING UP

GARBAGE AND RECYCLING

When it comes to kitchen waste, the eco-friendliest approach is to not create it in the first place. Reduce waste by composting food scraps, not buying overpackaged products or products packaged in nonrecyclable materials, and buying items in bulk. Give preference to products packaged in reusable or recyclable packaging.

When designing a new kitchen, plan for storage of recyclables as well as trash. If there's a readily accessible but out of sight place for recyclables, people are more likely to keep paper, cans, and bottles out of the trash. Design the location and number of receptacles to reflect the local municipality's collection program. A heavy-duty slide-out drawer with three bins—one for trash, one for paper, and one for bottles and cans—is a typical setup.

Garbage disposers are a nice convenience, but they are a bit wasteful. Not only do they require electricity and water to operate, but they send nutrient-laden food scraps down the drain. If you prefer to use the disposer, conserve water and energy by not running it any longer than necessary. Also, always use cold water; flushing the disposer with hot water wastes water-heater energy.

COMPOSTING

Many households forgo the disposer altogether and toss their food scraps in the garbage. But the greenest option is to compost food scraps. San Francisco has a greenwaste program for citywide curbside collection of food scraps and plant waste. The local garbage company gives residents three large bins on wheels: a blue bin for recyclable paper, metal, and plastic; a green bin for food scraps and yard waste; and a black bin for trash destined for the landfill. The greenwaste gets trucked to a municipal compost facility, where it is turned into loamy nutrient-rich compost that's coveted by local farms.

If your city doesn't offer food-scrap collection but you have some outdoor space, consider starting your own backyard compost pile. Compost bins are available that keep out pests and neatly contain the scraps.

If you have a compost pile in your yard or if your city picks up compostable waste, one nifty convenience is to include a cut-out in the kitchen counter to hold a small drop-in stainless-steel container with a lid. Vegetable trimmings can be easily swept into the container. The container can be lifted out when full and emptied into the compost bin.

Recycling and composting are easy when convenient storage is designed into the kitchen. Here, a container for vegetable scraps is inset into the butcher-block counter. It can be lifted out and dumped in the compost pile outside.

CLEANING PRODUCTS

Household cleaning products come in snazzy, colorful packaging that promises an easy route to a sparkling home, and, by implication, to a better life.

But the contents of those packages are often not quite so cheery. Many conventional cleaning products are made with hazardous chemicals such as chlorine bleach, ammonia, and lye. Fragrances are often added to conceal noxious chemical odors, but the fragrances themselves can trigger allergies or irritate the respiratory system. Some cleansers contain ingredients known to be carcinogens or neurotoxins, or they may cause hormone disruption. Others have components that don't break down in wastewater treatment systems, and wind up polluting our waterways and harming fish or aquatic plants.

Switching to less-toxic cleaning products is one of the simplest steps you can take toward a healthier kitchen. Read labels carefully; don't buy anything marked "Poison" or "Danger," and avoid chlorine- or ammonia-based products. If your local supermarket doesn't carry healthier, eco-friendly cleaning products, try a natural foods store or buy online. Look for products made by companies such as AFM, BioShield, Bon Ami, Ecover, Earth Friendly Products, and Seventh Generation.

You can also make your own cleaners using simple, safe household ingredients. Distilled white vinegar, baking soda, lemon juice, and liquid castile soap are good for general-purpose

◄ ▼
The trash and recycling bins are concealed in cabinets built into the wall. The kitchen's backsplash (below) has slots with chutes that drop into recycling and trash bins outside.

cleaning tasks. Grease and baked-on residue in the oven can be scrubbed with a paste of baking soda, water, and soap. Rather than using an ammonia-based window cleaner, fill a spray bottle with water and 1/4 cup of distilled white vinegar.

Don't use chemical drain cleaners; they are extremely caustic. If the kitchen sink's drain is clogged, try a plunger or a plumbing auger (known as a "snake").

For more detailed recommendations, check out The Green Guide's product report on household cleaning supplies at thegreenguide.com, or the Safer Cleaning Products Fact Sheet from the Washington Toxics Coalition (watoxics.org).

PESTICIDES AND OTHER POISONS

Sooner or later everyone has a problem with pests in the kitchen. I'm referring to bugs and rodents, of course, not family members. Don't reach for pesticides or rodenticides—these products are designed to be poisonous, and don't belong in a healthy home or garden. Instead, start with preventive steps like closing up any gaps to the outside that are larger than 1/4 inch, using garbage cans with tight lids, keeping kitchen surfaces clean, and storing food in critter-proof containers. If that doesn't do the trick, go to the Pesticide Action Network's online Pesticide Advisor guide at panna.org for nontoxic pest-control solutions.

▲
Adjacent to the kitchen is the original laundry porch, now a sunny enclosed seating area.

In Focus: Old Houses

MODERNIZED VICTORIAN KITCHEN

Although I'd spent less than an hour in Leslie Spring's company, as soon as I bit into the fresh tomato galette she served up for lunch, I wanted to ask her to be my friend for life. Spring grew up in San Francisco in the Queen Anne–style Victorian where she and her husband, architect Geoffrey Gainer, now live. Room by room, they are gradually renovating the three-story house, which was originally built in 1894. Given their zest for cooking, it's no surprise that the kitchen was a top priority.

The interior spaces had good bones, including original

Richlite counters, made from paper and resin, provide an attractive, durable work surface.

Victorian woodwork, large double-hung windows, and eleven-foot ceilings, but the kitchen was outdated and walled off from the dining room, inhibiting casual entertaining. The couple dreamed of having enough storage to accommodate their large collection of antique and modern cookware, as well as enough counter space to hold the profusion of organic produce they haul home from the city's farmers' markets on weekends.

Gainer removed interior walls between the old kitchen, dining room, and pantry to create an airy 450-square-foot space that's a dream in which to cook and entertain. Instead of demolishing the walls and hauling the splintered framing lumber to the landfill, which happens all too frequently in these tear-down-happy times, Gainer had the walls deconstructed.

The wall studs—old-growth Douglas fir harvested more than a century ago—were re-milled and joined to create a dramatic system of open shelves suspended from the ceiling. In keeping with the spirit of deconstruction, the shelving units, some of which have frameless glass doors, can be fully disassembled, the wood and hardware reused, and the metal and glass recycled.

Gainer's alterations provide a stylish reminder that greening an existing building has less to do with introducing novel products or offbeat technologies than it does with thoughtful reuse of what's already there.

Green Details

+ Interior walls were deconstructed and 100-year-old Douglas fir wall studs were re-milled and joined to create open shelves that provide much of the kitchen storage

Open shelves hold the couple's colorful cookware.
Glass doors on upper shelves keep items secure
and dust-free in this most-used kitchen.

▲
Above left: Gainer took care to retain the original window and door trim.
Above right: The island provides ample storage for the couple's kitchenware.
Drawers allow for easy access to items stored at the back.

+Additional reclaimed Douglas fir was purchased from a local salvage yard to complete the shelves and build the dining table
+The shelves can be fully disassembled, the hardware reused, and the stainless-steel tubing and glass doors recycled
+Glass doors on the upper shelves allow daylight to pass between the kitchen and dining area
+Broad-louvered shades painted white help reflect the east and south sun deep into the room; white paint on the walls and ceiling also bounce daylight into the room
+The flooring is a glueless-cork floating floor finished with a water-based polyurethane
+Counters are Richlite, a paper and resin composite
+Original Victorian features were preserved, including wood door and window trim

After removing interior walls that separated the kitchen and dining room, Gainer used the 100-year-old framing lumber for shelves. Old nail holes in the wood give evidence of its age.

+Perimeter walls are insulated with formaldehyde-free fiberglass
+Low-VOC paints were used

Project Credits
+Architect: Geoffrey S. Gainer, Actual-Size Architecture, San Francisco, California, actualsize.com.
+Builder: Simon Chambers.
+Cabinetmaker: David Brunges.
+Photographer: Linda Svendsen.

▶
The tabletop is made from salvaged Douglas fir.

The Beauty of Salvaged Wood

After more than twenty years in their rambling, 1890s Victorian in the heart of San Francisco's Haight-Ashbury neighborhood, Gregory Johnson and Michele Morainvillers were ready to overhaul their old kitchen. The couple, who raised their family in this house, are passionate cooks and vivacious hosts. They dreamed of a kitchen that would be as inviting as it was functional, with space enough for friends and family to relax during dinner preparations yet efficiently laid out so that multiple cooks could work together without stepping on each other's toes.

Johnson and Morainvillers drove the kitchen-design process, collaborating closely with talented local artisans. Early in the project, they accompanied their cabinetmaker, Ken Seidman of Seidman Woodworks, to a salvaged-woods showroom north of San Francisco. The trip proved fateful for the design of the kitchen.

Evan Shively, who runs the salvage outfit, tracks down trees in the region that have fallen or need to be removed from private properties—trees that would otherwise have gone for firewood or mulch—and hauls the logs back to his sawmill. The wood, primarily black acacia, bay laurel, redwood, claro walnut, and other local species, is custom milled and prepared according to each project's requirements. A chef who once plied his trade at Bay Area dining meccas, including Oliveto and Postrio, Shively now feeds the hunger of high-end furniture makers, builders, and designers who want to work with gorgeous wood but don't want to lose sleep wondering if it was irresponsibly or even illegally harvested. All the wood that Shively sells is salvaged from local sources; in addition to the salvaged trees, he procures wood from old buildings, huge wine casks, and other structures that are slated to be demolished.

Seidman and his clients were staggered by the beauty of the wood in Shively's showroom. Ultimately they selected oversized slabs of tightly grained old-growth redwood streaked with tones of yellow and amber, boards of mocha-colored claro walnut, and planks of multihued bay laurel. The redwood was so magnificent that they couldn't

◄

Open shelves hold the family's collection of well-used cookware. Work surfaces are designed to be functional, with a butcher-block cutting surface to the left of the sink and a stainless-steel counter to the right for stacking wet dishes.

▲

The floor is bay laurel, an abundant species native to the area that's rarely used in residential interiors. It came from Evan Shively's salvaged wood operation. Local craftsman Bart Lewis designed and built the custom range hood over the La Cornue range.

These eight-foot pantry doors were designed to showcase the beauty of the salvaged old-growth redwood.

The doors open to reveal pantry shelving and drawers.

bear the thought of cutting all of it into many small cabinet-door panels. They came up with a design that included eight-foot-tall pantry doors that kept a number of the redwood slabs intact. Claro walnut trim accents the redwood on all the cabinet and drawer faces.

The floor, also provided by Shively, is wind-felled bay laurel, a native species that's abundant in the region but is rarely used for residential interiors. The planks range in color from pale blond to chocolate brown, animating the floor with a sense of movement. Like everything about the kitchen, the floor is unique, spirited, and beautiful.

All the cabinets and drawers, as well as the refrigerator panels, are old-growth redwood with claro walnut trim. The wood came from salvaged trees that would otherwise have been chopped for firewood or chipped for mulch.

Green Details

- Cabinet and drawer faces are local wind-felled redwood and California claro walnut removed from an orchard that was being converted to a vineyard
- Floors are local wind-felled bay laurel
- On-demand (tankless) water heater
- Renovation of 110-year-old home in inner-city location

Project Credits

- Designer: Owners.
- Cabinetmaker: Seidman Woodworks, San Francisco, California, seidmanwoodworks.com.
- Salvaged wood source: Evan Shively, evan@arborica.com.
- Photographer: Linda Svendsen.

▼

Open stainless-steel shelves set into the wall provide utilitarian storage for large pots. The stained-glass windows here and next to the sink were made by Olivia Monteleone.

▲

The backsplash tiles and counter are limestone.

▲

The ironwork, including shelf brackets and pot hooks, was custom made by local craftsman Roger Yearout.

bibliography

Alevantis, Leon. *Building Material Emissions Study*. Sacramento, CA:
California Integrated Waste Management Board, 2003.

All About Tiling Basics. Des Moines, IA: Ortho Books, 2001.

Ardley, Suzanne. *The Kitchen Planner*. San Francisco, CA: Chronicle Books, 1999.

Baker-Laporte, Paula, Erica Elliott, and John Banta. *Prescriptions for a Healthy House*. Gabriola Island, BC: New Society Publishers, 2001.

Cahill, Coleen. *Simple Solutions: Kitchens*. New York, NY: Sterling Publishing Co., 2003.

California Energy Commission's Consumer Energy Center.
http://consumerenergycenter.org.

Cheng, Fu-Tung. *Concrete at Home*. Newtown, CT: The Taunton Press, 2005.

Chiras, Daniel D. *The New Ecological Home*. White River Junction, VT:
Chelsea Green Publishing Co., 2004.

Conran, Terence. *Kitchens*. New York, NY: Clarkson Potter, 2002.

Corson, Jennifer. *The Resourceful Renovator*. White River Junction, VT:
Chelsea Green Publishing Co., 2000.

Environmental Building News. Brattleboro, VT: BuildingGreen, Inc., 1992–2005.
http://www.buildinggreen.com.

Department of Health and Human Services, Centers for Disease Control and
Prevention. *Third National Report on Human Exposure to Environmental Chemicals*. Atlanta, GA: National Center for Environmental Health, 2005.
NCEH Pub. No. 05-0570.

Energy Information Administration. http://www.eia.doe.gov.

Goldbeck, David. *The Smart Kitchen.* 2nd ed. Woodstock, NY: Ceres Press, 1994

The Green Guide. http://www.thegreenguide.com/.

Health Care Without Harm. http://www.noharm.org.

Jeffries, Dennis. *The Flooring Handbook.* Buffalo, NY: Firefly Books, 2004.

Joint Center for Housing Studies of Harvard University. *The Changing Structure of the Home Remodeling Industry.* Cambridge, MA: President and Fellows of Harvard College, 2005.
http://www.jchs.harvard.edu/publications/remodeling/remodeling2005.html/.

Johnston, David and Kim Master. *Green Remodeling.* Gabriola Island, BC: New Society Publishers, 2004.

Krigger, John, and Chris Dorsi. *Residential Energy.* Helena, MT: Saturn Resource Management, 2004.

Langholz, Jeffrey and Kelly Turner. *You Can Prevent Global Warming (And Save Money!): 51 Easy Ways.* Kansas City, MO: Andrews McMeel Publishing, 2003.

McLellan, Tara. *Small Spaces, Beautiful Kitchens.* Gloucester, MA: Rockport Publishers, 2003.

Pearson, David. *The New Natural House Book.* New York, NY: Fireside, 1998.

Powell, Jane. *Linoleum.* Salt Lake City, UT: Gibbs Smith, Publisher, 2003.

Roberts, Jennifer. *Good Green Homes.* Salt Lake City, UT: Gibbs Smith, Publisher, 2003.

Roberts, Jennifer. *Redux.* Salt Lake City, UT: Gibbs Smith, Publisher, 2005.

Rocky Mountain Institute. "Home Energy Briefs: #8 Kitchen Appliances." Snowmass, CO: Rocky Mountain Institute, 2004. http://www.rmi.org/.

Spence, William P. *Installing and Finishing Flooring.* New York, NY: Sterling Publishing, 2003.

StopWaste.Org. *Multifamily Green Building Guidelines, Home Remodeling Green Building Guidelines, and New Home Construction Green Building Guidelines.* San Leandro, CA: Alameda County Waste Management Authority, 2004. http://www.stopwaste.org.

U.S. Department of Energy, Energy Efficiency and Renewable Energy. http://www.eere.energy.gov/consumer.

U.S. Department of Housing and Urban Development. *Kitchens & Baths: Volume 6 of the Rehab Guide.* Washington, DC., 1999. http://www.huduser.org/publications/destech/rehabgds.html/.

U.S. Environmental Protection Agency. http://www.epa.gov.

U.S. Green Building Council. *Rating System for Pilot Demonstration of LEED for Homes Program.* Washington, D.C.: 2005. http://www.usgbc.org.

Warde, John. *The Healthy Home Handbook.* New York, NY: Times Books, 1997.

Wilhide, Elizabeth. *Eco.* New York, NY: Rizzoli International Publications, 2003.

Wilson, Alex, Jennifer Thorne and John Morrill. *Consumer Guide to Home Energy Savings.* Washington, DC: American Council for an Energy-Efficient Economy, 2003.

Wilson, Alex and Mark Piepkorn, eds. *Green Building Products.* Gabriola Island, BC: New Society Publishers, 2005.

Winter, Ruth. *A Consumer's Dictionary of Household, Yard, and Office Chemicals.* New York, NY: Crown Publishers, 1992.

Thanks

In memory of my mother, Anita Roberts, who cooked like an angel.

And with thanks to all the homeowners, builders, architects, designers, cabinetmakers, manufacturers, and friends who were so generous with their time, photographs, ideas, inspiration, and enthusiasm. I'm also grateful to everyone at Gibbs Smith, Publisher, for their continuing support of books about eco-friendly design. Special thanks to Jonathan Cunha, Jay Vicar, and Ravi Wilson of Fusion Building Company for building my good green kitchen while I was writing this book.

project credits

V (bottom), 97 (top), 118–21
Architect: Sogno Design Group, sognodesigngroup.com. Builder: Cerami Builders. Photos © Linda Svendsen, lindasvendsen.com.

V (top), 92–93
Architect: Christopher C. Deam, cdeam.com. Builder: Fusion Building Co., fusion-buildingcompany.com. Photographer: Linda Svendsen, lindasvendsen.com.

VI (bottom), 24, 38, 59, 70–72, 131, 133
Architect: Todd Jersey Architecture, toddjerseyarchitecture.com. Builder: Beaman Construction, beamanconstruction.com. Interior design: Deborah Coburn, naturallyinspired.net. Photos © Linda Svendsen, lindasvendsen.com.

VI (top), 150–53, 156 (bottom)
Design: Owners. Cabinets: Seidman Woodworks., seidmanwoodworks.com. Salvaged wood: Evan Shively, evan@arborica.com.

VII (bottom), IX (bottom), XII, 60, 145–49, 156 (top)
Architect: Geoffrey S. Gainer, Actual-Size Architecture, actual-size.com. Builder: Simon Chambers. Cabinetmaker: David Brunges.
Photos © Linda Svendsen, lindasvendsen.com.

VII (top), 113
Design and construction: Spectrum Fine Homes, spectrumfinehomes.com. Photo © Spectrum Fine Homes.

VIII, 64, 105, 112
Designer: Emanate Design, emanatedesign.com.
Builder: Atsatt & Taddie General Contractors.
Photos © Paul Schraub.

IX (top), 95
© IceStone, icestone.biz.

X (top), 84 (top)
Cabinets and photo © AlterECO, bamboocabinets.com.
Counter: Counter Production, counterproduction.com.

X (bottom), 159 (bottom)
Design: Openspace Architecture Inc., openspacearchitecture.com. Photo © Linda Svendsen, lindasvendsen.com.

XI, 129

Architect: Thompson Naylor Architects, thompsonnaylor.com. Builder: Allen Associates. Photos © Emily Hagopian, essentialimages.us.

XIII

Architect: Arkin Tilt Architects, arkintilt.com. Builder: Sage Design/Build. Photo © Edward Caldwell, edwardcaldwell.com.

14

Builder: Drew Maran Construction/Design, drewmaran.com. Architect: Heidi Hansen. Interior design: Barbara Shoolery. Photo © Emily Hagopian, essentialimages.us.

15, 25, 86

© Neil Kelly Cabinets, neilkellycabinets.com.

16–17

Architect: Hays Ewing Design Studio, hays-studio.com. Builder: Craig DuBose Carpentry. Photos © Philip Beaurline.

18–19, 158 (*bottom*)

Builder: Fusion Building Co., fusionbuildingcompany.com. Photos © Todd Pickering

20, 87, 108

© AlterECO, bamboocabinets.com.

21

© 1996 Forest Stewardship Council A.C., fsc.org.

28, 158 (*top*)

Architect: Okamoto Saijo Architecture, os-architecture.com. Builder: Alan Bertolani. Photos © Lewis Watts.

32

Developer/architect/builder: Leger Wanaselja Architecture, lwarc.com. Photo © Leger Wanaselja Architecture. Counters: Counter Production, counterproduction.com.

33

Developer: Building Opportunities for Self-Sufficiency (BOSS), self-sufficiency.org. Architect: Babette Jee. General Contractor: Fine Line Construction. Photo © Linda Svendsen, lindasvendsen.com.

34–35, 125, 155

Architect/builder: Leger Wanaselja Architecture, lwarc.com. Photos © Linda Svendsen, lindasvendsen.com.

36–37, 161 (*top*)

Architect/builder: Timothy Mueller Architecture and Building, 510.540.5558. Photos © Linda Svendsen, lindasvendsen.com.

39, 73–75, 159 (*top*)

Architect: Henry Taylor. Builder: Gary Giesen Construction. Photographer: Linda Svendsen, lindasvendsen.com.

44

Designer/developer: Carol Solfanelli. Builder: Fusion Building Co., fusionbuilding-company.com. Photo © Fusion Building Co.

49, 55

© EcoTimber, ecotimber.com.

50

Design/construction: Gary Wolff. Photo © Linda Svendsen, lindasvendsen.com.

57, 58

Marmoleum flooring, themarmoleumstore.com. © Forbo Linoleum.

61

Architect: Arkin Tilt Architects, arkintilt.com. Photo © Linda Svendsen, lindasvendsen.com.

69, 116–17, 160 (*top*)

© EnviroGLAS Products Inc., enviroglasproducts.com.

76, 77

Cabinets: Woodshanti, woodshanti.com. Photos © Todd Semo.

78, 81, 89

Cabinets: Silver Walker Studios, silverwalker.com. Photo © Vanophoto.com.

79

© Berkeley Mills, berkeleymills.com.

84 (*bottom*)

Architect/Builder: Todd Jersey Architecture, toddjerseyarchitecture.com. Photo © Linda Svendsen, lindasvendsen.com.

85

Architect/Builder: Todd Jersey Architecture, toddjerseyarchitecture.com. Cabinets: Woodshanti, woodshanti.com. Photo © Todd Semo.

88

© SpectraDécor, spectradecor.com.

90–91, 160 (*bottom*)

Architect/builder: Chris Parlette, Wilson Associates, dswdesign.com. Photo © David Stark Wilson, dswdesign.com.

94, 97 (*bottom*)

Designer: Eco Interiors, ecointeriors.biz. Photo © Emily Hagopian, essentialimages.us.

96

© Eco Friendly Flooring, ecofriendlyflooring.com.

100, 101 (top)

Designer: Michael Heacock, LEED AP, mheacock@designarc.net. Builder: Creative Spaces, Inc. Photos © Emily Hagopian, essentialimages.us.

101 (bottom)

© Laguna Bamboo, lagunabamboo.com.

102

© Fireclay Tile, Inc., fireclaytile.com.

103

Architect: David Hertz Architects, syndesisinc.com. Photos © Linda Svendsen, lindasvendsen.com.

106

© Oceanside Glasstile, glasstile.com. Photo © Christopher Ray Photography

109

© Eleek, Inc., eleekinc.com.

115

© Coverings Etc., coveringsetc.com.

122–23, 161 (bottom)

Architect: Leger Wanaselja Architecture, lwarc.com. Builder: Owner. Photos © Linda Svendsen, lindasvendsen.com.

124

Developer/architect/builder: Leger Wanaselja Architecture, lwarc.com. Photo © Cesar Rubio, cesarrubio.com.

128

© Sun Frost, sunfrost.com.

132, 137

© Bosch, boschappliances.com.

141

© Rinnai, rinnai.us.

143–44

Architect: Arkin Tilt Architects, arkintilt.com. Photos © Arkin Tilt Architects.

glossary

acid rain	Rain that contains a high concentration of acids formed by the mixing of various pollutants—primarily sulfur dioxide and nitrogen oxides—in the atmosphere. It is harmful to plants and aquatic life.
advanced wood framing	Design and construction techniques that significantly reduce the amount of wood used to frame a building without compromising structural integrity. Includes strategies such as studs placed twenty-four inches on center rather than the standard sixteen inches on center, two-stud corners, engineered wood products, and roof or floor trusses.
asbestos	A mineral that separates into thread-like fibers and is used in certain products to increase strength or resist heat, fire, or chemicals. Very high levels of exposure to airborne asbestos fibers over long periods of time may cause cancer or asbestosis, a lung disease.
backdrafting	A reversal of the normal flow of combustion gases from combustion appliances, such that they spill into the home instead of flowing out the chimney or flue.
ballast	A device that provides a starting voltage for a lamp and limits the flow of electric current. Fluorescent lamps have electronic or electromagnetic ballasts; electronic ballasts are more energy efficient and don't flicker.
bamboo	A giant fast-growing grass with a hollow stem. Considered an environmentally friendly alternative to wood because it can be harvested every three to five years. Residential interior uses include flooring, cabinets, tabletops, and other furnishings.
biodegradable	Capable of being readily decomposed by microorganisms under natural conditions.

biodiversity	A contraction of biological and diversity. A wide range of living things in a particular region.
black water	Wastewater that contains sewage.
building envelope	A building's shell, including exterior walls, windows, doors, roof, and the bottom floor.
California cooler	*See* cool pantry.
cellulose insulation	Insulation made from wood fiber, primarily recycled newspaper, treated with nontoxic chemicals to retard fire, mold, and insects. Loose-fill cellulose can be blown into attic spaces or packed into wall cavities. Damp-spray cellulose is a damp mix of cellulose and adhesives that is sprayed into wall cavities before hanging drywall.
ceramic-glass cooktop	Cooktops with a smooth surface made of a ceramic-glass material that is very strong and withstands quick temperature changes. The heat source may be electric radiant ribbons, halogen lamps, electromagnetic induction technology, or sealed gas burners.
certified wood	Wood certified by an independent third-party certification program to have been grown and harvested using environmentally responsible forestry practices.
cistern	A tank, often underground, used to collect and store rainwater for later use.
cohousing	Collaborative housing planned, owned, managed, and maintained cooperatively by the residents, who live in their own private dwellings but share extensive common facilities.
color rendering index (CRI)	A measurement system that indicates the relative ability of a light source to render color. CRI ranges from 1 to 100. In general, people and objects look better under light sources with higher CRIs.
color temperature	A measurement of a light source's color appearance in degrees Kelvin. Lamps with a color temperature of 3,500 K or less appear warm or reddish yellow. Lamps with a color temperature of 3,500 K to 4,000 K appear neutral or white, while those with a color temperature of 4,000 K or higher appear cool or bluish white.
combustion appliance	Any appliance or device that burns fuel for heating, cooking or decorative purposes, such as gas ranges, furnaces, fireplaces, clothes dryers, and water heaters.
community-supported agriculture	A cooperative arrangement whereby people who wish to support local agriculture become members or shareholders in a local farm, paying a fee in advance to help finance the farm's operations and in return receiving regular distributions of the harvest.
compact fluorescent lightbulb (CFL)	A type of fluorescent lightbulb designed to be compatible with standard lightbulb sockets. CFLs are three to four times more energy efficient and last eight to ten times longer than an incandescent bulb.
compost	A mixture of vegetable scraps, other decomposing plant matter, and sometimes manure used to fertilize and condition soil.
convection oven	A gas or electric oven with an internal fan that circulates hot air around the food. Temperatures and cooking time can be decreased compared to a conventional oven, reducing energy use by 20 to 30 percent.
cool pantry	An insulated cabinet used to keep food cool without refrigeration. Often built into a perimeter wall on the cooler side of the kitchen and equipped with screened vents to circulate cool air from the basement or outside.

cork flooring	Flooring made from cork, which is harvested from the outer bark of cork oak trees without having to fell the trees. Cork oaks regenerate their bark and can be reharvested in about ten years.
cotton insulation	Insulation made from post-industrial recycled cotton textile trimmings. Typically treated with a nontoxic fire retardant and sold as batts that fit between framing studs.
daylighting	The controlled use of natural light (as opposed to electric light) to illuminate a space. The goal is typically to create a stimulating, appealing environment while reducing energy use from electric lighting.
deconstruction	Disassembling rather than demolishing a building so that its components can be reused.
dioxin	A group of chemicals that is highly persistent in the environment and among the most toxic known. Dioxin is an unintentional by-product of many industrial processes involving chlorine. A potent human carcinogen, dioxin accumulates in animal fat and increases in concentration as it travels up the food chain.
double-glazed (or double-pane) window	A window with two panes of glass separated by an airspace. Also known as an insulating window. Compared to single-glazed windows, double-glazed windows significantly reduce heat and sound transmission. Some double-glazed windows contain a gas such as argon or krypton in the air gap to provide additional insulation.
efficacy	A measurement of how efficiently a light source converts electricity into light, expressed in lumens per watt.
electromagnetic field	An invisible force surrounding an electrical wire or device, with two components: an electric field that is produced by voltage, and a magnetic field that results from the flow of current through wires or electrical devices.
emissivity	The capacity of a surface to radiate energy.
energy efficiency	Using less electricity or fuel than a conventional technology to perform the same task.
Energy Factor (EF)	A measure that indicates the efficiency of a variety of appliances, including water heaters and dishwashers.
Energy Star	A program sponsored jointly by the U.S. Environmental Protection Agency and the U.S. Department of Energy that promotes energy-efficient products, homes, and technologies for consumers and businesses. Energy Star–qualified products and new homes are 10 to 50 percent more efficient than their conventional counterparts.
EnergyGuide label	A label required by U.S. law on certain new household appliances, including dishwashers, refrigerators, and freezers. The label provides the unit's estimated annual energy use and allows consumers to compare the projected energy use of various models.
engineered floor	Flooring made with three to five thin sheets of wood stacked in a cross-grain arrangement and glued together under heat and pressure. The top surface is typically a veneer of finish-grade hardwood. Easier to install and less likely to be affected by changes in humidity than solid wood flooring.
engineered lumber	Building products, including beams, framing studs, and floor and roof joists, made from wood fibers bound with adhesives. The wood typically comes from plantation-grown trees, thus reducing demand for old-growth trees. In general, engineered wood products result in less wood waste than solid-sawn lumber products.

engineered stone	A man-made countertop material consisting of a blend of stone aggregate (usually quartz), plastic resin, and pigments.
EPA-certified fireplace insert	A product designed to fit within an existing masonry fireplace opening. It converts a wood-burning fireplace into a more efficient, less-polluting heating system.
fiber-cement countertop	A countertop material made from a blend of cement and cellulose fiber formed into thick slabs.
fluorescent lightbulb	A lamp with a sealed glass tube coated on the inside with a fluorescent substance. Electric current energizes the substance, causing it to give off light. Fluorescent lamps are very energy efficient, converting most of the electricity they consume into light rather than heat.
fly ash	A waste product from coal-fired electric power plants that can be used as a substitute for portland cement in some concrete mixtures. Portland cement manufacturing is an energy-intensive process, producing significant carbon dioxide (CO_2) emissions that contribute to global warming. Substituting fly ash for the portland cement in concrete reduces CO_2 emissions.
footprint	In architecture, the area of land covered by a building. The term *ecological footprint*, on the other hand, is sometimes used to indicate the number of acres of productive land necessary to support the resources a person consumes.
Forest Stewardship Council (FSC)	An international certification organization that has established voluntary environmental forest management standards. FSC accredits independent third-party organizations that monitor and certify the compliance of forestry operations with FSC standards. FSC-labeled wood products give consumers assurance that the wood comes from trees grown and harvested in an environmentally and socially responsible manner.
formaldehyde	A colorless pungent gas used in many glues, adhesives, preservatives, and coatings. It also occurs naturally. Products and materials containing formaldehyde can offgas the chemical into the air; products containing urea formaldehyde typically offgas at much higher levels than products containing phenol formaldehyde. According to the U.S. Environmental Protection Agency, exposure to formaldehyde may cause allergic reactions, respiratory problems, or cancer in humans.
fossil fuel	A fuel, such as natural gas, oil, or coal, formed from the decomposition of animals and plants millions of years ago.
FSC	*See* Forest Stewardship Council.
full cutoff fixture	An outdoor light fixture that directs light downward instead of toward the sky.
geothermal heating system	Also known as ground-source or water-source heat pump. Water circulates through a coil buried in the ground or sunk in a nearby water source such as a pond. The system uses the difference between the ground (or water) temperature and the indoor air to cool and heat the home. Can also be used for domestic water heating. The systems are expensive to install but very efficient to operate.
glazing	Transparent or translucent material, such as glass or plastic, that lets light into a building.
global warming	The long-term warming of the planet caused by heat being trapped in the lower atmosphere by greenhouse gases. These gases are being emitted primarily as a result of human activities, including burning fossil fuels.

glulam	Contraction of glued laminated. An engineered wood product consisting of thin layers of wood, usually less than two inches thick, bound with an adhesive and formed into structural beams that can be used instead of solid-sawn lumber.
gray water	Household wastewater that doesn't contain sewage and can be reused for irrigation. Gray water typically comes from showers, dishwashers, and clothes washing machines.
green building	Building design and construction practices that use energy, water, and other resources wisely so that present and future generations can live well without needlessly damaging the environment. Also called sustainable, eco-friendly, or environmentally responsible building.
green roof	A roof that has a layer of soil or other growing medium on top of a waterproofing membrane. May be planted with sedum, grasses, wildflowers, or other ground cover. Also known as a living, eco, or vegetated roof.
greenhouse gas	Gases that trap heat in the atmosphere, contributing to global warming. Greenhouse gases, which are primarily the result of human activities such as burning fossil fuels, include carbon dioxide, methane, nitrous oxide, and hydrofluorocarbons.
greenwashing	Falsely claiming that a product, service, or company is environmentally responsible.
halogen cooktop	A cooktop that uses tungsten halogen lightbulbs under a glass surface to generate heat. It heats up and responds to adjustments in temperature settings very quickly, but is not significantly more energy efficient than radiant and electric-coil cooktops.
halogen lightbulb	A type of incandescent lightbulb that is filled with halogen gas. It lasts longer than a standard incandescent bulb and provides a crisp white light, but it gets very hot and is less energy efficient than a fluorescent lightbulb.
heat exchanger	An energy-saving device that takes waste heat from one process and reuses it in another process. For example, an air-to-air heat exchanger (also known as a heat-recovery ventilator) captures heat from indoor air that's about to be vented from a home and transfers that heat to fresh air that's being drawn in from the outside.
heat gain	Heat from the sun, people, electric lights, or appliances that cause the temperature in a space to rise.
heat loss	The decrease of heat in a space as a result of heat escaping through the building's walls, windows, roof, and other building envelope components.
high performance	A building or building component that provides a substantial improvement over a comparable conventional building or component, either in terms of energy or resource use, health, durability, comfort, or other desirable features.
incandescent lightbulb	A lightbulb that consists of a filament inside a glass bulb. Passing electric current through the filament causes it to heat up and produce light. Standard household lightbulbs are incandescent bulbs; they are very inefficient because up to 90 percent of the energy they consume results in wasted heat instead of useful light.
indoor air quality	The level of air pollutants inside a building. Indoor air pollution sources include tobacco and wood smoke; certain building materials and furnishings; certain cleaning, maintenance, and personal care products; dust mites; pet dander; mold; radon; pesticides; and outdoor air pollution. Inadequate ventilation and high humidity levels can also contribute to indoor air quality problems.

induction cooktop	Also known as magnetic-induction cooktop. A very energy-efficient cooking technology consisting of heating elements that transfer electromagnetic energy directly to the pan. The cooking surface does not heat up, so less heat is wasted. It can only be used with ferrous metal cookware, such as stainless steel and cast iron.
infill development	Building on empty or underutilized lots in cities or older suburban areas instead of building in an undeveloped area. Reduces pressure to develop agricultural lands and wildlands.
infiltration	The movement of outdoor air into a building through cracks and other defects around doors, windows, walls, roofs, and floors.
insulated concrete form (ICF)	Plastic foam shaped into hollow blocks, panels, or planks and used as a form to create a concrete wall. After positioning the foam forms, rebar is typically inserted into the cavities to reinforce the walls, and then concrete is poured in. Once the concrete cures, the foam remains in place to insulate the walls. Exterior siding and interior wall finishes are attached to the ICFs.
insulation	A material that has a high resistance to heat flow. Used to increase comfort and reduce the energy needed to heat and cool the home.
kilowatt (kW)	A unit of electrical power equal to 1,000 watts.
laminate flooring	Flooring product consisting of a printed layer of paper glued to a fiberboard core and sealed under heat and pressure. The printed image is topped with a clear melamine wear layer for protection. Typically fabricated into planks that snap together and install easily.
lead-based paint	Lead was a common additive to oil-based paints before 1978. Inhalation or ingestion of lead-based paint chips or dust can pose a serious health risk, particularly for infants and children.
LEED Green Building Rating System	A voluntary, consensus-based national standard for high-performance, sustainable buildings. Developed and administered by the U.S. Green Building Council. LEED is an acronym for Leadership in Energy and Environmental Design.
light pollution	Excess light that escapes into the night sky rather than illuminating the intended surfaces.
linoleum	A smooth floor covering typically used in kitchens and bathrooms. True linoleum is made from natural renewable resources, including pine rosin, sawdust, linseed oil, natural pigments, and jute. Vinyl flooring, sometimes mistakenly called linoleum, is made from polyvinyl chloride (PVC), which is derived from petrochemicals.
low-e (low-emissivity) window	A window with a special coating that allows daylight to enter a building but reduces the flow of heat. The appropriate type of low-e glazing for a home will depend on the climate and the window's orientation.
lumen	A measurement of the light output of a lamp.
material safety data sheet (MSDS)	A standardized form designed to provide workers and emergency personnel with information about the hazards associated with a substance or product, and how to safely handle the product.
medium-density fiberboard (MDF)	A composite board made of sawmill waste bound with urea formaldehyde or other synthetic resins. Similar to particleboard but made with smaller wood particles so it mills cleanly. Used in place of wood boards for cabinets, furniture, molding, and the like. Medite II, an MDF product made by SierraPine, is made without added formaldehyde.

melamine	A type of plastic laminate that is fused to an underlying core using heat and pressure. Often used to line the interior of cabinets to create a moisture- and abrasion-resistant surface.
natural cooling	Cooling a building through passive means rather than mechanical systems such as air-conditioning. Natural cooling strategies include shading, cross ventilation, and the use of thermal mass to moderate temperatures inside a space.
natural oil finish	Also called plant-based oil finish. Finish made primarily from vegetable oils and waxes, used as a protective coating on wood flooring, trim, furniture, and other wood products.
natural ventilation	The introduction of outside air into a building by using passive means such as open windows and cross ventilation, rather than using mechanical systems such as air conditioners, heating systems, or fans.
nonrenewable resource	A natural resource that does not replenish itself or is consumed at a faster rate than it is replaced in the environment. Primarily refers to oil, minerals, gas, and coal.
nontoxic	Not posing a significant risk to people or the environment.
offgas	The release of vapors from a material through the process of evaporation or chemical decomposition. Many building products, furnishings, floor and wall coverings, and other products brought into the home offgas formaldehyde, volatile organic compounds (VOCs), or other potentially troublesome chemicals.
old-growth tree	A tree that has been growing for approximately 200 years or longer.
on-demand hot-water recirculation pump	A small pump used to move hot water to sinks, showers, and other household water fixtures to reduce waiting time for hot water. It is typically installed at the fixture farthest from the water heater. Pushing an activation button at any fixture engages the pump.
organic gardening	Gardening without synthetic pesticides, herbicides, or fertilizers, instead using environmentally responsible techniques and substances like compost, mulch, and manure to build healthy soils, manage pests, and encourage healthy plant growth.
oriented strand board (OSB)	An engineered wood panel made from strands of wood arranged in crisscrossing layers and bound with an adhesive. In homes, used for subflooring and sheathing.
parallel strand lumber	An engineered wood product made from strands of wood glued together under pressure and cut to form beams, columns, and other structural building components.
particulate	Very fine particles in the air, such as smoke, dust, soot, or pollen.
passive solar heating	A building specifically designed to collect and store the sun's heat, and release that heat into the interior spaces to help warm the rooms naturally. Depending on the design and climate, passive solar heating can be the sole source of heat for the building or can be supplemented with a heating system.
perfluorooctanoic acid (PFOA)	A synthetic chemical used to make Teflon and other products such as breathable waterproof clothing. PFOA has been found in low levels in the environment and in the blood of people worldwide, according to the U.S. EPA. Studies have shown that it causes developmental and other adverse effects in laboratory animals. It is not yet known whether PFOA poses a health risk to humans.

permaculture	An approach to agriculture and the design of human habitats that emphasizes examining and following nature's patterns.
phantom load	The small amounts of electricity consumed by many appliances and equipment—such as TVs and stereos with remotes, ovens with digital clocks, cell phone chargers, and answering machines—even when they're not in use.
photovoltaic (PV) cell	A material that converts light directly into electricity.
phthalate	A group of synthetic chemical compounds primarily used as plasticizers to increase the flexibility of plastics, including PVC.
pisé	An acronym for pneumatically impacted stabilized earth. Pioneered by David Easton of Rammed Earthworks in Napa, California. Pisé is a system of building thick earthen walls using a high-pressure air hose to spray a damp soil mix against one-sided formwork.
polyvinyl chloride	Also known as vinyl or PVC. A family of plastics, derived from vinyl chloride, with a wide range of forms and uses. PVC is used extensively in building products, consumer goods, and industrial applications. There has been considerable debate about the environmental impacts related to PVC manufacturing and the eventual disposal of products made from PVC. Some groups have called for phasing out PVC production or limiting its use.
portland cement	A component of concrete, made from limestone, sand, and clay that is fired at an intense heat in a kiln.
post-consumer recycled content	Materials that have been used and discarded by a consumer and are then reprocessed as raw material for a new product. Post-consumer recycled content has been diverted from landfills or incinerators, usually as part of residential or commercial recycling programs, and is environmentally preferable to pre-consumer recycled content.
pre-consumer recycled content	Waste material from a manufacturer or processor, including scrap, trimmings, and overruns, used as the raw material to make a new product. For many manufacturers, the reuse of pre-consumer waste is a normal part of doing business. This type of waste is not as likely to end up in landfills as post-consumer waste is.
PVC	*See* polyvinyl chloride.
radiant floor heating system	A space heating system consisting of heating tubes embedded in a concrete floor slab or attached to the subflooring beneath the finish floor. Heat from the tubes travels through the floor and is slowly released to the room, providing a comfortable, quiet, gentle warmth that doesn't stir up dust or create drafts. While hot water is the most frequent heat source, some radiant floor systems use electricity or hot air.
radon	A radioactive gas derived from the natural decay of uranium. Radon is emitted by some soils and rocks, and can enter a home through cracks and holes in the foundation or through well water.
rainwater harvesting	Collecting rainwater from a catchment area such as a roof and storing it in cisterns or other containers to use for watering a yard or garden, or for other purposes.
reclaimed material	A material that's put to a new beneficial use after it's no longer needed for its original use, such as wood removed from an abandoned building and used to construct a new building.
recycling	Taking a material that would otherwise become waste and processing it into raw material for a new product.

renewable energy	Energy generated from replenishable resources, such as sunlight, wind, and agricultural products.
renewable resource	A material that can be replenished in a relatively short period of time after it is harvested or used.
sealed-combustion appliance	A gas-burning appliance (such as a furnace or fireplace) with a sealed combustion chamber. Fresh air is supplied directly to the combustion chamber from outside instead of being drawn from inside the room. Harmful combustion gases are kept out of the home because the combustion exhaust vents directly to the outside.
skylight	A translucent or transparent window set into a roof to allow daylight into a building.
solar collector	A device used to capture solar energy to heat water. A typical system used for heating household water consists of one or more collectors; the collector is often a glass-topped insulated box that contains a black metal panel designed to absorb heat. Collectors are typically mounted on a roof and angled to face south. Liquid circulates in tubes through the collectors, where it heats up when the sun is shining. In some systems, the liquid is potable water that's stored in a tank until needed. In other systems, the liquid is an antifreeze solution that flows through a heat exchanger to heat potable water.
solar electricity	Electricity generated from sunlight. Also called photovoltaic or PV power.
solar heat gain coefficient (SHGC)	An indication of how much of the sun's heat will enter through a window. An SHGC of 0.40, for example, means that 40 percent of the sun's heat gets through the window.
solar orientation	The relationship of a building, or a window or other building component, to compass direction and consequently to the sun's position. Careful solar orientation is a fundamental aspect of passive solar design and daylighting.
solar water heater	*See* solar collector.
solid-disk cooktop	A cooktop consisting of cast-iron disks on top of electric resistance wires. They are less energy efficient than electric coil and ceramic-glass electric cooktops.
solid-surface countertop	A synthetic countertop material typically made from minerals and acrylic or an acrylic/polyester blend. Unlike laminates, which consist of a thin sheet of plastic laminated to a wood-fiber substrate, solid-surface counters are manufactured in thicker slabs and have their colors and patterns running all the way through the material.
sone	A measurement of loudness. The lower the sone, the quieter the source of noise is.
stack effect	Planned ventilation design that naturally cools a home by taking advantage of the high- and low-pressure zones created by the rising of warm air. An exit vent near the top of the house, sometimes in a tower, draws warm air out of the building, while fresh cool air is pulled in through vents located at lower levels in the home.
standby heat loss	A measure of the heat that escapes from a water heater tank. It is the ratio of heat lost per hour to the heat content of the stored water above room temperature, expressed as a percentage.
storm-water runoff	Water that flows off of buildings and paved surfaces and over land during a rain storm or as a result of snowmelt.

straw bale construction	A construction method that uses straw bales to form walls. The bales can be load-bearing, meaning that they carry some or all of the roof's weight. More commonly, however, the bales are stacked within a structural framework to provide insulation. Straw is an agricultural waste product—it's what's left after harvesting rice, wheat, barley, and other grains.
strawboard	A panel product made primarily from compressed straw, an agricultural waste product. Typically made without formaldehyde binders. Used for cabinet boxes, floor underlayment, furniture, paneling, and other interior applications.
structural insulating panel (SIP)	An alternative to framing with wood studs and joists. SIPs can be used to build well-insulated floors, walls, and roofs. They are prefabricated panels that typically consist of rigid foam insulation sandwiched between two panels of oriented strand board or plywood.
sustainability	Meeting the needs of the present without compromising the ability of future generations to meet their own needs (as defined by the World Commission on the Environment and Development).
tankless water heater	A water heater that saves energy by heating water as it is needed rather than storing hot water in a tank. Also known as demand or instantaneous water heater.
terrazzo	A surfacing material, either poured in place or precast, that combines small chips of marble, granite, quartz, glass, or another aggregate in a cement- or resin-based matrix.
thermal mass	The ability of a material to absorb and retain heat. Materials with a high thermal mass, such as rocks, earth, and concrete, have the capacity to absorb heat during the day and release it when temperatures cool.
thermofoil	In kitchen cabinets, thermofoil is a thin decorative sheet of PVC that is heat-fused onto the cabinet surface, creating a look similar to a painted cabinet.
thinset	A tile-setting mortar formulated to be applied in a thin layer. May be cement-based or an organic mastic.
toxic	Capable of adversely affecting organisms.
truss	A structural framework for supporting roofs or floors. Prefabricated trusses are shipped to the building site ready to install. They are typically fashioned of small pieces of wood joined with metal plates into a triangulated form. They use less wood, and save time and money compared to site-built rafters and joists.
tubular skylight	A circular skylight that's much smaller than typical skylights, designed to illuminate interiors with daylight while keeping out excessive heat. It consists of a small roof-mounted dome attached to a tube lined with reflective material. Light is reflected down the tube and is transmitted into the room through a translucent ceiling fixture.
U.S. Green Building Council	A voluntary coalition of building industry professionals working to promote buildings that are environmentally responsible, profitable, and healthy places to live and work. Administers the LEED Green Building Rating System.
universal design	An approach to designing a product or a building to make it more easily usable by people of all ages and diverse physical abilities.
utility grid	The network of transmission and distribution lines that provides electricity to the vast majority of homes and buildings in the United States.
vegetated roof	*See* green roof.

ventilation	The process of bringing outside air into an indoor space by natural or mechanical means.
vinyl	*See* polyvinyl chloride.
volatile organic compound (VOC)	A class of organic chemicals that readily release gaseous vapors at room temperature. VOCs occur naturally in many materials, and can also be manufactured and added to materials and products. VOCs are released ("offgassed") into a home by common furnishings and building materials, including many types of particleboard, paint, solvents, carpets, and synthetic fabrics. Exposure to VOCs can cause symptoms ranging from short-term nausea, eye irritation, and headaches to more severe, longer-lasting effects.
weatherstripping	A material used to reduce air and water leaks around doors and windows. Typically made of foam, felt, metal or vinyl. Includes pliable gaskets, tension strips, door sweeps, and door shoes.
wheatboard	*See* strawboard.
work triangle	A kitchen planning concept that represents the lines between the kitchen's main activity zones, usually the sink, stove, and refrigerator.

index

a

n

o

p

priorities, whole house green building, 26–28; identifying green, 30

Pyrolave, 114

r

radon, 22, 27, 114

range hood ventilation, 23, 30, 33, 135–36

recycled material: in insulation, 16; for a green kitchen, 20, 33; post-consumer vs. pre-consumer, 20, 110; certification of, 23; in flooring materials, 45–47, 61–62, 66–68; in subfloor materials, 69; in cabinets, 82, 86, 88; in countertops, 96, 98–99, 102–4, 107–11, 114; in paints, 117; in sinks, 140

recycling: of construction waste, 27, 43, 103, 109–10; of kitchen waste, 29, 143–44; of appliances, 29, 109, 127, 129

redecorating: as eco-friendly, 29; cost effectiveness of, 33; of cabinets, 82

Rediscovered Wood, 23

refacing, of cabinet doors, 29, 83

refrigerators: proliferation of, 20, 130; energy-efficient, 33, 124, 126–28; recycling of, 109, 129; drawer style, 128; choosing the best, 129; getting the best performance from, 129; water filters in, 140

remodeling: eco-friendly, 10, 26, 29–30; for energy-efficient kitchen, 16–17; for resource-efficient kitchen, 20–21; for healthy kitchen, 22–26; of whole house, 26–28; featured kitchens, 118–23, 145–53

rescued wood, 48

resources, rapidly renewable: types of, 20; bamboo as, 45, 54, 87, 101; cork as, 45, 59

restoration of existing flooring, 42–43

reverse osmosis water treatment, 139

Richlite, 75, 94, 108, 119, 146, 148

Rodda Horizon Interior, 117

Rogers, Kathryn, 118–21

root cellar, 130

rubber: asbestos in, 43; as flooring material, 44, 60–61

s

safety: recommendations for kitchen, 24; considerations for floor, 42, 65

salvage materials: for shelves, x, 146; for cabinets, xi, 28, 73, 81, 83, 87, 129, 152; for doors and windows, 19, 120; for kitchen remodeling, 20, 27, 30, 123, 140; sources of, wood, 21, 23, 48–49, 155; sources of, building materials, 34, 37; for countertops, 35, 98–99, 100–102, 113–14, 123; for flooring, 41–43, 45–46, 51–52, 65–68, 123, 151; for backsplashes, 70; for furnishings, 73, 90, 148

Sandhill Industries, 94, 97, 107

Scientific Certification Systems, 23, 86

sealants: for wood floor finishing, 53; for stone, 111

seasonal affective disorder (SAD), 23

Seidman, Ken, 151

selective-cut wood, 48

Seventh Generation, 143

shading for natural cooling, 16, 26

Sherwin-Williams Harmony, 117

Shively, Evan, 151

shoes, pollution and contaminants from, 22, 44

SierraPine, 86–88, 94

Silestone, 105

Silver Walker Studios, 35, 78, 88–89

sinks, 110, 140, 142

t

u